S0-DTK-828

Better Homes and Gardens

HOLIDAY COOK BOOK

MEREDITH PRESS
New York Des Moines

Printed in the United States of America.
Tenth Printing, 1970.

Grand finale for a circus birthday party—Mint-balloon Cake, pink ice cream, and circus cocoa (float tiny colored marshmallows atop). Toy clown offers each guest a take-home balloon

Contents

Our Test Kitchen seal means recipe goodness

Every recipe in your Holiday Cook Book is *endorsed* by the Better Homes and Gardens Test Kitchen. Each was tested over and over till it rated superior—in both practicality and deliciousness.

Better Homes and Gardens
TEST KITCHEN

Entertaining?

The secret's in planning before you tie on your apron: Scan the check list of tips at right. Then choose from our jackpot of no-fuss foods, simple serving ideas, decorations!

Consider self-service—

The buffet, luau, and smorgasbord rate high with every hostess who likes to enjoy her own party. All the flurry is over before guests arrive.

Do it with flair—the easy way!

Balance your guest list

Don't include everyone you know or owe at one party (except for occasions like a golden wedding tea). The easiest formula: Invite folks who already know and like each other.

The more experienced hostess may want to try a bolder combination. Here's a tip: Aim at a balance of personalities within a framework of not-too-different interests and backgrounds. Choose some shy guests, some outgoing (and see that they meet). Your best bet—people genuinely interested in others.

For pre-schoolers' parties, invite only as many guests as years in the child's age.

Create party atmosphere

This helps people relax and catch the mood for fun. Just grouping chairs for easy conversation helps a formal occasion. For a casual party, try seating guests on pillows. Or roll up the rug to encourage dancing.

Lighting is important, too. Use lamps and the glow from candles and fireplace. Skip harsh overhead lights.

Teen-age and birthday parties call for as much "fancy" decorating as you wish.

Plan activities

Start the party off with something that will invite each guest to participate. Dancing, games, lively conversation, listening to records, coming in costume—anything that makes people feel they have a part.

For young children, alternate quiet games with lively ones and restore calm with singing just before refreshments. (Do be sure *each* child has a "prize" to take home.)

Never put off having a party because you can't do it in the same style as someone else. Do things in keeping with your own budget and surroundings—your entertaining will have a flavor all its own.

Make your schedule flexible

It's essential to the success of a party not to plan anything that has to be done "on the dot." The good hostess keeps a finger on the pulse of her party.

For instance, at a dinner party, there's a "right" time to eat—the moment before conversation lags or appetites become ravenous.

Be ready to end a children's party early, while everyone's still having a good time.

These things you do beforehand spell success for your party—

- Invitations—Send them out one week to 10 days ahead of time for most parties. But plan on two to three weeks during the holidays.
- Be sure to tell guests what to wear, and whether there will be any special activity.
- If you're new at entertaining, organize your party early. List the major jobs which must be done ahead. Examples are: Deciding what to serve, groceries to buy, how you want the table set, and when to cook the food. Plan a schedule and check off each item as you do it.
- Pick one or more dishes you can fix ahead of time—ready-to-heat casserole, molded salad, refrigerator dessert. Complete as much early preparation on other foods as possible.
- Serving something new? It's a good idea to try the recipe first. Unless you know your guests well, it's best not to serve anything that's *too* unusual. As a rule, men like simple food and women take to "something different."
- Keep track of special days as themes for party refreshments, festive family desserts.
- You'll save dishwashing if you count on smart ovenware and electric skillets that can travel from kitchen to table.
- Before the party, decide how to split duties between the host and hostess.
- Budget your time—save a precious hour before guests arrive to relax.

Carnival of snacks offers Stuffed Edam with fruit, Blue-cheese Fluff and hatful of dunkers, Garlic Cheese Dip on ferris wheel, and platter merry-go-round with Guacamole, . . .

. . . Ham and Cheese Dip, Cla Cheese Dunk. For foreign flavor — Rio Grande Dip; and Batter-fried Shrimp with Oriental-style dunks; Water Chestnuts With Chicken Livers, pages 104 and 105

New Year's Eve

For your midnight party—easy snacks and trims

Offer tangy caviar canapes, dip

You'll make a big splash as hostess with caviar on the snack table! It's delicious. Quick, too.

Caviar Canapes are make-your-own. Nestle caviar—right in the jar—in a bed of ice. Guests spread it on crisp melba rounds or fingers of pumpernickel. Offer lemon to dash on top. Next—a sprinkling of finely chopped onion, hard-cooked egg white and/or egg yolk.

For zippy *Caviar-Cheese Dip*, combine 1 cup sour cream and one 3-ounce package softened cream cheese. Add 1 teaspoon grated onion. *Gently* stir in one 2-ounce jar lumpfish caviar. Pass with crisp crackers.

Quick spicy warm-ups with cider, tea

Ready in a minute, *Hurry-up Hot Mulled Cider* is so good you'll serve it to fireside sitters all winter long!

Set out pretty mugs. Poke a long cinnamon stick through clove-studded orange slice to stand in each. Pour in *hot, hot* cider. Guests sip through cinnamon "straws," sample warm French doughnuts and walnuts toasted in the shell.

For *Speedy Spiced Tea*, put 1½ teaspoons sugar in each mug and poke cinnamon sticks through clove-studded lemon slices. Pour in *very hot* tea (quick with instant); sample through cinnamon "sippers."

Dramatic—"timely" centerpiece

Spark your watch-party table with a handsome carnation clock. Red flower stands for midnight, white blossoms mark other hours.

Position pottery clock hands. (Or use hands cut from plastic foam.) Place beribboned flower at base.

Clock-design plates, black cloth, and white napkins are smart props for a midnight party any time.

Another quick table trim—Place your punch bowl on round mirror, then garland mirror with wide band of bright Christmas ornaments. Pin more ornaments to plastic-foam balls suspended from ceiling.

Party dips and dunks

When you invite folks in for late refreshments, or plan an open house, call on these easy-on-the-hostess snacks—so good they'll be the talk of the party!

Offer a choice of dips, and of dunkers—crisp crackers, potato or corn chips, carrot and celery sticks, pineapple chunks. Folks help themselves, leave you free to chat.

Quick Dips

Ham and Cheese Dip: With electric mixer, blend one 5-ounce jar pimento-cheese spread, one 2¼-ounce can deviled ham, ½ cup salad dressing, 2 tablespoons minced parsley, 1 tablespoon minced onion, dash monosodium glutamate, 4 drops Tabasco sauce. Chill.

Garlic Cheese Dip: Soften two 3-ounce packages cream cheese. Blend in 2 cups dairy sour cream. Add 1 package garlic-cheese salad-dressing mix, dash Tabasco; beat smooth.

Braunschweiger-Onion Special: Blend one 8- or 10-ounce package Braunschweiger, 1 cup dairy sour cream, 1 envelope onion-soup mix, 1 teaspoon Worcestershire sauce, and a dash Tabasco sauce.

Cottage Chip Dip: Blend one 12-ounce carton cream-style cottage cheese, 1 tablespoon mayonnaise, and 1 teaspoon salad-spice-and-herb mix in mixer till almost smooth. Chill. Top with parsley snips. Makes 1½ cups.

Appetizer Ham Ball

2 4½-ounce cans deviled ham
3 tablespoons chopped stuffed green olives
1 tablespoon prepared mustard
Tabasco sauce to taste
1 3-ounce package cream cheese, softened
2 teaspoons milk

Blend deviled ham, olives, mustard, and Tabasco. Form in ball on serving dish. Chill. Combine cream cheese and milk, and frost ball with mixture. Keep chilled; remove from refrigerator 15 minutes before serving time. Trim with parsley. Makes about 1 cup.

Rio Grande Dip

2 1-pound cans (4 cups) pork and beans in tomato sauce, sieved
½ cup shredded sharp process American cheese
1 teaspoon garlic salt
1 teaspoon chili powder
½ teaspoon salt
Dash cayenne pepper
2 teaspoons vinegar
2 teaspoons Worcestershire sauce
½ teaspoon liquid smoke

• • •

4 slices crisp-cooked bacon, crumbled

Combine all ingredients except bacon; heat in chafing dish or double boiler. Top with crumbled bacon. Serve hot with corn chips or potato chips. Makes about 4 cups.

Parmesan Cheese Snack

1 8-ounce package cream cheese, softened
¼ cup shredded Parmesan cheese
2 teaspoons horseradish
⅓ cup chopped stuffed green olives

• • •

¼ cup finely chopped dried beef *or* chopped parsley

Blend together first 3 ingredients. Stir in olives. On waxed paper, shape into two 1½x5-inch rolls. Roll in chopped dried beef or parsley. Wrap carefully; chill several hours or overnight. To serve, slice and pass with assorted crackers.

Clam Cheese Dunk

1 8-ounce package cream cheese, softened
1 4-ounce package blue cheese, crumbled
⅓ cup drained minced clams
1 tablespoon chopped chives
¼ teaspoon salt
Tabasco sauce to taste

Combine ingredients. Keep chilled; remove from refrigerator about 15 minutes before serving time. Offer assorted crackers and potato chips. Makes 2 cups.

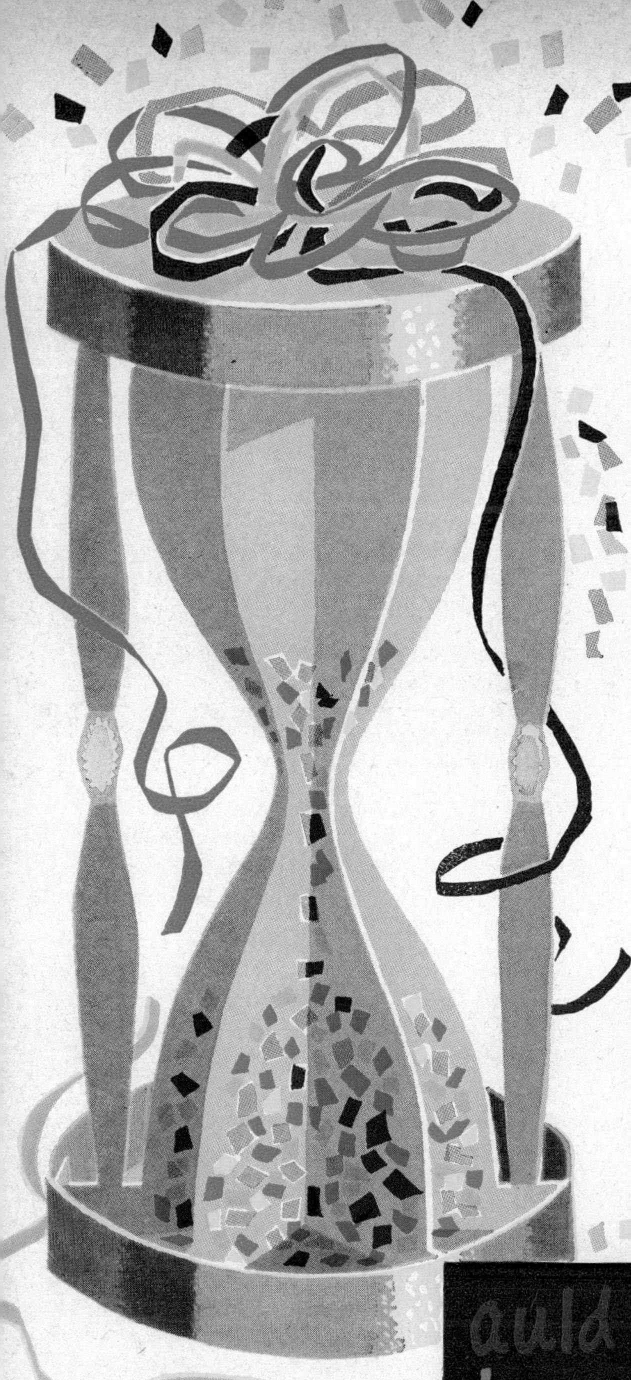

Get set to ring in the new!

To welcome the New Year—a midnight snack, a festive table! Set the stage with a giant hourglass to measure out the last bright minutes of the Old Year. Bank balloons behind it, lavishly scatter paper serpentine—you'll have a show stealer! Hourglass is made from heavy Bristol board, confetti, and stout rubber cement. Experiment with trims—we show notary seals, foil paper, ribbon.

Hourglass is easy paper "sculpture"—

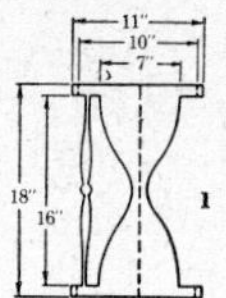

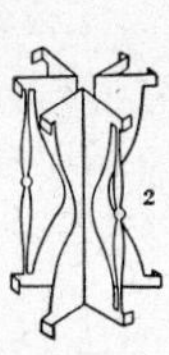

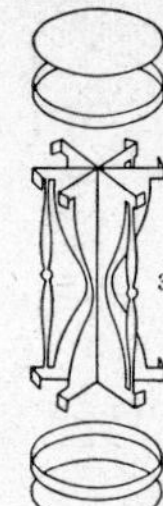

Draw pattern shown in figure 1. Use to cut 3 pieces from Bristol board. Crease each piece down center. "Paint" sand-shape with glue; scatter confetti on it immediately. When dry, repeat on back of each piece. Sew the pieces together through the creases, in two places (figure 2). Fold back ½-inch tabs at top and bottom of each section.

Cut two paper strips 1½x31 inches; curve around tabs at top and bottom; glue; staple into rings. Cut two 10-inch circles; glue confetti to center of bottom one. Fasten to rings with cellophane tape or ribbon (figure 3).

12 o'clock place mats—easy, inexpensive

auld lang syne

← Each mat is a 12x18-inch sheet of colored construction paper.

Fold serpentine to make Auld Lang Syne or numerals; glue on; add confetti.

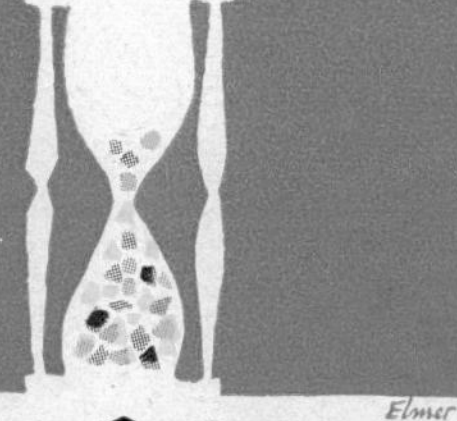

Hourglass, balloons, and confetti set the mood for a New Year's buffet table ↓

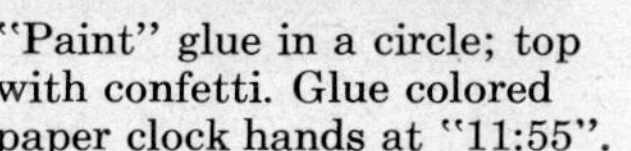

"Paint" glue in a circle; top with confetti. Glue colored paper clock hands at "11:55".

↑ Cut hourglass from a 6x12-inch piece of white paper. Glue on confetti "sand." Glue hourglass to colored paper.

For cutout effect, glue hourglass half on end of mat, half off.

Pickup snacks—easy hostessing!

Goobersnap

1 8-ounce package corn-muffin mix

• • •

1 cup coarsely chopped salted peanuts
½ cup grated Parmesan cheese
1 teaspoon garlic salt
3 tablespoons butter or margarine, melted

Prepare corn-muffin mix according to package directions; spread evenly in well-greased 15½x10x1-inch jelly-roll pan. Sprinkle with peanuts, cheese, and garlic salt; drizzle butter over top. Bake in moderate oven (375°) about 25 minutes or till crisp and lightly browned. Immediately cut in squares; cool slightly, remove from pan.

Curried Wheat Snacks

⅓ cup butter or margarine
½ teaspoon curry powder
¼ teaspoon onion salt
⅛ teaspoon ginger
3 cups (about 25) spoon-size shredded-wheat biscuits

Melt butter in large skillet. Blend in seasonings. Add shredded wheat and toss. Heat about 5 minutes over low heat, stirring frequently. Drain on paper towels. Serve warm.

Scramble

2 pounds mixed salted nuts
1 12-ounce package bite-size shredded-wheat squares
1 10½-ounce package crisp doughnut-shaped oat cereal
1 6-ounce package bite-size crisp rice squares
1 7-ounce package small pretzel twists
1 5¾-ounce package slim pretzel sticks
1 4½-ounce can pretzel bits
2 cups salad oil
2 tablespoons Worcestershire sauce
1 tablespoon garlic salt
1 tablespoon seasoned salt

Mix all ingredients in very large roaster or large pans. Bake in very slow oven (250°) 2 hours, stirring and turning mixture with wooden spoon every 15 minutes (be careful not to crush cereals).

Makes about 9 quarts.

Crisp Rye Curls

With very sharp knife or slicer, slice tiny "icebox" rye loaf *paper-thin.* Place in single layer on baking sheet; heat at 300° till crisp and edges curl, about 30 minutes. Dip in hot garlic butter to serve.

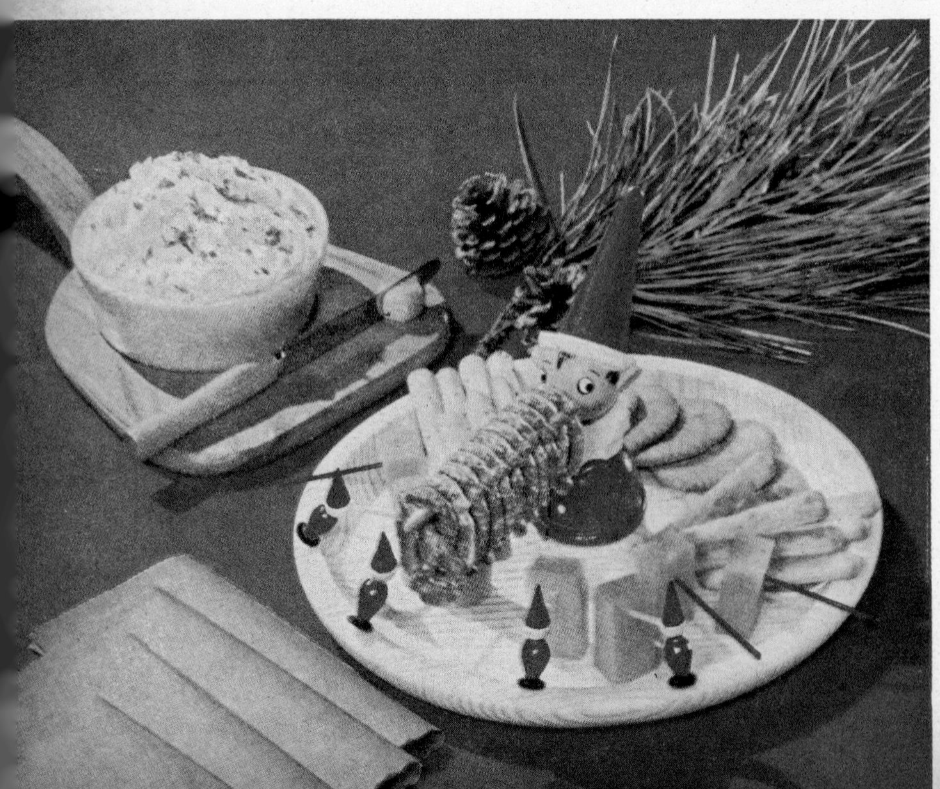

With Blue-cheese Fluff, offer a choice of dunkers

Blue-cheese Fluff: Soften two 3-ounce packages cream cheese. Add ½ cup crumbled blue cheese (2 ounces), ¼ teaspoon garlic salt, and 3 tablespoons milk. Blend. Mound in serving bowl; sprinkle with parsley.

Pinocchio offers pretzels for dunking. Or try crisp crackers or bread sticks. Picks hold bite-size chunks of Cheddar.

Another snack idea—liverwurst cubes on pretzel sticks, with barbecue sauce for dip.

Ready-in-a-minute food for little parties

These Sizzling Ripe Olives are chafing-dish *hot!* Offer chilled ripe olives, too. Slice a variety of cheeses to circle a Baby Gouda, cut poinsettia-style. (There's a second cheese underneath, waiting for the second round.) Serve with crisp crackers and marmalade, hot punch.

Stuffed Edam

1 round Edam or Gouda cheese
Onion juice
Prepared mustard
Light cream or milk

Have cheese at room temperature. Press cooky or biscuit cutter into top of cheese, cutting deep circle. Remove circle of cheese, then scoop out center leaving ¼-inch wall. Notch edge of cheese shell with sharp knife.

Whip the cheese with electric mixer or mash with fork; add onion juice and prepared mustard to taste. Beat in enough light cream to make of spreading consistency. Mound cheese in shell. Chill several hours to blend flavors.

Remove from refrigerator 1 hour before serving. Poke a spreader or two in top; arrange on tray with crackers, fresh fruit.

Stuffed Mushrooms

1 tablespoon finely chopped onion
1 tablespoon butter or margarine
1 2¼-ounce can deviled ham
¼ cup soft bread crumbs
¼ teaspoon seasoned salt
¼ teaspoon Worcestershire sauce

• • •

1 6-ounce can (1⅓ cups) mushroom crowns, drained
Melted butter or margarine

Cook onion in 1 tablespoon butter over low heat till tender but not brown. Combine with deviled ham, crumbs, seasoned salt, and Worcestershire.

Stuff mushrooms with mixture; brush with melted butter. Broil, stuffed side up, 5 to 8 minutes or till heated through. Keep hot in chafing dish.

Sizzling Ripe Olives

1 7-ounce can pitted ripe olives
1 to 2 cloves garlic, minced

• • •

2 tablespoons salad oil

To undrained olives in can, add the garlic. Refrigerate several days. To serve, heat olives in small amount of the olive liquid, with salad oil added. Spear on toothpicks.

Burger Canapes

10 slices enriched bread
Softened butter or margarine

• • •

1 pound ground beef
2 tablespoons grated onion
1 tablespoon Worcestershire sauce
1 teaspoon salt

• • •

¼ cup chili sauce

Toast bread on one side; cut four 1½-inch rounds from each slice. Lightly butter rounds on untoasted side. Combine remaining ingredients except chili sauce. Shape mixture in 40 marble-size balls (1 heaping teaspoon each) and place one on buttered side of each bread round, leaving border of bread showing. Make indentation in center of balls.

Broil 4 inches from heat 5 to 6 minutes or till meat is done and edges of bread are toasted. Fill indentations with chili sauce. Serve hot.

Herbed Chips

Place large potato chips on baking sheet; sprinkle with marjoram, thyme, or basil. Heat in moderate oven (350°) 5 minutes.

Glamorous punch for open house

Tomato Consomme

1 46-ounce can (about 6 cups) tomato juice
1 can condensed consomme
1 teaspoon grated onion
1 teaspoon prepared horseradish
Dash pepper
1 teaspoon Worcestershire sauce

• • •

1 lemon, sliced
Whole cloves

In saucepan, combine juice, consomme, onion, horseradish, pepper, and Worcestershire. Stud lemon slices with cloves; add to juice and heat just to boiling. Serve immediately, with lemon slices as floaters in each cup. Makes 8 to 10 servings.

Brazilian Chocolate

3 tablespoons instant coffee
¼ cup sugar
2 cups milk or water
1 pint chocolate ice cream
½ cup heavy cream, whipped and sweetened
Shaved unsweetened chocolate

Combine coffee, sugar, and milk; stir to dissolve. Add ice cream; stir till almost smooth. Place an ice cube in each of 4 tall glasses. Pour in chocolate mixture. Top with fluffs of whipped cream and shaved chocolate.

French Chocolate

2½ 1-ounce squares unsweetened chocolate
½ cup water
⅔ cup sugar
½ teaspoon salt
½ cup heavy cream, whipped
1 quart hot milk

Heat chocolate and water over low heat, stirring till chocolate melts. Add sugar and salt. Bring to boiling, reduce heat, and simmer 4 minutes. Cool to room temperature. Fold in whipped cream.

To serve, place 1 heaping tablespoon chocolate "batter" in each cup; fill with hot milk; stir. Makes 8 to 10 teacup servings.

Hot Cranberry Punch

(as served at Publick House)

2 tablespoons whole cloves
1 tablespoon whole allspice
12 inches stick cinnamon, broken
¼ cup brown sugar
4 cups water
¼ teaspoon salt
4 cups pineapple juice (canned unsweetened)
2 1-pound cans (4 cups) jellied cranberry sauce

• • •

Few drops red food coloring
Few bits butter
Cinnamon sticks

Tie whole cloves and allspice in small piece of cheesecloth. Combine in a saucepan the spice bag, cinnamon pieces, brown sugar, 1 cup of water, and salt. Bring slowly to a boil. Add the pineapple juice and 3 cups of water. Crush the cranberry sauce with a fork and add. Bring to a boil again and simmer for 5 minutes; remove spices.

Add a few drops of red food coloring. Pour into a heated punch bowl. Add a few bits of butter. For trim, float clove-studded orange slices, cut in half. Serve in mugs with cinnamon sticks as stirrers. Makes about 10 to 12 cups.

Holiday Eggnog

(from Williamsburg's Colonial Capitol)

¼ cup sugar
¼ teaspoon cinnamon
¼ teaspoon ginger
¼ teaspoon ground cloves
6 well-beaten eggs
2 quarts orange juice, chilled
½ cup lemon juice, chilled

• • •

1 quart vanilla ice cream
1 quart ginger ale, chilled
Nutmeg

Beat sugar and spices into beaten eggs. Stir in chilled orange and lemon juices. Cut ice cream in chunks; place in punch bowl. Slowly pour ginger ale down side of bowl. Gently stir in egg mixture. Sprinkle with nutmeg. Makes about 20 servings.

Sunshine Toddy—cheerful perk-up on a blustery day

Sunshine Toddy: In saucepan, combine 4 cups orange juice, ⅓ to ½ cup sugar, 6 inches stick cinnamon, 2 teaspoons whole cloves, and 2 teaspoons grated orange peel.

Bring to boiling, then simmer 5 minutes. Strain. Pour into heated punch bowl and float orange slices atop. Makes about 8 servings.

Here punch is served with Ribbon Sandwiches.

To serve hot beverage in glass punch bowl, (like this red-striped one) first heat bowl with warm water. Pour out water and place large metal spoon in bowl. Then pour beverage slowly onto spoon.

Eggnog

- ⅓ cup sugar
- 2 egg yolks
- ¼ teaspoon salt
- 4 cups milk, scalded
- 1 teaspoon vanilla or 2 tablespoons cooking sherry
- 2 egg whites
- 3 tablespoons sugar
- 1½ teaspoons sugar
- ½ cup heavy cream, whipped

Beat ⅓ cup sugar into egg yolks. Add salt; slowly stir in milk. Cook in double boiler over *hot, not boiling water*, stirring constantly, till mixture coats spoon. Cool. Add vanilla. Beat egg whites till foamy. Gradually add 3 tablespoons sugar, beating till soft peaks form. Add meringue to custard and mix thoroughly. Chill 3 or 4 hours. Pour into punch bowl.

Fold 1½ teaspoons sugar into whipped cream—dot eggnog with "islands" of it. Sprinkle with nutmeg. Makes 6 to 8 servings.

Pineapple Wassail

- 4 cups unsweetened pineapple juice
- 1 12-ounce can apricot nectar
- 2 cups cider
- 1 cup orange juice
- 6 inches stick cinnamon, broken
- 1 teaspoon whole cloves
- 4 cardamom seeds, crushed

Combine ingredients. Heat to boiling; simmer 15 to 20 minutes. Serve hot. Makes 2 quarts.

Hot Pineapple Cider

- ½ cup mint leaves
- 4 cups cider
- 2 cups unsweetened pineapple juice
- 1 large bottle ginger ale (not chilled)
- Crab apples, fresh or spiced

Crush mint; add cider and pineapple juice. Bring to boiling. Strain. Bring to a boil again. Add ginger ale. Serve immediately with crab apples afloat. Makes 12 servings.

February days

Honor St. Valentine, Lincoln, and Washington

Lacy trim—Valentine Ribbon Tree

Paint a round 1-pint freezer carton and a 2-foot piece of ¼-inch doweling red. Make holes in center of carton lid and bottom; fill carton with pebbles; cover, and insert dowel. Fold six 10-inch red foil doilies in half, right sides together. Glue outside of folds to dowel at top, pressing to widen edges of folds. Glue half of one doily to half of next, back-to-back, making six wings.

Cut three 5-foot lengths of pink ribbon; pin centers to top of doweling. Crown with ribbon bow. Arrange the ribbon streamers between wings of doilies; notch ends and pin to tablecloth. Cut hearts from 3-inch squares of red paper; glue near ends of streamers.

Cherry Tricorn Tarts for February 22

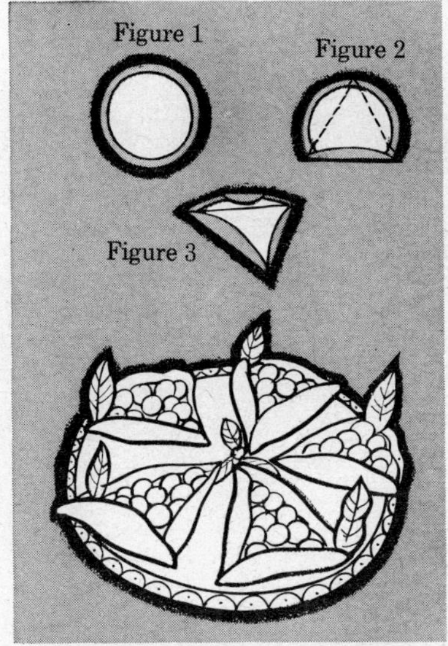

For 5 tarts, use 1 stick pastry mix or 1 recipe plain pastry calling for 1½ cups flour. Roll the pastry to ⅛ inch. Cut in 5-inch circles, using saucer or canister cover as a guide. Lightly press each pastry round on a 5½-inch circle of heavy-duty foil (figure 1). Prick pastry with fork. With edge of ruler, press three fold lines in pastry circle to form triangle.

Holding pastry and foil together, fold the three sides in form of tricorn (figure 2). Moisten insides of corners; pinch together to depth of 1¼ inches. Turn edges of foil down over edges of pastry—that way tart shell keeps its shape (figure 3).

Bake on cooky sheet at 450° 10 to 12 minutes or till golden brown. Cool on rack; remove foil. Fill with canned cherry-pie filling (or make filling for Red Cherry Pie, page 19). Tuck green leaf in one corner of each tricorn for "plume" as shown. Pipe a rosette of softened cream cheese atop each tart, if desired.

Heart-shaped cake—two ways to cut it

Cut cake crosswise in six slices. For 11 pieces (lower right): Cut cake in half *to* (*not through*) slice at tip of heart. For 13 slices (left): Cut first, fourth, and fifth slices in half; second and third slices in three pieces.

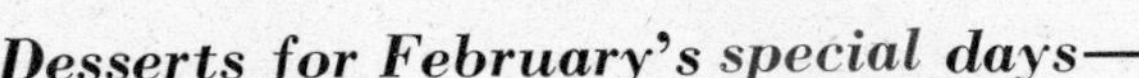

Desserts for February's special days—

On Valentine's Day, choose Pink Meringue Hearts, Chocolate Chiffon Pie, or Frozen Valentine Rounds. For February 22, pick Red Cherry Pie, Washington Pie, or chocolate cake with ½ cup chopped maraschino cherries baked in (try with Red Devil's Food Cake, page 139). Make Lincoln Log (not pictured) on February 12.

Valentine Cake

1 package white-cake mix
1 package fluffy instant-frosting mix
Red food coloring
⅓ cup flaked coconut

Mix cake batter according to package directions. Pour into 2 paper-lined heart-shaped pans and bake at 350° for 25 to 30 minutes.

Prepare frosting mix according to directions on label; tint pink with red food coloring. Tint coconut pink (see how, page 124). Frost cooled cake. Leaving a 2½- to 3-inch border around top of cake, trace a heart (freehand or from pattern) in frosting; fill in design with tinted coconut.

Valentine ensemble—pink and pretty hearts

Valentine Cake or Strawberry Hearts—there's no more delicious way to say "Be mine"! You fix them fast with mixes and simple ingredients. The easy final touches make them fancy.

Strawberry Hearts

1 10-ounce package frozen strawberries, thawed
1 package strawberry-flavored gelatin
2 cups heavy cream, whipped
9 Gelatin Heart Cutouts

Drain strawberries, reserving syrup. Add water to syrup to make 1 cup; heat to simmering. Dissolve gelatin in hot liquid; add drained strawberries. Chill till partially set. Fold whipped cream into gelatin mixture.* Pour into heart-shaped individual molds, chill till set. Unmold. Top with Gelatin Heart Cutouts. Makes about 9 servings.

*To match picture, save out a few drained strawberries, and a little whipped cream; fold together and spoon over hearts.

Frozen Valentine Rounds

1 No. 2½ can (3½ cups) fruit cocktail
1 package lemon-flavored gelatin
1 cup hot water
¼ cup maraschino-cherry syrup
2 tablespoons lemon juice
2 3-ounce packages cream cheese
½ cup mayonnaise or salad dressing
1½ cups tiny marshmallows
¼ cup drained quartered maraschino cherries
1 cup heavy cream, whipped
Few drops red food coloring
12 Gelatin Heart Cutouts

Drain fruit cocktail, reserving 1 cup syrup. Dissolve gelatin in hot water; add reserved fruit-cocktail syrup, maraschino-cherry syrup, and lemon juice. Chill till partially set.

Soften cream cheese; add mayonnaise and beat smooth. Add to gelatin mixture, mixing well. Stir in fruit cocktail, marshmallows, and cherries. Fold in whipped cream. Tint pink with red food coloring. Pour into two No. 2 or 2½ cans. Freeze several hours or overnight. Use can opener to cut around bottom of can. Push salad out. Slice and place on lettuce. Top with Gelatin Heart Cutouts. Makes 12 generous servings.

Gelatin Heart Cutouts

Dissolve 1 package cherry- *or* strawberry- *or* raspberry-flavored gelatin in 2 cups hot water. Pour into shallow dish—gelatin should be a little less than ½ inch deep. Chill till firm. Cut out hearts with cooky cutter. Use to trim salads, desserts.

Pink Meringue Hearts

Make Pink Meringue: Beat 3 egg whites with 1 teaspoon vanilla, ¼ teaspoon cream of tartar, and dash salt till frothy. Add 1 cup sugar, a small amount at a time, beating till stiff peaks form and sugar dissolves. Tint delicate pink.

Cut heart pattern from a 4½-inch square of paper. Cover baking sheet with plain paper; draw 6 hearts from pattern. Spread meringue over each heart shape, making ¼-inch layer. With pastry tube, pipe on rim about ¾ inch high. Bake at 275° for 1 hour. For crisper meringues, turn off heat; let dry in oven (door closed) 1 hour.

To serve: Fill meringues with scoops of vanilla ice cream (takes 1 quart). Top with 1 pint fresh strawberries, sugared and sliced (*or* use one 10-ounce package frozen strawberries, barely thawed).

Washington Pie

Make cake batter according to recipe for French Pastries, page 140 *but bake in two paper-lined 9x1½-inch round pans at 350° 25 to 30 minutes.* Cool.

Decorate top layer with Glaze and Chocolate Spiral Trim below.

Put layers together with *Vanilla Cream Filling:* Prepare 1 package vanilla pudding, *using only* 1¾ cups milk. Cover. Chill. Beat till fluffy and smooth.

For make-ahead dessert, put together 1 to 3 hours before serving time, keep chilled.

Glaze and Chocolate Spiral Trim

(for Washington Pie)

1 cup sifted confectioners' sugar
1 tablespoon *warm* water
1½ teaspoons light corn syrup
¼ teaspoon vanilla
Chilled canned chocolate syrup

Combine first four ingredients; stir till blended. Leaving a ½- to ¾-inch border of cake, quickly spread frosting over top layer. Immediately add Chocolate Spiral:

Start at center of cake. Using a teaspoon, pour chocolate syrup from the tip in a thin stream to form spiral. Quickly run tip of spatula from center of cake to edge, "pulling" each band of chocolate slightly. Repeat, making 16 to 24 spokes, evenly spaced. (Wipe spatula with damp cloth after each stroke.) See picture, page 14.

"Holiday" refreshments for February

Cherry Chocolate Cookies

½ cup shortening
¼ cup brown sugar
½ teaspoon salt
1 egg yolk
1 1-ounce square unsweetened chocolate
1 cup sifted enriched flour
1 slightly beaten egg white
1 cup broken California walnuts
⅓ cup cherry preserves

Cream together shortening, sugar, salt, and egg yolk till fluffy. Melt chocolate; blend into creamed mixture. Stir in flour. Chill ½ hour. Shape in 1-inch balls; dip in slightly beaten egg white; roll in nuts. Place 2½ inches apart on greased cooky sheet; press centers with thumb. Bake at 350° 8 minutes; press centers again. Bake about 8 minutes longer. Cool slightly; remove from pan. At serving time, fill centers with cherry preserves. Makes 3 dozen.

Chocolate Chiffon Pie

Soften 1 envelope unflavored gelatin in ¼ cup cold water. In saucepan, combine ½ cup water, 1 teaspoon instant coffee, and two 1-ounce squares unsweetened chocolate. Stir over low heat till blended. Remove from heat. Add softened gelatin; stir to dissolve. Beat 3 egg yolks till thick and lemon-colored; gradually beat in ½ cup sugar; add ¼ teaspoon salt and 1 teaspoon vanilla. Slowly stir in chocolate mixture. Chill till partially set. (Mixture should mound when spooned.)

Stir till smooth. Beat ½ cup sugar into 3 stiff-beaten egg whites. Fold into chocolate mixture. Fold in 1 cup tiny marshmallows, if desired. Pile into cooled baked 9-inch pie shell. Chill till firm.

All-American cherry pie

We can thank George Washington and his hatchet for the custom of serving delicious cherry treats in February.

Top on the list is Red Cherry Pie. Peek-a-boo crust shows off bright red filling; flavor's a perfect blend of tart and sweet.

Red Cherry Pie

¾ cup juice from cherries
¾ cup sugar
1½ tablespoons quick-cooking tapioca
Dash salt
2½ cups drained canned pitted tart red cherries*
Few drops red food coloring
1 tablespoon butter or margarine

• • •

1 recipe Plain Pastry

Combine the juice, sugar, tapioca, salt, cherries, and food coloring; let stand 20 minutes. Line 9-inch pie plate with pastry. Fill with cherry mixture. Dot with butter.

Make Lattice Crust: Trim lower crust ½ inch beyond edge of pie plate. Cut strips of pastry dough ½ to ¾ inch wide with pastry wheel or knife. Lay lengthwise strips on top of filled pie at 1-inch intervals. Fold back alternate strips to help you weave crosswise strips over and under, placing them on the diagonal. Trim lattice even with outer rim of pie plate; dampen edge of pastry lightly with water; fold lower crust over strips. Seal; crimp edge high.

Bake at 450° 10 minutes. Reduce heat to 350°; continue baking about 30 minutes.

*Or use 2½ cups drained frozen pitted tart red cherries, decreasing sugar to ¼ cup and omitting food coloring.

Plain Pastry

2 cups sifted enriched flour
1 teaspoon salt
⅔ cup shortening
5 to 7 tablespoons cold water

Sift together flour and salt; cut in shortening with pastry-blender or blending fork till pieces are the size of small peas. Sprinkle water, a tablespoon at a time, over part of mixture. Gently toss with fork; push to one side of bowl. Sprinkle next tablespoon water over dry part; mix lightly; push to moistened part at side. Repeat till all is moistened. Gather up with fingers; form into ball.

For double-crust pie, divide dough for lower and upper crust. Form each in ball. Flatten ball slightly and roll ⅛ inch thick on lightly floured surface. If edges split, pinch together. Always roll from center out to edge. Use light strokes. Makes enough pastry for one 8- or 9-inch lattice-top pie or one 9- or 10-inch double-crust pie.

Lincoln Log

5 egg whites
½ teaspoon cream of tartar
½ cup sugar

• • •

5 egg yolks
½ cup sugar
¼ cup sifted enriched flour
3 tablespoons cocoa
¼ teaspoon salt
1 teaspoon vanilla

• • •

1 quart pink peppermint ice cream

• • •

1 recipe Chocolate Glaze
Broken California walnuts

Beat egg whites and cream of tartar till stiff but not dry. Gradually beat in ½ cup sugar. Beat egg yolks till thick and lemon-colored. Sift together remaining ½ cup sugar, flour, cocoa, and salt; fold into egg yolks till blended; stir in vanilla. Carefully fold yolk mixture into egg-white mixture.

Line bottom and sides of 15½x10½x1-inch jelly-roll pan with waxed paper; grease paper lightly. Spread batter evenly in pan. Bake in slow oven (325°) 25 minutes, or till cake springs back when lightly touched.

Cool 5 minutes; turn out onto towel sprinkled with sifted confectioners' sugar. Peel off waxed paper quickly but carefully so you won't tear cake. Cool to lukewarm. Trim off side crusts with very sharp knife. Roll cake with towel, jelly-roll fashion. When cake is cool, unroll.

Stir ice cream just to soften; gently spread on cake. Roll up as jelly roll. Wrap in waxed paper; freeze. Remove waxed paper and spread with Chocolate Glaze; dot with walnuts. Serve at once or keep in freezer till serving time. Makes about 12 servings.

Chocolate Glaze

(for Lincoln Log)

1 6-ounce package (1 cup) semisweet chocolate pieces
1 6-ounce can (⅔ cup) evaporated milk

Combine ingredients in small saucepan. Cook over low heat, stirring constantly, till blended and mixture comes to a boil. Lower heat; cook gently 3 to 5 minutes, till thick, stirring constantly. Cool, stirring occasionally. Frost Lincoln Log.

St. Patrick's Day

How about a bow to the Irish?

Slice corned beef thin

Carve across the grain of corned-beef brisket. Since the grain goes in several directions, you will need to switch course, too!

Don't hesitate to have 3 sides "in business" at one time. Slice *thin* and at a slight angle. Meat will be easy to eat, tender.

It's easiest to carve firsts ahead on a board in the kitchen, carve seconds at the table.

Horseradish Sauce—

It's a spunky accent for corned beef; another time for pot roast.

Soften one 8-ounce package cream cheese and fluff it with electric mixer. Beat in 2 to 3 tablespoons of prepared horseradish. Makes 1½ cups. Chill if sauce is made ahead of time.

Mound in pretty bowl and add this touch of green—parsley, snipped fine with kitchen scissors.

Blarneystones to eat!

Turn cupcakes into Blarneystones! (Nice for birthdays, too—poke tiny candle in each.)

Make cupcakes from your favorite mix, according to package directions. Cool. Frost all over with fluffy instant frosting mix or Snowy 7-minute Frosting (page 112). Cover with green-tinted coconut (see how to tint coconut on page 124).

← *Old-fashioned goodness—corned beef and cabbage*

Corned beef is a fine choice for entertaining—it offers lots of hearty flavor, little fixing. Cook Irish potatoes, cabbage, and carrots with the meat—they'll take on savory flavor. Jumbo potatoes are a dandy stand-in for posies. Trail greenery among them; add beribboned clay pipes.

Irish favorites –a salute to St. Patrick's day

Let dessert carry out "wearing o' the green." Serve Perfect Apple Pie warm from the oven with clover leaves of cheddar, hot coffee!

Tomato Refresher

Combine 1 No. 2 can (2½ cups) tomato juice, 3 tablespoons lemon juice, 1 teaspoon sugar, ¼ teaspoon celery salt, and 1 teaspoon Worcestershire sauce. Chill.

Stir. Makes five 4-ounce servings.

Cheese Straws

Thoroughly cream ¼ cup butter with ¼ teaspoon Tabasco sauce; blend in ¾ cup shredded sharp process cheese, ⅔ cup sifted flour. Chill 1 hour. On lightly floured surface, roll into 15x6-inch rectangle, ⅛ inch thick. Cut in strips 6x¾ inches. Bake on ungreased baking sheet at 350° 10 to 12 minutes. Serve warm. Makes 20.

Corned-beef Dinner, Irish Style

3 to 4 pounds corned-beef brisket
2 onions, sliced
2 cloves garlic, minced
6 whole cloves
2 bay leaves

• • •

6 small to medium potatoes, pared
6 small carrots, pared

• • •

1 medium head cabbage, cut in 6 wedges

Place corned beef in Dutch oven and barely cover with hot water; add onion, garlic, cloves, and bay leaves. Cover and simmer (*do not boil*) 1 hour *per pound* of meat, or till fork tender. Remove meat from liquid; add potatoes and carrots. Cover; bring to boiling and cook 10 minutes. Then add cabbage wedges; continue cooking 20 minutes longer or till vegetables are done.

To carve corned beef, cut at slight angle across the grain, making thin slices. (See how on page 21.)

Spice Glaze: If you like, glaze the corned beef while vegetables cook. Spread fat side of meat lightly with prepared mustard. Then sprinkle with mixture of ¼ cup brown sugar and ¼ teaspoon ground cloves. Place in shallow pan. Bake in moderate oven (350°) 15 to 20 minutes or till nicely glazed.

Perfect Apple Pie

5 to 7 tart apples
¾ to 1 cup sugar
2 tablespoons enriched flour
1 teaspoon cinnamon
¼ teaspoon nutmeg
Dash salt
1 recipe Plain Pastry, page 19
2 tablespoons butter or margarine

Pare apples and slice thin. Combine sugar, flour, spices, and salt; mix with apples. Fill 9-inch pastry-lined pie plate; dot with butter. Adjust top crust;* sprinkle with sugar for sparkle. Bake in hot oven (400°) 50 minutes or till done.

*A strip of aluminum foil or pie tape around edge of crust will keep juices in pie instead of running over oven; also guards against overbrowning.

Quick Apple Pie: Substitute 2 No. 2 cans (5 cups) sliced pie apples, drained, for tart apples in recipe above.

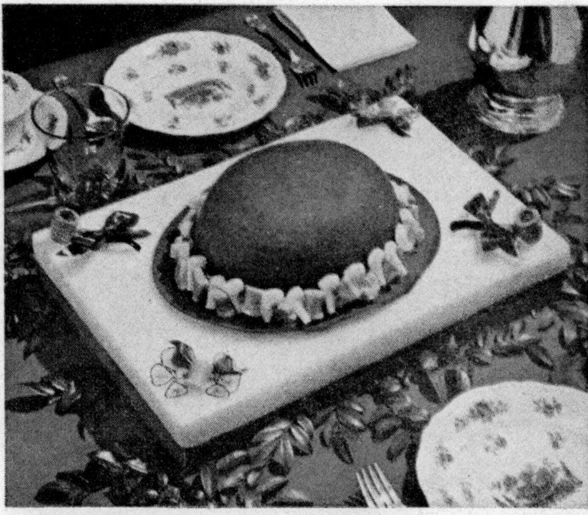

All hats off to Erin—

Simple centerpiece—a green bowler on a plastic-foam "isle." Band is string of candy pipes and harps in saran wrapping. Be-ribboned favors decorate the base.

Emerald Isle Dessert Cups

Perfect refreshment for the bridge club—

1 cup white cream mints
¾ cup milk
Few drops green food coloring
1 cup heavy cream, whipped

• • •

1 7-ounce package solid chocolate-mint candy wafers, *or* 1 6-ounce package (1 cup) semisweet chocolate pieces
2 tablespoons shortening

Make *Mint Ice Cream:* Combine mints and milk. Cook over low heat, stirring frequently, about 15 minutes or till mints are melted. Cool to room temperature. Stir in food coloring; fold in whipped cream. Pour into refrigerator tray and freeze till firm.

Serve in *Chocolate Cups:* Melt chocolate-mint candy wafers or semisweet pieces with shortening over *hot, not boiling*, water, stirring till smooth. Cool to room temperature. Place paper baking cups in muffin pans. With a teaspoon, swirl chocolate mixture around inside cups, covering entire surface with a thin layer of chocolate. Chill.

When chocolate cups harden, tear off paper. Fill with rounded scoops of Mint Ice Cream. Top each dessert with a chocolate-mint wafer. Makes 8 servings.

Note: Another time, use commercial peppermint, vanilla, chocolate, or coffee ice cream in place of the Mint Ice Cream.

Easter

Try springy salads and pretty hams

Crisp salad baskets

To make Combination-salad Baskets (like those served at McDonald's Tea Room), fit two lettuce cups together. Fill with tossed salad. Split green-pepper ring for handle. Top with dressing and crumbled blue cheese.

Trim with "marigolds": Notch carrot slice; top with carrot chunk; spear both on toothpick.

Tips for scoring ham

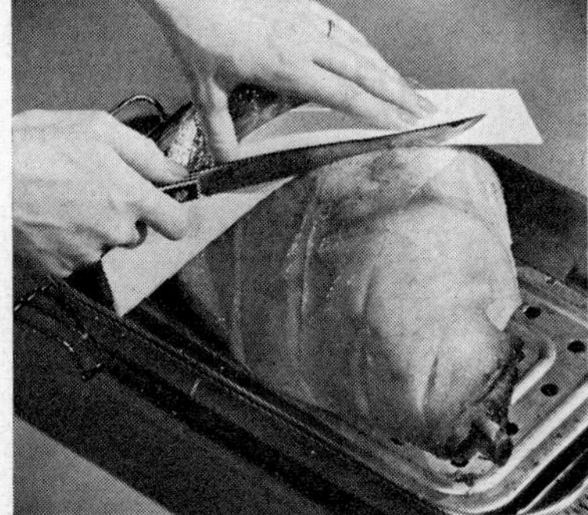

A strip of heavy paper, 12x2 inches, makes it a snap to cut parallel lines when scoring.

Cuts should be only ¼ inch deep. Repeat lines at an angle to make diamonds.

Pour drippings from pan and score ham half an hour before end of baking time. Glaze scored ham and bake 30 minutes more.

Dad—Carving's done!

Ask meatman to slice a canned ham and tie it with heavy cord. (Take shallow baking pan to market for easy carrying.)

Bake ham at 325° about 20 minutes *per pound* for a 6-pound canned ham; 15 minutes *per pound* for larger hams. Last 30 minutes, glaze with marmalade. Place on platter; remove cord.

← *Gala Easter buffet follows the season's tradition*

Easter-egg tree, a symbol of new life, sets the stage! Ham—beautifully glazed and trimmed with a candied-orange daisy—is the star of this dinner. Spring-y accompaniments—frilly leaf-lettuce salad, asparagus with almond topper, Parsleyed New Potatoes. Serve hot rolls, coffee.

Easter dinner that bows to Spring

Fruit-filled Oranges

Slice tops from large oranges. With grapefruit knife or paring knife, remove orange sections. Combine orange sections with banana slices and strawberry halves. Refill orange shells. Pour over chilled ginger ale. Trim with mint sprigs.

Baked Easter Ham

Place whole ham, fat side up, on rack in shallow pan. Insert meat thermometer in center of thickest part, tip not touching fat or bone. Bake in slow oven (325°)—see timetable for baking time and internal temperature for the kind of ham (uncooked or cooked) you've chosen. Half an hour before ham is done, remove from oven and pour fat drippings from pan.

If desired, score ham fat, making cuts only 1/4 inch deep. Spoon orange marmalade over ham. Continue baking about 30 minutes or till well glazed. Allow 1/2 to 3/4 pound uncooked-type ham for each serving or 1/3 pound cooked, ready-to-eat type.

To match picture, page 90, trim ham with *Candied Orange Daisy:* Cut petals from orange peel; cook in hot water 10 minutes. Drain; again cover with hot water; simmer till tender. Cook in syrup of 2 cups sugar and 1 cup water till translucent. Drain. Arrange petals on ham; fasten in place with cloves. Center flower with green gumdrop.

Baked-ham timetable

Set oven at 325°. Times are for chilled hams taken right from refrigerator—

Uncooked (cook-before-eating type)	**Time** (per lb.)	**Time*** (total)
Half ham, 6-8 lbs. 8-lb., for example	25 min.	3 hrs.
10-12-lb. ham 10-lb., for example	18-20 min.	3 1/2 hrs.
12-14-lb. ham 12-lb., for example	16-18 min.	3 3/4 hrs.
14-16 lbs. and over	14-16 min.	3 3/4 hrs.
Round boneless half ham 8-lb., for example	30 min.	4 hrs.
whole ham 10-lb., for example	25 min.	4 hrs.

**Cooking times are approximate only. If you use a meat thermometer, cook ham to an internal temperature of 160°.*

Cooked (fully-cooked type)	**Time** (per lb.)	**Time†** (total)
Half ham, 6-8 lbs. 8-lb., for example	18-24 min.	2 1/2 hrs.
Whole ham, 12-14 lbs. 12-lb., for example	12-15 min.	3 hrs.
Boned, rolled half ham 8-lb., for example	20 min.	2 1/2 hrs.
whole ham 12-14-lb., for example	18 min.	4 hrs.

†Cooking times are approximate only. If you use a meat thermometer, heat to 130°.

Canned	**Time** (per lb.)	**Time** (total)
Small (about 6 lbs.)	20 min.	2 hrs.
Large (8 to 13 lbs.)	15 min.	2-3 1/4 hrs.

Fresh Asparagus with Almonds

Wash stalks of asparagus thoroughly and scrub gently with vegetable brush; if sandy, scrape off scales. To remove woody base, break stalks instead of cutting. Stalk will snap at point where tender part starts.

Fasten asparagus in a bundle—easy with a band of foil. Stand upright in about 1 inch boiling salted water in glass percolator, double boiler, or deep keetle. If needed, crumple extra foil and place in bottom of pan to prop asparagus. Cover. Cook 10 to 15 minutes, or till just tender.

Sprinkle hot buttered asparagus with toasted blanched almond halves.

Asparagus left over? Marinate in French or Italian dressing; serve next day in salad.

EASTER-BEST DINNER

Fruit-filled Oranges
Baked Easter Ham
Parsleyed New Potatoes
Fresh Asparagus with Almonds
Spring Salad   Cloverleaf Rolls
Easter Basket Desserts
Milk   Hot Coffee

Spring Salad Bowl

1 bunch leaf lettuce, torn in bite-size pieces
2 cups tiny spinach leaves
2 tomatoes, cut in wedges
24 carrot curls
4 green onions with tops, chopped
12 pitted ripe olives, sliced
Radish roses (optional)
Italian dressing

Combine greens. Add remaining ingredients. Toss with dressing. Makes 6 servings.

Parsleyed New Potatoes

1½ pounds (about 15 tiny) new potatoes
¼ cup butter or margarine
¼ cup minced parsley
1 tablespoon lemon juice (optional)

Scrub or scrape potatoes. Cook in boiling salted water till just tender, 15 to 20 minutes; drain. Peel if desired. Meanwhile, melt butter in saucepan; stir in parsley and lemon juice. Pour over hot potatoes. Makes 4 to 6 servings.

Cloverleaf Rolls

1 package active dry yeast *or* 1 cake compressed yeast
¼ cup water
1 cup milk, scalded
2 tablespoons shortening
2 tablespoons sugar
1 teaspoon salt
1 egg
3¼ to 3½ cups sifted enriched flour
Melted butter

Soften active dry yeast in *warm* water (110°), compressed yeast in *lukewarm* water (85°). Combine milk, shortening, sugar, salt; cool to lukewarm. Add 1 cup flour; beat well. Add softened yeast and egg; beat well. Gradually stir in the remaining flour to form a soft dough.

Cover with damp cloth and let rise in warm place till double (about 1½ hours). Punch down. Turn out on lightly floured surface. Cover and let rest 10 minutes.

Form 3 balls of dough to fill each greased muffin pan half full. Brush with melted butter. Let rolls rise till almost double, about 30 minutes.

Bake in hot oven (400°) 10 to 12 minutes. Makes about 2 dozen rolls.

Know-how makes you a master carver

Cut a steady base

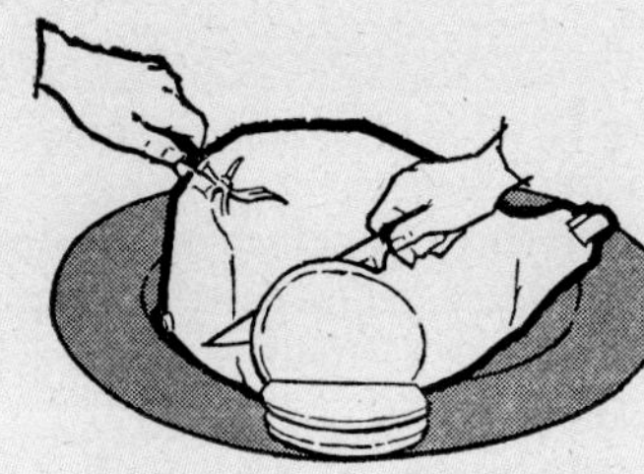

1 Place ham on the platter so shank (smaller end) will be to the carver's right.

For a left ham (the large round side faces away from carver), cut a few slices from the near side.

If ham is a right one (round side toward the carver), slice from far side.

Turn ham up and slice evenly

2 To steady the ham, turn it onto the flat surface you've just cut.

Get a good grip on the ham with carving fork. Then, cut a small wedge, about 6 inches from end of shank. Remove it to platter. Now cut thin slices down to the leg bone, as shown.

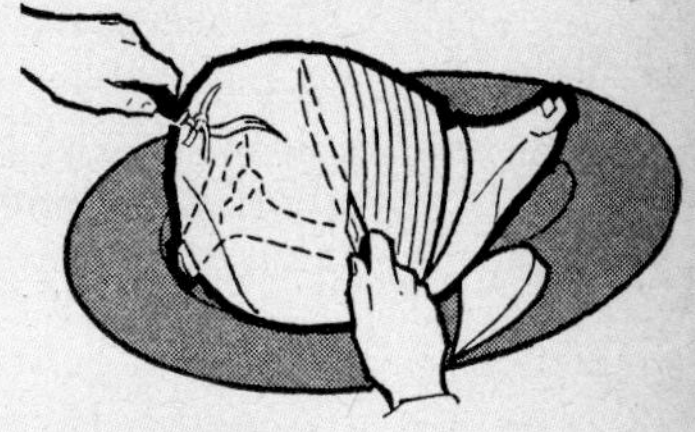

Release the slices

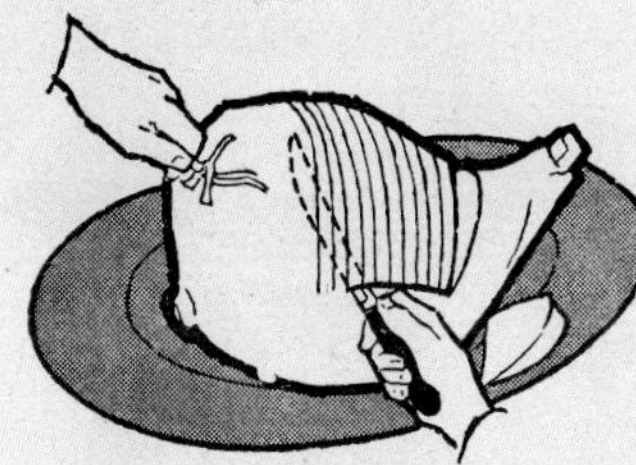

3 When you have a slice for everyone, run knife along leg bone as shown. Slices are released quickly and easily at one fell swoop!

Lift slices to one side of the platter or onto an extra plate and serve.

Turn ham to cut the side slices

4 Time for seconds? Turn ham back to the position shown in first sketch.

Cut slices at right angles to bone, then slide knife along it to free all the pieces at once. These slices are just as tender as the larger ones.

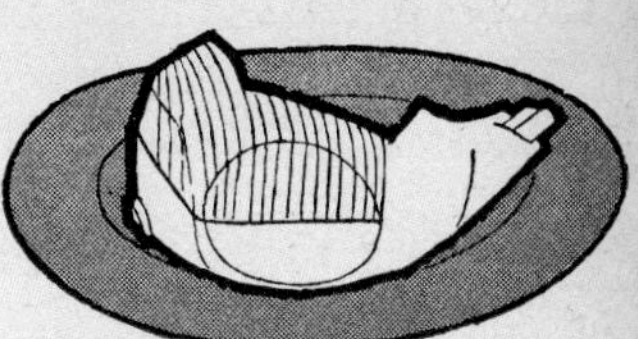

Fresh-as-spring desserts and garnishes

Easter Basket Desserts

Make Meringue Shells; cool. From 1 pint each strawberry, chocolate, and pistachio ice cream, make 15 balls (5 of each flavor), using a small ice cream scoop.

Fill each Meringue Shell with 3 balls of ice cream—one of each flavor. For topping, pass frozen strawberries, thawed, but with a *few ice crystals remaining*. Makes 5 servings.

Meringue Shells: Beat 3 egg whites, 1 teaspoon vanilla, ¼ teaspoon cream of tartar, dash salt till frothy. Gradually add 1 cup sugar, beating till stiff and sugar dissolves.

Cover cooky sheet with plain paper. Using a pastry bag with No. 7 star tube, make 5 large individual shells on the paper. Bake at 275° for 1 hour. Turn off heat and let shells dry in oven (door closed) 1½ hours.

Easter Bonnets

For cooky brims, bake 3-inch Sugar Cookies, using recipe on page 64. Cool.

Drop marshmallows (one per cooky) in hot milk to soften outside. Then roll each in tinted flaked coconut (page 124) to cover sides and *one* end. Don't cover other end of marshmallow—the sticky surface helps it cling to cooky. Place coconut-trimmed marshmallows, sticky side down, in center of the cookies, for crowns.

Hatband and bow are confectioners' sugar icing—tinted if you like. (Add just enough milk to sifted confectioners' sugar to make icing of the consistency to put through a pastry tube.)

Tuck a fresh mint-sprig feather in the hatband before the icing sets.

Show-off meringue shells star ice cream trio, fruit topper

There's little fixing to Easter Basket Desserts. Shells are make-aheads. At last minute, heap with ice cream (scoop balls ahead and freeze).

Jiffy toppers—frozen strawberries or raspberries.

Easter-bonnet cookies —

Start with sugar cookies from our recipe, or use big ones from a package. To change the "frills upon it," vary color of coconut trim and frosting bows, ribbons.

Lemonade Angel Dessert

1 envelope (1 tablespoon) unflavored gelatin
½ cup sugar
Dash salt
2 beaten eggs
½ cup water

• • •

1 6-ounce can frozen lemonade concentrate
1 14½-ounce can evaporated milk, chilled *icy cold* and whipped
1 10-inch tube angel cake

Mix gelatin, sugar, and salt; add eggs and water. Cook and stir till gelatin dissolves; remove from heat. Stir in concentrate. Chill till partially set; fold in whipped milk. Add a few drops yellow food coloring.

Rub brown crumbs off cake; tear cake in bite-size pieces. Cover bottom of a 10-inch tube pan with a thin layer of gelatin mixture. Loosely arrange ⅓ of cake on top. Pour ⅓ of remaining gelatin over. Repeat. Chill till firm. Unmold. Makes 12 servings.

Strawberry Shortcake

2 cups sifted enriched flour
1 tablespoon sugar
3 teaspoons baking powder
½ teaspoon salt
⅓ cup shortening
1 beaten egg
⅔ cup milk

• • •

Soft butter or margarine
3 to 4 cups sugared sliced strawberries
1 cup heavy cream, whipped

Sift together dry ingredients; cut in shortening till mixture is like coarse crumbs. Combine egg and milk; add all at once to dry ingredients, stirring only to moisten.

Turn dough out on floured surface; knead gently for ½ minute. Pat or roll dough to ½ inch. Cut 6 biscuits with floured 2½-inch round or fluted cutter. Bake on ungreased baking sheet in very hot oven (450°) about 10 minutes.

Split shortcakes; butter bottom layers. Fill and top with strawberries and whipped cream. Serve warm.

Rich Shortcake: In above recipe, increase sugar to 2 tablespoons; use ½ cup butter or margarine for the shortening, and light cream in place of the milk.

Perky Platter Trims

Turnip Lily: Cut two *thin* turnip slices; curve to shape flower. Slip in carrot-stick for center. Anchor with toothpicks. Crisp lilies in ice water. Arrange with parsley.

Deviled-egg Flowers: Notch small end of each egg to make petal-like opening. Remove yolks; make deviled filling. Refill whites, using pastry tube. Slice piece off bottom if egg is wobbly. Chill till serving time.

Cranberry Tulips: Using a tulip cooky cutter, stamp out shapes from slices of canned jellied cranberry sauce. Place each cranberry tulip atop a slice of canned pineapple.

For your Easter table—colorful centerpiece you can make

Graduated squares, made of narrow painted slats (joined with brads) can be interlocked as shown, or telescoped or zigzagged.

Paint plastic foam eggs and string on ribbons; fasten to squares. Slide eggs up and down to most interesting position. Arrange flowers where squares join.

Fresh as hyacinths—that's the way you'll find this Easter eye-opener!

Start with a salad of orange sections and strawberries (pass powdered sugar for "dressing"). You may bake the Eggs in Toast Cups, or poach eggs and slide them into their holders as we did. Bacon can cook in the oven or a skillet—your choice. Bunnies hide hot Pink Cereal.

Sunny Easter breakfast

Eggs in Toast Cups

Trim crusts from slices of day-old bread. Brush both sides with melted butter or margarine. Fit each into a custard cup or large muffin-pan cup. Toast in slow oven (325°) 15 minutes. Remove from oven.

Break an egg into each toast cup. Season with salt and pepper and dot with butter. Cover with foil. Return to oven and bake 12 to 15 minutes or till done. With spatula, loosen toast from sides of cups or muffin pans. Serve hot.

Note: Or poach eggs; serve in toast cups.

Toast Blintzes

16 slices enriched sandwich bread
3 tablespoons milk
1 cup drained large-curd cream-style cottage cheese
3 tablespoons melted butter or margarine

• • •

2 cups sweetened sliced strawberries or 2 10-ounce packages frozen strawberries

Cut 3-inch rounds from bread, using a cooky cutter. Brush top edge of all bread rounds with milk. Put 2 tablespoons cottage cheese in center of each of 8 rounds. Place plain round, milk-brushed side down, over cheese; press edges together. Brush tops with butter.

Toast on a baking sheet in hot oven (400°) about 10 minutes or till golden brown. Serve hot with berries to spoon over. Makes 8 Blintzes or 4 servings.

Oven Bacon

Separate slices and place on rack in shallow baking pan. Bake at 400° 10 minutes. There's no need to turn or drain oven bacon.

Pink Cereal

Prepare farina or creamy rice cereal according to package directions. Add few drops red food coloring to tint the white cereal pink. Serve hot, topped with strawberry jam, preserves, or currant jelly.

Jiffy Hot Cross Buns

(*For traditional recipe, see next page*)

1 package active dry yeast *or* 1 cake compressed yeast
¾ cup water
1 egg yolk
2½ cups packaged biscuit mix
⅓ cup currants
2 tablespoons sugar
½ teaspoon cinnamon

• • •

1 slightly beaten egg white
½ teaspoon vanilla
Sifted confectioners' sugar

Soften dry yeast in *warm* water or compressed yeast in *lukewarm* water. Add next 5 ingredients; beat vigorously 2 to 3 minutes. Turn out on surface well-dusted with biscuit mix. Knead till smooth, about 25 strokes. Roll out to ½ inch. Cut with floured 2½-inch biscuit cutter; shape in buns. Place in greased 11x7x1½-inch baking pan. Cover with damp cloth.

Let rise in warm place till almost double, 1 to 1¼ hours. If desired, cut shallow cross in each bun with scissors. Brush tops with slightly beaten egg white. Bake in hot oven (400°) 12 to 15 minutes or till done. Remove to cooling rack.

Add vanilla and confectioners' sugar (about 1 cup) to the remaining egg white. Use this as frosting for piping crosses on warm buns. Makes about 1 dozen.

EASTER BREAKFAST

Morning Salad of Fruit
Eggs in Toast Cups
Oven Bacon
Pink Cereal — Cream
Jiffy Hot Cross Buns
Hot Coffee — Milk

Especially-for-Easter breads

Skillet Warm-up for Buns

To reheat Hot Cross Buns, put 2 tablespoons water in large skillet. Place trivet or wire rack in skillet and lay cold buns or rolls on top. Place over medium heat about 5 minutes. Don't cover skillet—frosting will melt.

Hot Cross Buns—a favorite

These rich rolls of "one-a-penny, two-a-penny" fame came from England along with Mother Goose. We give traditional recipe, above, and quick version (page 31).

Hot Cross Buns

2 packages active dry yeast *or* 2 cakes compressed yeast
⅓ cup water
⅓ cup milk, scalded
½ cup salad oil or melted shortening
⅓ cup sugar
¾ teaspoon salt
3½ to 4 cups sifted enriched flour
½ to 1 teaspoon cinnamon
3 beaten eggs
⅔ cup currants
1 slightly beaten egg white
Sifted confectioners' sugar

Soften active dry yeast in *warm* water or compressed yeast in *lukewarm* water. Combine milk, salad oil, sugar, and salt; cool to lukewarm. Sift together *1 cup of the flour* and the cinnamon; stir into milk mixture. Add eggs; beat well. Stir in softened yeast and currants. Add remaining flour (or a little more or less to make a soft dough). Cover with damp cloth; and let rise in warm place till double (about 1½ hours). Punch down.

Roll or pat out to ½ inch on lightly floured surface. Cut in rounds with 2½-inch biscuit cutter; shape in buns as shown on opposite page. Place on a greased baking sheet about 1½ inches apart. Cover and let rise in warm place till almost double (about 1 hour). If desired, cut shallow cross in each bun with *sharp* scissors or knife. Brush tops with egg white. Bake at 375° about 12 minutes, or till done. Add confectioners' sugar (about ¾ cup) to the remaining egg white. Use this as a frosting for piping crosses on warm buns, as shown. Makes about 2 dozen.

Blueberry Breakfast Bread

Prepare batter from one package blueberry-muffin mix, according to package directions for coffeecake or loaf cake. Pour into a greased 8½-inch round baking dish.

Mix ½ cup sugar, ¼ cup enriched flour; cut in 2 tablespoons butter with pastry-blender till crumbly. Sprinkle over batter.

Bake at 400° 30 minutes or till done. Cut in 6 to 8 wedges. Serve warm with butter.

Easter Braid

1 package active dry yeast *or* 1 cake compressed yeast
¼ cup water
1 cup milk, scalded
½ cup sugar
2 teaspoons salt
½ cup softened butter, margarine, or shortening
4½ to 5 cups sifted enriched flour
2 eggs
2 teaspoons grated lemon peel
¼ teaspoon mace (optional)
1 cup seedless raisins, dark or golden
Sugar Glaze

Soften active dry yeast in *warm* water, compressed yeast in *lukewarm* water. Combine milk, sugar, salt, and butter. Cool to lukewarm. Stir in about 2 cups of the flour; add eggs and mix well. Stir in softened yeast. Add lemon peel, mace, the raisins, and remaining flour to make a soft dough. Let rest 10 minutes.

Knead on lightly floured surface till smooth and elastic. Place in lightly greased bowl, turning once to grease surface. Cover and let rise in warm place till double (about 1½ hours). Punch down; let rise till almost double (about 1 hour). Divide and round dough into 2 balls, one for each loaf. Let rest, covered, 10 minutes.

For each loaf: Divide one ball in fourths. Shape 3 parts into strands 12 inches long, tapering ends. Line up strands 1 inch apart on lightly greased baking sheet. Braid loosely without stretching dough, beginning at middle and working toward either end (see picture, page 35). Seal ends well. Divide remaining dough in thirds. Shape in strands 8 to 9 inches long, tapering ends. Braid loosely and place atop large braid, tucking ends of small braid into large one (see page 35). Cover and let rise till double.

Bake loaves in moderate oven (350°) about 25 to 30 minutes. While warm, spread with Sugar Glaze. Makes 2 loaves.

Sugar Glaze

To 2 cups sifted confectioners' sugar, add ¼ cup hot water and 1 teaspoon butter or margarine; mix till well blended.

Use as is to brush over warm Hopping Bunnies (next page), or thin with a teaspoon or so more water to drizzle over warm Easter Braid.

Know-how for Hot Cross Buns

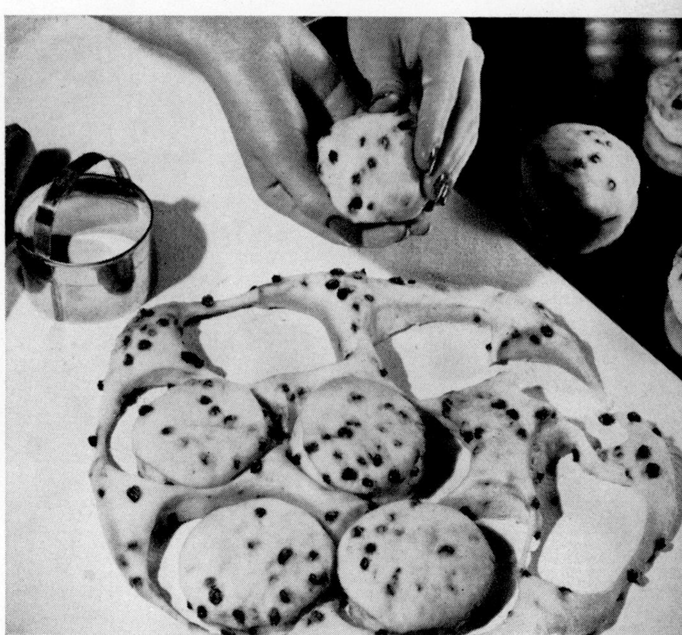

Cut dough with 2½-inch biscuit cutter; shape in buns as shown. Place on greased baking sheet. Cover and let rise. Snip a *shallow* cross in top of each bun. Brush with beaten egg white. Bake.

Let buns cool, then fill crosses with confectioners'-sugar icing. Use pastry tube, or make paper cornucopia: Roll paper into cone, fill, fold top to fasten, and cut off a little of tip on slant.

Give yeast dough a fancy twist —make cute Hopping Bunnies or raisin-filled Easter Braid

Children will be saucer-eyed over these Hopping Bunnies. Just for fun, arrange with candy eggs on nest of coconut, tinted green.

For the grownups, glazed Easter Braid—so good you'll make it all year round! (Recipe, page 33; how to shape, page 35.)

Hopping Bunnies

- 1 package active dry yeast *or* 1 cake compressed yeast
- ¼ cup water
- 1 cup milk, scalded
- ⅓ cup sugar
- ½ cup shortening
- 1 teaspoon salt
- 5 to 5½ cups sifted enriched flour
- 2 beaten eggs
- ¼ cup orange juice
- 2 tablespoons grated orange peel

• • •

- 1 recipe Sugar Glaze, page 33

Soften active dry yeast in *warm* water; compressed yeast in *lukewarm* water. Blend milk, sugar, shortening, and salt. Cool till lukewarm; stir in about *2 cups* of flour; beat well. Add eggs; mix well. Stir in softened yeast. Add orange juice, peel, and remaining flour to make soft dough. Let rest 10 minutes.

Knead dough 5 to 10 minutes on lightly floured surface till smooth and elastic. Place in lightly greased bowl, turning once to grease surface. Cover; let rise in warm place till double (about 2 hours). Punch down; cover and let rest 10 minutes.

To start bunnies, roll dough in rectangle ½ inch thick, on lightly floured surface. Cut dough in strips about ½ inch wide and roll between hands to smooth. Shape in curlicue or twist bunnies as directed at right.

Cover and let rise in warm place till light and nearly double (45 to 60 minutes). Bake at 375° 12 to 15 minutes. Frost while warm with Sugar Glaze. Makes about 2½ dozen.

Twist bunnies: (center of tray in picture): For each, you'll need a 14-inch strip of dough. On lightly greased cooky sheet, lap one end of strip over other to form a loop; now bring end that's underneath up over top end, letting one extend to each side for ears. Pat tips of ears to shape in point.

Roll small ball of dough for tail; place atop dough at bottom of loop. Let bunnies almost double before you put them in oven.

Curlicue bunnies: (other bunnies in picture): For each, you'll need a 10-inch strip of dough for body and a 5-inch strip for head. On lightly greased cooky sheet, make a loose swirl of the body strip. Swirl strip for head and place close to body (they'll "grow" together as dough rises).

For ears, pinch off 1½-inch strips and roll between hands till smooth and cigar-shaped. Let point make tip of ear; snip off opposite end and place ear next to head. Pinch off a bit of dough and roll in ball for tail. Let bunnies almost double; bake.

Pineapple Turnover Biscuits

Combine ½ cup crushed pineapple, drained, ¼ cup brown sugar, 2 tablespoons butter, melted, and ½ teaspoon cinnamon; divide in 10 muffin cups; center each with a California walnut half. Add 1 teaspoon pineapple syrup to each cup; top with a refrigerated biscuit (takes 1 package biscuits).

Bake at 425° 12 to 15 minutes. Invert pan immediately on serving plate. Cool 1 minute before removing from pan.

For Hopping Bunnies, measure off strips of dough, shape in bunny figures, as directed in recipe. Add balls for tails. Let rise.

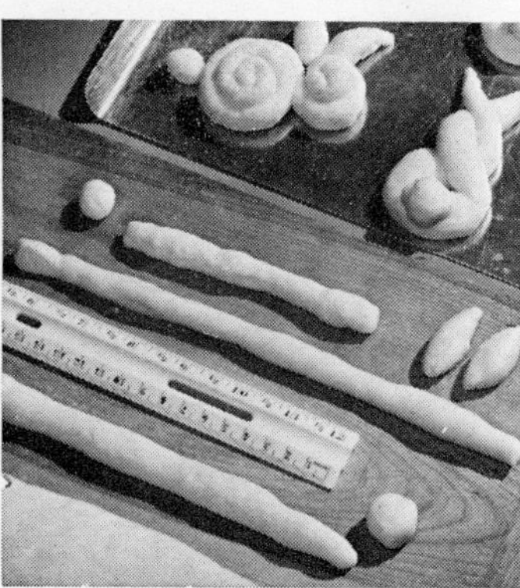

For Easter Braid, you make two braids —the bottom one larger than the top. Chef's tip: Braid from the center toward each end for professional look.

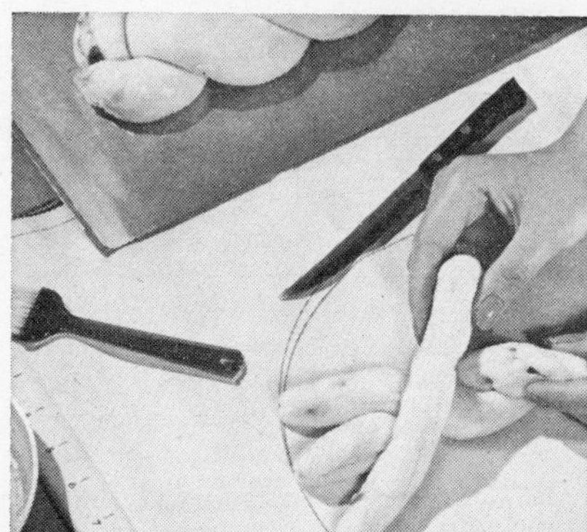

Seal ends of each braid by pinching firmly. Place small braid atop big one, tucking ends of top braid into braid below. Cover, let rise.

Easter eggs—

Party dress for your Easter table—bright colored eggs, shell shadow boxes, handsome favors

Eggs with a touch of elegance—

Dainty shadow boxes make lovely pendants (see how-to at right). Hang several on graceful branch for "tree."

For impressive favors, tint plastic-foam eggs. Trim with gold lace, tiny artificial flowers, cake decorations, decals, or "jewels." Stand on ribbon wheels or boxes.

Choose well-shaped eggs—dye them blown, hard-cooked, or out-of-shell

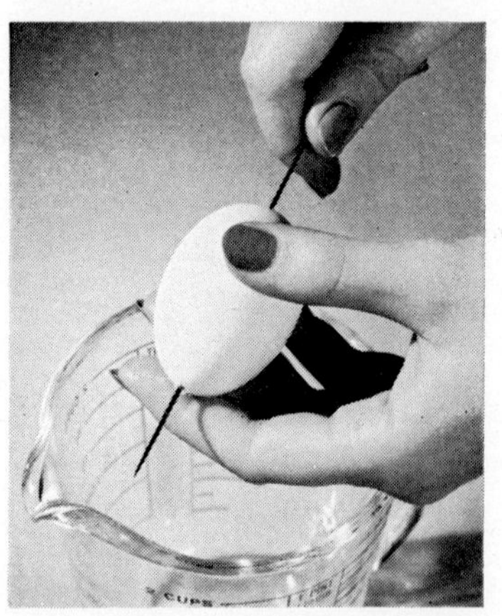

Blown eggshells—First wash egg. Make small hole at both ends with pin or tiny skewer; enlarge the holes slightly. Run pin through center of egg to break yolk.

Hold egg over bowl; blow gently in one hole. Rinse empty shell in cold water; let dry thoroughly. For even color: Just before dyeing, rinse in hot water and dry.

Hard-cooked, solid-color eggs—Wash eggs (white color's best). Cover with water; cook 15 minutes just below simmering. Cool quickly in cold water; dry.

Prepare dye solutions according to package directions.

While still warm, immerse eggs in coloring till dyed. Dry on rack. Polish with wax or oil.

Colored, out-of-shell eggs—pretty salad garnish! Dissolve 1 envelope summer-drink powder in 1 cup water. Add peeled hard-cooked eggs; let stand till tinted desired color. Dry on rack.

Or use pickled beet juice for pink color. Add shelled eggs; cover; chill 2 hours.

fun and fancy

Shadow Boxes

Make blown eggshells as shown at left—skip the dyeing for now. Draw an oval on side of shell; pierce center of penciled oval with skewer or large pin. Using manicure or other sharp, small scissors, cut in curve from center to pencil line and cut around it.

Now, if you want a colored ornament, dye according to directions for blown eggs. Dry.

To preserve shell, coat the inside with clear nail polish. Let dry.

Planning to hang your shadow box? Knot ends of gold cord; pull loop through tiny cardboard disk, then through hole at top of egg from inside. Or, omit cord loop; stand egg on colored posterboard collar.

Now you're ready for decorating. Glue center of gold paper doily inside egg for background. Use a toothpick to paste gold braid around edge of opening.

Pour few drops melted paraffin into bottom of egg; stick in tiny figurine and artificial flowers. Hide wax with cotton.

Glue edge of gold doily around braid. Top with row of plastic pearls (available by the yard). Glue sequins, small beads to outside.

Easter Tree

Select a graceful branch with several twisting finger-twigs. Clip branch to shape. Nail it from below to a board, or secure to a needlepoint holder—make sure the highest tip points straight up from center.

Paint branch and hang dyed blown eggs or Shadow Boxes from twigs. Place flowers in low dish at base—conceal dish with foliage. (See picture, page 24.)

Egg Treasures

Children will be all agog over these surprise eggs from the Easter bunny.

Dye blown eggshells according to directions on opposite page. Dry. Enlarge one hole to about ½-inch diameter. Fill each egg with tiny candies. Cover hole with gummed Easter label. Hide eggs, or nest in Easter grass at each place for favors.

Eggs—after Easter!

If you plan to eat those hard-cooked Easter eggs, refrigerate them till hunt time and again right afterward.

Eggs a la King: To 2 cups medium white sauce, add 6 sliced hard-cooked eggs, one 3-ounce can (⅔ cup) broiled sliced mushrooms, drained, and 2 tablespoons catsup. Heat. Pour over hot buttered toast; top with thick broiled tomato slices. Makes 6 servings.

Egg Sandwiches: Chop hard-cooked eggs and stuffed green olives; mix with salad dressing. Spread on rye bread; add lettuce.

Quick Salad: Arrange egg slices and chilled cooked asparagus spears on lettuce. Top with pimiento strips. Pass French dressing.

Chef's Bowl: Make deviled eggs—your favorite recipe. Arrange in lettuce-lined bowl with ham and cheese strips, chilled cooked peas, and radishes. Pass garlic dressing.

Gay setting for Easter brunch table

Hard-cooked eggs in vibrant colors, atop a black lacquer board, make a striking decoration. Matching eggs go in "nests" at each place. (For colors of this intensity, use India inks.) Added drama—a repeat of black in place mats. Painted wooden birds add a note of whimsey to the setting.

Halloween

Droll Outer-space Man will make spirits rise—

When jack-o'-lantern time rolls around, conjure up your own designs or try one of these. For this man from Mars, cut V-shaped lid off pumpkin; scoop out seeds. Continue line to form V-shaped eyes, as shown. Place big ripe olives where eyes meet. Cut nose with potato parer.

Cut mouth; poke in twisted-macaroni teeth. Ears are carrots, halved lengthwise, fastened with toothpicks. Curly carrot tops make hair.

Start with butternut squash for Slap-happy Sam

There's no reason to use a pumpkin every time! Pick a squash and fashion this jolly comic. First cut opening in back of squash—top stays intact. Scoop out. With apple corer, carve eyes and teeth (easy if you sketch features on first). Finish eyes, mouth with paring knife. For tongue, anchor half a large radish in mouth with toothpick.

Cut nose and push piece out slightly at bottom; secure with toothpicks. Make strands of hair with carrot tops or fluffs of parsley. For jaunty hat: Cut a hole in paper coaster and push over stem. Glue an upside-down nut cup atop to form the crown.

Daffy Devil has carrot horns, eyebrows of celery

Light a candle inside this pumpkin-head and set in window to greet little "tricksters," or use it to keynote a Fall buffet.

Choose a tall pumpkin. Cut the lid V-shape with the point in front. (Slant knife inward so lid will be smaller at bottom and won't fall in pumpkin.) Remove contents. Cut triangular features as shown. From the eye cutouts, carve flat triangles and pivot slightly in openings so they project for eyelids; secure with toothpicks.

Cut mouth; attach mouth piece with pins or toothpicks to form lower lip. Attach small leafy celery stalks for eyebrows. Toothpick big carrots in place for horns (slant ends to fit against pumpkin).

Saucer-eyed Goblin Girl will invite smiles

Try a jack-o'-lantern lass for once! You'll need a round pumpkin with a long stem. Draw zigzag line around top for the hair; cut along line and remove lid. Scoop out contents.

Make eyes with apple corer. Carve out mouth with paring knife. Poke toothpicks into the radish nose from inside pumpkin. Gently press in upper edge of pumpkin—the "Italian haircut" will stand out when lid's in place. Now tie a wide-ribbon bow on stem.

←*Spicy specials that "taste like Fall"—*

Here are new and old-fashioned favorites aplenty! Tiptop in picture are Sugared Nuts for nibbling; Gingerbread Boys on crisp apples make party favors or treats for doorbell ringers; cinnamon doughnuts (and holes!) are wonderful with Hot Mulled Cider. When it's dessert time, cut warm Gingerbread squares or wedges of Spice Layer Cake.

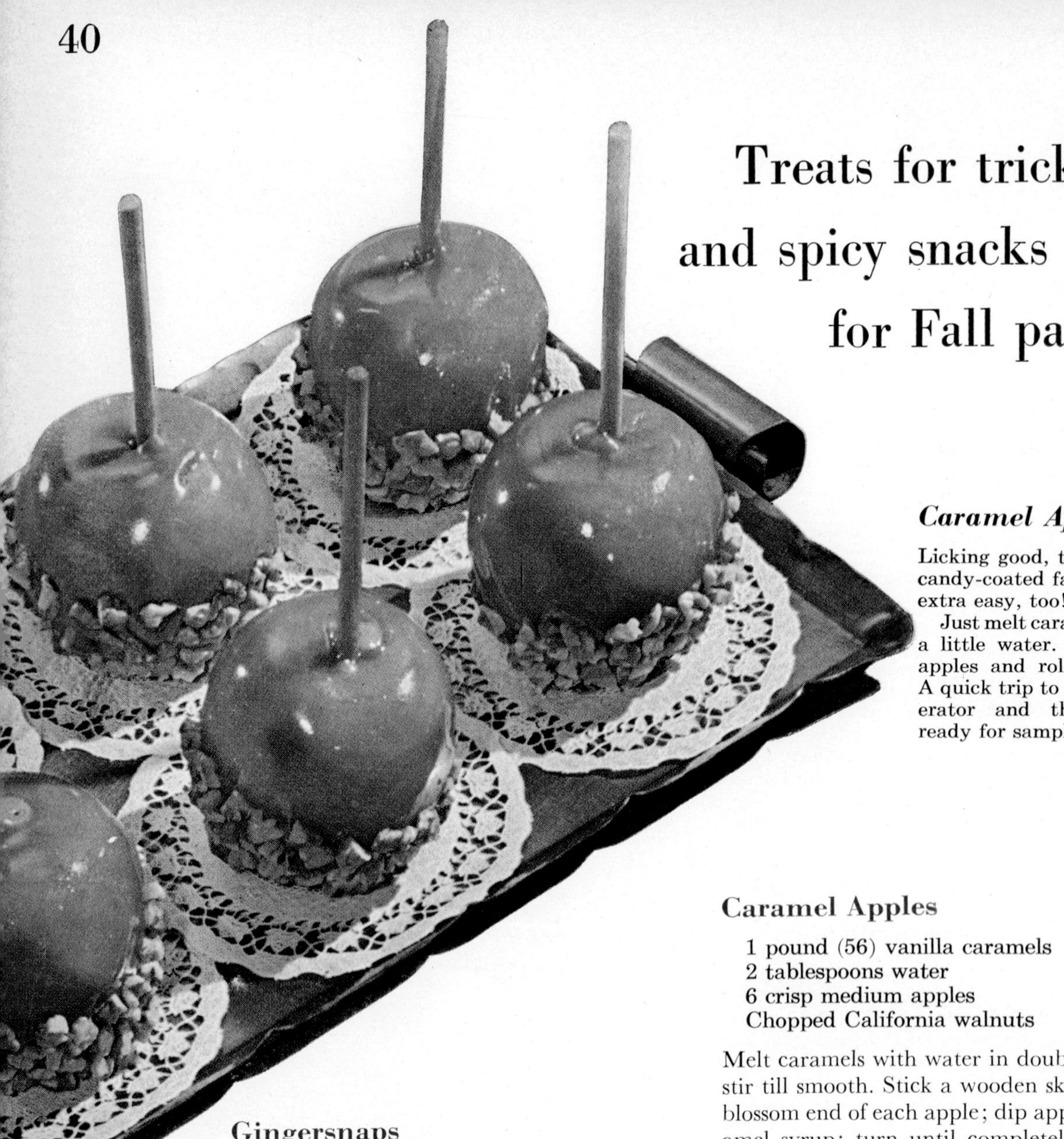

Treats for tricks and spicy snacks for Fall parties

Caramel Apples—

Licking good, these crisp candy-coated favorites—extra easy, too!

Just melt caramels with a little water. Then dip apples and roll in nuts. A quick trip to the refrigerator and they're all ready for sampling!

Caramel Apples

1 pound (56) vanilla caramels
2 tablespoons water
6 crisp medium apples
Chopped California walnuts

Melt caramels with water in double boiler; stir till smooth. Stick a wooden skewer into blossom end of each apple; dip apple in caramel syrup; turn until completely coated. (If syrup is too stiff, add few drops water.) At once roll bottom half of each apple in chopped nuts. Set on cooky sheet covered with waxed paper. Chill till coating's firm.

Gingersnaps

¾ cup shortening
1 cup brown sugar
¼ cup molasses
1 egg
2¼ cups sifted enriched flour
2 teaspoons soda
½ teaspoon salt
1 teaspoon ginger
1 teaspoon cinnamon
½ teaspoon ground cloves

Cream together shortening, brown sugar, molasses, and egg till light and fluffy. Sift together dry ingredients; stir into molasses mixture till blended. Form in small balls. Roll in granulated sugar and place 2 inches apart on greased cooky sheet. Bake in moderate oven (375°) about 10 minutes. Cool slightly; remove from pan. Makes 5 dozen.

Hot Mulled Cider

½ cup brown sugar
¼ teaspoon salt
2 quarts cider
1 teaspoon whole allspice
1 teaspoon whole cloves
3 inches stick cinnamon

Combine brown sugar, salt, and cider. Tie spices in small piece of cheesecloth; add. Slowly bring to boiling; simmer, covered, 20 minutes. Remove spices. Serve hot. Float clove-studded orange slices atop. Serves 10.

Gingerbread Boys

1 cup shortening
1 cup sugar
½ teaspoon salt
1 egg
1 cup molasses
2 tablespoons vinegar

• • •

5 cups sifted enriched flour
1½ teaspoons soda
1 tablespoon ginger
1 teaspoon cinnamon
1 teaspoon ground cloves

Thoroughly cream shortening, sugar, and salt. Stir in egg, molasses, and vinegar; beat well. Sift together dry ingredients; stir into molasses mixture. Chill (about 3 hours).

On lightly floured surface, roll to ⅛ inch. Cut with gingerbread-boy cutter (or draw your own pattern). Place 1 inch apart on greased cooky sheet. Use red hots for faces and buttons.

Bake in moderate oven (375°) about 6 minutes. Cool slightly; remove from cooky sheet. When thoroughly cool, use confectioners'-sugar frosting to pipe on trims.

To make cookies stand up, fasten each on skewer with cellophane tape and stick end into plump red apple.

Makes about 8 dozen.

Gingerbread

½ cup shortening
½ cup sugar
1 egg
½ cup light molasses

• • •

1½ cups sifted enriched flour
¾ teaspoon salt
¾ teaspoon soda
½ teaspoon ginger
½ teaspoon cinnamon
½ cup boiling water

Stir the shortening to soften. Gradually add sugar, creaming till light and fluffy. Add egg and molasses; beat thoroughly. Sift together the dry ingredients; add to molasses mixture alternately with boiling water, beating after each addition until smooth.

Bake in greased 8x8x2-inch pan in moderate oven (350°) about 45 minutes. Serve warm. Cut in squares and top with whipped cream and a pear half, if desired. For pink blush on pear, sprinkle with red sugar.

Sugared Nuts

Add 2 tablespoons cold water to 1 slightly beaten egg white. Stir in ½ cup sugar, ½ teaspoon salt, and ¼ teaspoon *each* cinnamon, ground cloves, and allspice. Mix well.

Add 1 cup California walnut halves and 1 cup blanched whole almonds; stir to coat. Place nuts, flat side down, on greased cooky sheet. Bake at 250° about 1 hour. Cool.

Spice Layer Cake

¾ cup shortening
2¼ cups sifted cake flour
1 cup granulated sugar
1 teaspoon baking powder
1 teaspoon salt
¾ teaspoon soda
¾ to 1 teaspoon cinnamon
¾ to 1 teaspoon cloves
¾ cup brown sugar
1 cup buttermilk
3 eggs

Stir shortening just to soften. Sift in flour, granulated sugar, baking powder, salt, soda, and spices. Add brown sugar and buttermilk. Mix till all flour is dampened. Then beat vigorously 2 minutes. Add eggs and beat 2 minutes longer. Bake in 2 paper-lined 9x1½-inch round pans at 350° 30 to 35 minutes. Cool. Frost with Brown-sugar Frosting.

Brown-sugar Frosting

2 egg whites
¾ cup granulated sugar
¾ cup brown sugar
1½ teaspoons corn syrup *or*
¼ teaspoon cream of tartar
⅓ cup cold water
Dash salt
1 teaspoon vanilla
½ cup chopped pitted dates
½ cup broken California walnuts

Place first 6 ingredients in top of double boiler. Beat 1 minute with electric mixer or rotary beater. Place over boiling water; beat constantly till mixture forms peaks, *about* 7 minutes (*don't overcook*). Remove from boiling water. Add vanilla; beat till of spreading consistency, about 2 minutes. Add dates and nuts to about 1 cup of frosting; fill between layers of cooled Spice Layer Cake. Swirl remaining frosting on cake. Press broken walnuts on sides, if desired.

Halloween funny faces for spooky parties

Lollipop Clowns

3 cups sugar
¾ cup light corn syrup
3 tablespoons vinegar
⅓ cup boiling water
¼ cup butter or margarine
Dash salt
Wooden skewers
Fruit-flavored hard-candy circles

Combine sugar, corn syrup, vinegar, water; stir till sugar dissolves. Cook to hard-crack stage (300°). Remove from heat; add butter and salt. Cool until mixture thickens slightly. Quickly drop from tablespoon over skewers placed 5 inches apart on greased cooky sheet to form 3-inch lollipops. Make faces with the candy circles. Makes about 16.

Jolly Owls are popcorn balls

Popcorn Owls don't give a hoot if you eat them. Their eyes are fruit-flavored hard-candy circles and ends cut from black jelly strings. Owls' characteristic V markings are jelly-string strips; wings, candy orange slices.

To make stands for owls (or Spooky Cats), cut tops off paper cups; invert.

Goblin Frosties hold sherbet →

These happy pumpkin heads are orange cups. Scoop out the fruit and fill shells with lime sherbet (or pumpkin ice cream).

Stick in eyes of licorice drops held with toothpicks. Give each goblin a nose and mouth of whole cloves. Deck the jaunty hats with bright maraschino-cherry topknots.

← *Lollipop Clowns in apples*

The youngsters will get in some good licks on these! Make faces of fruit- or mint-flavored hard-candy circles. Dress them up with perky bow ties made of paper ribbons.

Stick lollipops in crisp apples—a double treat! Serve with mugs of cold milk and sugared spiced doughnuts warmed in the oven.

Popcorn Owls or Spooky Cats

5 quarts hot popped corn
2 cups sugar
1½ cups water
½ teaspoon salt
½ cup light corn syrup
1 teaspoon vinegar

Keep popped corn hot in slow oven (325°). Butter sides of saucepan. In it combine remaining ingredients; cook to hard-ball stage (250°). Pour slowly over popped corn, mixing well. Form in Owls *or* Spooky Cats.

Popcorn Owls: Form a little more than half the popcorn mixture into 5 balls for bodies of owls; remainder in slightly smaller balls for heads (butter hands if necessary).

Press heads on bodies while popcorn is warm. For wings, cut candy orange slices in half lengthwise; press 2 pieces in place on body. (If needed, use toothpicks.) Cut licorice jelly strings in fourths lengthwise; use 2 strips to make a chevron on each head. Make eyes of orange-flavored hard-candy circles centered with ends cut from jelly strings. Makes 5 Popcorn Owls.

Spooky Cats: Form popcorn in 10 balls. For ears, cut candy orange slices in half lengthwise; split each half crosswise and press pieces in place on balls. For bow ties, press 2 candy orange slices at base of each. Make eyes and nose of licorice jelly beans. Use colored toothpicks for whiskers.

Goblin Frosties

4 medium oranges
7 licorice candy drops
Whole cloves
1 to 1½ quarts lime sherbet
4 maraschino cherries with stems

With a sharp knife, cut off thin slice of peel from one end of each orange to make it stand firmly. For hat, cut off thick slice, about ¼ to ⅓ way down from top. With spoon, scoop out pulp and white membrane from rest of orange (save to use in fruit cup or salad). Use licorice drops for the eyes, whole cloves for nose and mouth.

Fill orange shells with sherbet, mounding it above rim. Place hats atop sherbet at jaunty angle. With toothpick, stick maraschino cherry in hat; anchor end of toothpick in sherbet. Place in freezing compartment of refrigerator or in freezer till serving time. Makes 4.

Little Ghosties

Make spice cupcakes, using mix or your favorite recipe. Frost tops and sides with Snowy 7-minute Frosting (page 112).

Press on eyes and nose of fruit-flavored hard-candy circles. For mouths, cut licorice jelly strings in half; curve in a smile.

Peanut Punkins

½ cup chunk-style peanut butter
⅓ cup shortening
¾ cup sugar
1 egg
2 tablespoons milk
1½ cups sifted enriched flour
1 teaspoon soda
½ teaspoon salt

Cream together peanut butter, shortening; gradually add sugar; mix thoroughly; beat in egg and milk. Sift together flour, soda, and salt; add to creamed mixture. Shape in balls, using rounded teaspoon of dough for each. Flatten on ungreased baking sheet. Bake at 375° 10 to 12 minutes. Cool.

Add enough milk to 1 cup sifted confectioners' sugar to make of spreading consistency. Tint orange with a little red and yellow food coloring; spread on *flat* sides of 2 cookies; sandwich together. Make faces with semisweet chocolate pieces. Stick peanut half in top for stem. Makes about 18.

Thanksgiving

Pretty trimmings of the season—

Golden touch for turkey

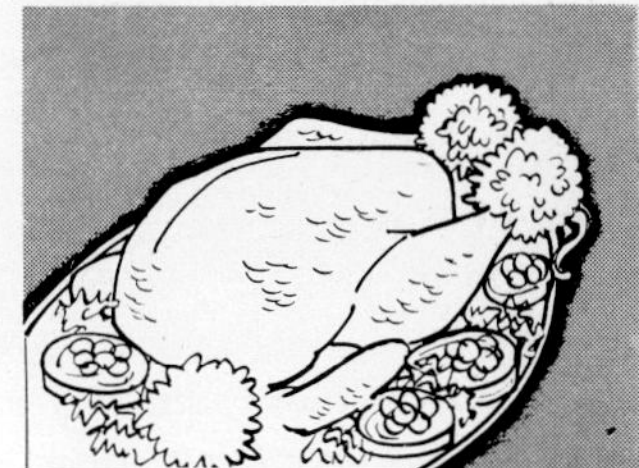

Fluffy yellow chrysanthemums make the turkey drumsticks festive. (Snip some from your living-room bouquet!)

Platter garnish—one more flower plus pineapple rings topped with small bunches of sugared green grapes.

Colorful accent—crab apples

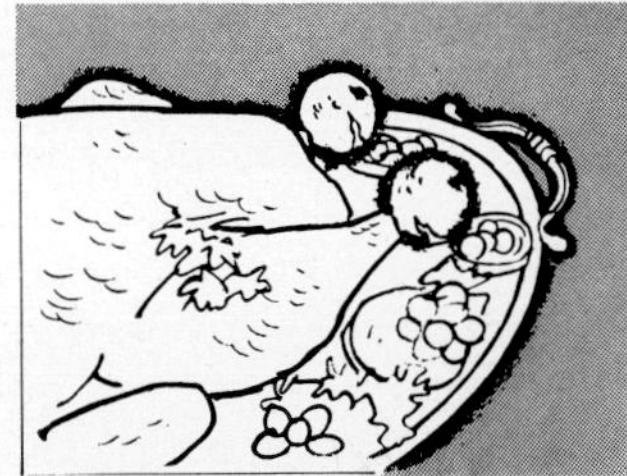

Remove cores from stem end of spiced crab apples; poke on ends of drumsticks. Or, anchor fluffs of parsley to drumsticks.

Quick platter trim—rounds of jellied cranberry sauce, topped with pineapple rings, split and twisted in S-shape.

Pumpkin-pie cornucopias . . .

Cut slice of American process cheese in half on diagonal; roll each piece on long side. Anchor cornucopias with whole cloves. Arrange in pinwheel shape in center of pie (one per piece).

. . . or whipped-cream "daisy"

Each snowy petal takes 1 large spoonful of whipped cream. To make petal, turn spoon sideways and flip oval island of whipped cream onto pumpkin pie. Form five or six petals—one for each serving.

For spicy flavor accent, dice candied ginger and sprinkle over daisy.

← *Set for holiday feasting—turkey's on the table!*

While Dad carves the turkey and spoons out fragrant stuffing, Mother serves buttery mashed potatoes, passes Giblet Gravy and Cranberry Sauce. Harvest vegetables, crisp fruit salad, and Pumpkin Pie are "trimmings." Small family? Have an 8-pounder—or drumsticks around.

For Thanksgiving–poultry favorites

Foil-wrapped Roast Turkey

Truss and wrap: Tie drumsticks to tail. Press wings to body so tips are flat against sides of breast. Use heavy foil (the thin tears too easily). Place turkey, breast up, in center of foil. (Foil should be wide enough to extend 5 to 6 inches beyond leg and breast ends of bird; if it isn't, join 2 pieces together with drugstore or lock fold, pressing to make leakproof joining.) Bring one end of foil snugly over top of turkey; bring opposite end up, lapping over first (overlap should be 2 to 3 inches). Now fold foil down snugly at breast and legs; press remaining two sides of foil up (foil should come high enough to prevent drippings from running into pan, burning).

To roast: Place foil-wrapped bird, breast up, in bottom of shallow pan (broiler pan is convenient)—do not use rack. Roast at constant, *high temperature*. See chart.

When turkey has cooked to within *15 to 20 minutes of total cooking time* given in the foil-wrapped-turkey roasting chart, *remove from oven*. Quickly slit foil with scissors or knife and fold away from bird to edge of pan. (If you use a meat thermometer, insert it in center of inside thigh muscle adjoining cavity.) Return turkey to oven. Continue roasting till turkey is tender (tests done in usual ways, or meat thermometer registers 190°). When turkey's done, lift from foil to warm platter. Make gravy from drippings.

THANKSGIVING TURKEY DINNER

Hot Tomato Starter
Roast Turkey   Herb Stuffing
Cranberry Sauce
Orange-glazed Sweet Potatoes
Buttered Green Beans
Apple-Pineapple Slaw
Hot Biscuits   Butter
Pumpkin Pie   Hot Coffee

Roast Stuffed Turkey

Stuff and truss: Stuff turkey just before roasting. Allow ¾ to 1 cup stuffing per pound ready-to-cook weight. Stuff wishbone cavity and skewer neck skin to back. Tuck wing tips behind shoulder joints. Rub large cavity with salt. Spoon in stuffing. Shake bird to settle stuffing; do not pack. Close opening by placing skewers across it and lacing shut with cord. Tie drumsticks securely to tail. (If opening has band of skin across, push the drumsticks underneath, and you won't need to fasten opening or tie legs.)

Grease skin thoroughly. If you use a meat thermometer, insert it in the center of the inside thigh muscle adjoining the cavity.

To roast: Place bird breast up on rack (but breast down on a V-rack) in shallow pan; leave in this position for entire roasting time. Cover with loose "cap" of foil—press it lightly at drumstick and breast ends, but *avoid having it touch top or sides*. Roast at constant *low temperature*. See chart.

When turkey is about two-thirds done according to turkey roasting chart, cut the cord or band of skin so heat can reach inside of thighs.

Doneness tests: About 20 minutes before roasting time is up, test doneness by pressing thick part of drumstick between fingers (protect hand with paper towel). Meat should feel very soft. Also move drumstick up and down; it should move easily or twist out of joint. (If you use a meat thermometer, it should register 195°.) When turkey is done, remove from pan and keep warm while you make gravy from drippings (simmer drippings first to concentrate). Let turkey stand 20 minutes before carving for neater slices.

Frozen Stuffed Turkey

These birds weigh 5 to 20 pounds and are already stuffed for your convenience.

Unwrap and roast the turkey. (And stew the giblets.) *Keep turkey frozen* till ready to cook it—however turkey may be transferred from freezer to refrigerator night before cooking; this cuts roasting time about 1 hour. *Follow directions that come with bird.*

Turkey roasting timetable

Set oven at 325°. Times are for chilled turkey stuffed just before roasting—

Ready-to-cook weight (before stuffing)	*Time* (total)*
6 to 8 lbs.	3½ to 4 hrs.
8 to 12 lbs.	4 to 4½ hrs.
12 to 16 lbs.	4½ to 5½ hrs.
16 to 20 lbs.	5½ to 7 hrs.
20 to 24 lbs.	7 to 8½ hrs.

Foil-wrapped-tu[illegible] roasting timetable

Set oven at 450°. Times are for unstuffed chilled turkeys. For stuffed turkey, add 30 to 45 minutes to total roasting time.

Ready-to-cook weight (before stuffing)	*Time* (total)*
8 to 10 lbs.	2¼ to 2½ hrs.
10 to 12 lbs.	2¾ to 3 hrs.
14 to 16 lbs.	3 to 3¼ hrs.
18 to 20 lbs.	3¼ to 3½ hrs.
22 to 24 lbs.	3¼ to 3¾ hrs.

**Cooking times are approximate only. Meat thermometer should register 195° (for Foil-wrapped Roast Turkey, 190°).*

Frozen Turkey (*unstuffed*)

Thaw frozen unstuffed turkey in original wrapping just before time to cook. In refrigerator (at 40°), a 4- to 12-pound turkey will thaw in 1 to 2 days; a 12- to 20-pound bird in 2 to 3 days; and a 20- to 24-pound bird in 3 to 4 days. After thawing, follow recipe for roast or foil-wrapped turkey.

Note: To speed up thawing, you can place wrapped turkey under cold running water. See label directions that come with turkey.

Herb Stuffing

3 quarts slightly dry bread cubes
1½ teaspoons ground sage
1½ teaspoons thyme
1½ teaspoons rosemary
1½ teaspoons salt
⅓ cup chopped parsley
⅓ cup finely chopped onion
⅓ cup butter or margarine, melted
1 cup canned chicken broth*

Combine bread, seasonings, parsley, onion, and butter. Add broth and toss lightly to mix. Makes 8 cups, or enough stuffing for a 10-pound turkey.

*Or, you can use 2 chicken-bouillon cubes dissolved in 1 cup hot water.

Oven-fried Turkey

Cut in pieces one 3½- to 6-pound (ready-to-cook weight) fryer-roaster turkey. Sprinkle pieces with salt, pepper. Melt 1¼ cups butter; dip turkey pieces in butter; roll in 2 cups crushed packaged herb-stuffing. Place skin-side up in jelly-roll pan. Drizzle half of remaining butter over turkey; sprinkle with rest of crumbs. Bake at 350° about 1 hour and 40 minutes. After 1 hour of baking, drizzle with remaining butter. Serves 4 to 7.

Carve with sharp knife and showmanship

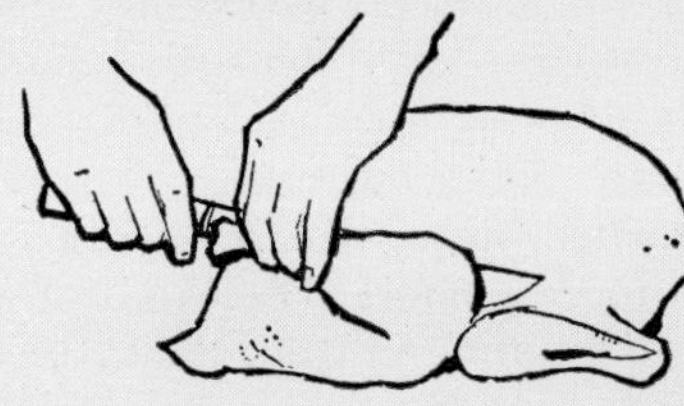

1 Place the turkey with legs to your right. First, carve the side toward your audience. Hold the drumstick with your fingers. Then cut through joint that joins the leg to the backbone.

2 Hold leg on plate. Cut joint to separate the drumstick and thigh. Slice drumstick as shown, turning for slices that are even. Carve thigh in slices parallel to the bone.

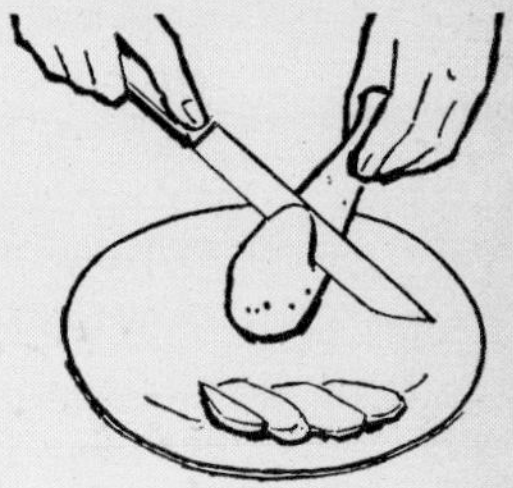

3 To carve the white meat, first make a deep cut into the breast to body frame, parallel to and as close to the wing as possible. Anchor the turkey with a fork. (A sturdy fork and big platter are musts.)

4 Starting halfway up the breast, thinly slice the white meat down to the cut made at wing level.

Spoon the stuffing from opening in turkey where the leg was removed.

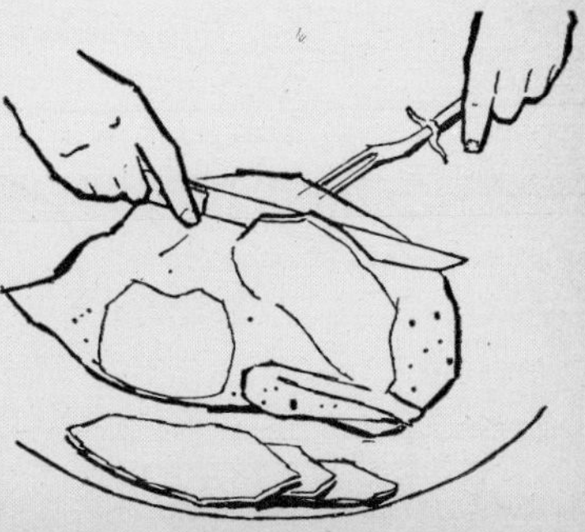

CHICKEN-DINNER SPECIAL

Cups of Hot Oyster Stew
Roast Chicken — Giblet Gravy
Creamed Onions — Green Peas
Cranberry Ring — Corn Bread
Country-kitchen Mince Pie
Hot Coffee

Roast Chicken

Select 3- to 4-pound ready-to-cook broiler-fryer. Wash outside with cold water; wipe inside with damp cloth; dry thoroughly.

Stuff loosely with 3 cups stuffing. Skewer opening shut; lace with cord. Fold neck skin over back; fasten with skewer. Fold wings across back; tie together with cord. Tie drumsticks to tail or push under strip of skin, if present. Place breast up on rack in shallow pan (or breast down, if using V-rack). Brush with melted butter. Roast uncovered at 400° 1¾ to 2½ hours. (For unstuffed bird, cut 15 to 20 minutes from total roasting time.)

When bird is about ⅔ done, cut string, or strip of skin, between drumsticks and tail. If roasted breast down, turn breast up to brown. Baste occasionally with drippings.

Roast till drumstick will move up and down easily. Let stand few minutes; carve.

Roast Rock Cornish Game Hens

4 1-pound ready-to-cook Rock Cornish game hens
Salt and pepper
⅓ cup melted butter or margarine
• • •
¼ cup canned condensed consomme
¼ cup light corn syrup

Season the hens inside and out with salt and pepper. Stuff each with ¼ cup stuffing, if desired. Place, breast side up, on rack in shallow pan and brush well with melted butter.

Roast uncovered in a hot oven (400°) about 45 minutes, or till tender. During the last 15 minutes of baking time, baste several times with mixture of consomme and syrup. Makes 4 servings. Serve on platter with Browned Rice or Mushroom Wild Rice.

Giblet Gravy

In covered pan, simmer (don't boil) giblets till tender in lightly salted water to cover—add a few celery leaves and onion slices to the water. Let giblets cool in broth; chop.

Turkey heart and gizzard take 2 to 2½ hours; turkey liver, 30 minutes. Simmer heart and gizzard of *broiler-fryer chicken* 1 to 1½ hours; liver, 5 to 10 minutes.

Transfer roasted bird to platter. Leave crusty bits in pan; pour pan liquid into measuring cup. When fat rises, skim it off.

For *each cup gravy*, measure 2 tablespoons fat back into roasting pan. Add 2 tablespoons flour; blend. Cook and stir over low heat till frothy. (For richer flavor, color, add a little kitchen bouquet.) Remove from heat; add 1 cup lukewarm liquid (juices from roasting, plus giblet broth). Stir smooth, return to heat; cook, stir till thick. Add cooked giblets. Simmer 5 minutes. Season.

Three corks, a coaster, and a bit of fabric make a pilgrim place card or favor

To make shoulders for pilgrim, split 1¾-inch cork lengthwise; glue large ends together. Cut off center hump, making flat surface for head. Cut 2½-inch fabric or paper circle for collar; cut out wedge; glue in place over shoulders.

For head, cut ⅜ inch off small end of a second cork, slanting the cut slightly. Glue cork, narrow end down, to collar. For hat brim, glue cork coaster atop. Glue on third cork, large end down. Add black paper hat buckle and nailhead eyes.

Tender Rock Cornish game hens make any meal festive! You baste birds with mixture of corn syrup and canned consomme — bake to a beautiful golden brown. Platter trim is fresh kumquats.

Mushroom Wild Rice

½ cup packaged wild rice

• • •

1 6-ounce can (1⅓ cups) broiled sliced mushrooms
½ teaspoon salt
1 4⅝-ounce package (1⅓ cups) precooked rice

• • •

2 tablespoons butter or margarine

Prepare wild rice according to package directions (allow over an hour). Drain mushrooms, reserving liquid. Add enough water to mushroom liquid to measure 1⅓ cups; add salt; use as the liquid for preparing precooked rice—heat according to package directions.

Combine drained wild rice and hot precooked rice, mushrooms, and butter. Cover; heat briefly over *low* heat. Serves 4 to 6.

Note: To short cut, use *canned* wild rice (1½ to 2 cups).

Browned Rice

Spread 1 cup rice in shallow pan; brown at 350° about 15 minutes, stirring occasionally. Combine 1 can condensed consomme and 1 can water, bring to boiling; add rice and cook till tender; drain. Makes 3 cups.

FEAST FOR THANKSGIVING

Harvest Fruit Cup
Roast Rock Cornish Game Hen
Mushroom Wild Rice
Asparagus Spears With Lemon Wedges
Baked Butternut Squash
Waldorf Salad
Pumpkin Chiffon Tarts   Hot Coffee

Dinner accents

–appetizers, salads

Apple-Pineapple Slaw

3 cups shredded crisp cabbage
1 9-ounce can (1 cup) pineapple tidbits, drained
1 cup diced unpared apples
1 cup tiny marshmallows
½ cup chopped celery
½ cup mayonnaise or salad dressing
Lettuce

Combine and toss till mayonnaise coats all ingredients. Serve in lettuce-lined bowl; trim with lemon-juice-sprinkled unpared apple wedges. Makes 4 to 6 servings.

Cranberry Ring

1 package strawberry-flavored gelatin
1 cup hot water
1 10½- or 11-ounce can (about 1 cup) frozen cranberry relish
1 13½- or 14-ounce can (1½ cups) crushed pineapple
1 package lemon-flavored gelatin
1¼ cups boiling water
2 cups tiny marshmallows
1 3-ounce package cream cheese, softened
½ cup mayonnaise or salad dressing
½ cup heavy cream, whipped

First layer: Dissolve strawberry-flavored gelatin in hot water. Add cranberry relish, dash salt. Pour into 6½-cup ring mold. Chill till firm. *Second layer:* Drain pineapple, reserving syrup. Dissolve lemon-flavored gelatin in boiling water; add marshmallows and stir till melted; add reserved syrup. Chill till partially set. Blend cream cheese, mayonnaise, dash salt; add to marshmallow mixture. Stir in pineapple. (If mixture is thin, chill till it mounds slightly when spooned.) Fold in whipped cream. Pour over first layer; chill firm. Unmold. Serves 10 to 12.

Hot Tomato Starter—delicious cup o' kindness that's quick!

"Done" in 2 minutes, this speedy appetizer is made of two soups, seasonings. Float parsleyed cracker.

Other speedy meal starters from a can—frozen Oyster Stew and Cream of Shrimp Soup.

Fresh-flavored and colorful, gala salads complement the holiday bird

Cranberry Ring—pretty two decker—has a tart-sweet cranberry ribbon atop rich pineapple layer.
Apple-Pineapple Slaw has marshmallow accent.

Hot Tomato Starter

1 can condensed tomato soup
1 can condensed beef broth
1 can water
¼ teaspoon marjoram
¼ teaspoon thyme
Butter

Combine ingredients except butter; simmer 2 minutes. Dot with butter. Top each cupful with toasted saltine, parsley fluff. So cracker floats, hold by opposite sides close to soup; let go. Another trim—use cooky cutter to cut turkey shape from a process cheese slice; slide gently onto soup.

Harvest Fruit Cup

Combine chilled canned fruit cocktail with red apple wedges, orange sections, and avocado balls. Serve with cheese crackers.

Shrimp Cocktail

¾ cup chili sauce
¼ cup lemon juice
1 to 2 tablespoons horseradish
1 teaspoon minced onion
2 teaspoons Worcestershire sauce
4 drops Tabasco sauce
Dash salt
Cooked, cleaned shrimp, chilled

Combine ingredients except shrimp. Chill thoroughly. Makes 1 cup cocktail sauce.

Spoon sauce into individual cocktail cups. Hook shrimp over rims of glasses. For trim, snip pointed fans from romaine and poke several into sauce in each glass.

Speedy Shrimp Dip

Blend ½ cup mayonnaise and ¼ cup spicy meat sauce. Serve with shrimp.

With the bird—vegetables and other

Cranberry Sauce

2 cups sugar
2 cups water
1 pound (4 cups) cranberries

Combine sugar and water in saucepan; stir to dissolve sugar. Heat to boiling; boil 5 minutes. Add cranberries; cook till skins pop, about 5 minutes. Remove from heat. Serve sauce warm or chilled. Makes 4 cups.

Orange-glazed Sweet Potatoes

6 medium sweet potatoes
¾ cup boiling water
1 teaspoon salt
3 tablespoons butter or margarine

• • •

½ tablespoon grated orange peel
1 tablespoon orange juice
¾ cup light or dark corn syrup
¼ cup brown sugar
3 or 4 orange slices, cut in half

Pare and halve sweet potatoes. Add boiling water and salt. Simmer in covered skillet until tender, about 15 minutes. Drain off liquid, leaving ¼ cup in skillet. Dot potatoes with butter. Combine remaining ingredients. Add to potatoes.

Cook uncovered over low heat until glazed, about 15 minutes—baste frequently, turning potatoes once. Makes 6 servings.

Creamed Onions

18 to 20 medium onions

• • •

⅓ cup salad oil
3 tablespoons enriched flour
1½ cups milk
1 cup shredded process American cheese
Peanuts, chopped

Peel onions and cook in a large amount of boiling, salted water until tender; drain. Blend salad oil and flour; stir in milk and cook slowly until thick, stirring constantly.

Add the cheese and stir until melted. Add the onions and heat through. Place in vegetable bowl and sprinkle with chopped peanuts. Makes 6 to 8 servings.

Pickled Beets and Onion Rings

2 tablespoons butter or margarine
1 1-pound jar (2 cups) sliced or whole pickled beets, drained
1 cup onion slices separated in rings
2 teaspoons sugar
½ teaspoon salt
Dash pepper

Melt butter or margarine in skillet. Add beets and onion rings. Sprinkle with sugar, salt, and pepper. Cook over low heat, stirring occasionally, till hot and onions are tender, about 15 minutes. Makes 4 servings.

For tradition's sake, serve time-honored Creamed Onions

To lots of folks, it's not Thanksgiving unless this specialty is on the table.

Our version has two Southern accents—cheese to enrich the sauce, peanuts for crunch and their own good flavor.

Remember Corn Bread, best so hot the butter melts right in!

.rimmings

Offer a winter garden of vegetables

Lazy Susan is a pretty frame for pimiento-dotted whole-kernel corn, Orange-glazed Sweet Potatoes, buttered peas and carrots, rosy spiced crab apples. In covered bowl — fluffy potatoes.

Butternut Squash with Parmesan

(*as served at Publick House*)

Cut squash in serving pieces and scoop out seeds and stringy part. Leave rind on. Parboil 15 minutes in boiling salted water. Remove; drain thoroughly. Season well with salt and pepper, dot with butter, sprinkle generously with grated Parmesan cheese. Bake at 375° for 15 to 20 minutes or till done.

Celery Oriental

(*as served at Neiman-Marcus*)

Cut 6 to 8 large, outside celery stalks diagonally or "Oriental julienne." Cook in a little boiling salted water till just crisp-done (you have to taste); drain.

Saute 1 cup sliced fresh mushrooms in 3 tablespoons butter; add the celery and ¼ cup toasted almond halves. Toss around lightly till heated. Makes 4 to 6 servings.

Peas and Tiny Onions

Cook 3 cups (2 packages) frozen green peas and ¾ cup tiny onions separately till tender; drain, combine. Dot with butter.

Corn Bread

1 cup sifted enriched flour
¼ cup sugar
4 teaspoons baking powder
¾ teaspoon salt
1 cup yellow corn meal
2 eggs
1 cup milk
¼ cup soft shortening

Sift together flour, sugar, baking powder, and salt; stir in corn meal. Add eggs, milk, and shortening. Beat with rotary or electric beater till just smooth, about 1 minute. (Do not overbeat.) Pour into greased 9x9x2-inch pan. Bake at 425° 20 to 25 minutes.

Happy ending delicious pie for dessert

Pumpkin Pie

Taste the filling before you add all the spice, then you can season it to suit yourself—

1½ cups canned or mashed cooked pumpkin
¾ cup sugar
½ teaspoon salt
½ to 1* teaspoon ginger
1 to 1¼* teaspoons cinnamon
¼ to ½* teaspoon nutmeg
¼ to ½* teaspoon cloves
• • •
3 slightly beaten eggs
1¼ cups milk
1 6-ounce can (⅔ cup) evaporated milk
• • •
1 9-inch unbaked pastry shell

Thoroughly combine the pumpkin, sugar, salt, and the spices. Blend in eggs, milk, and evaporated milk. Pour into unbaked pastry shell (have edges crimped high because amount of filling is generous).

Bake in hot oven (400°) 50 minutes, or till knife inserted halfway between center and outside edge comes out clean. Cool. Garnish with circle of walnut halves. Or, try the trims shown on page 45.

For a special treat, serve with plump wedges of aged Cheddar.

*Use first spice measurement for golden mildly spiced pie; use starred measure for richly spiced pie.

Three kinds to choose from—

← Country-kitchen Mince Pie, at top, boasts fragrant mincemeat with rich sour-cream layer and pastry trims. Pumpkin Pie is luscious, creamy, spiced to your liking. In front—Cranberry Mince Pie, tart-sweet and bright as calico.

Country-kitchen Mince Pie

Here mincemeat bakes with rich topper, rates a pretty pastry trim—

2 cups prepared mincemeat *or* 1 9-ounce package
• • •
1 unbaked 9-inch pastry shell
• • •
2 beaten eggs
2 cups dairy sour cream
2 tablespoons sugar
1 teaspoon vanilla

If using packaged mincemeat, prepare according to package directions. Spoon mincemeat into unbaked pastry shell; bake in hot oven (425°) for 20 minutes.

Meanwhile combine eggs, sour cream, sugar, and vanilla. Remove pie from oven and pour sour-cream mixture over mincemeat. Continue baking 6 to 8 minutes, or till topping is almost set. Cool pie. Chill. Just before serving, trim with circle of prepared mincemeat and pastry acorns and oak leaves*, if desired.

**For pastry trims*, cut out designs from scraps of rolled dough, prick with fork. Bake on a cooky sheet in very hot oven (450°) 3 to 4 minutes. Cool.

Cranberry Mince Pie

Filling's tangy with fruit, lusciously spiced—

1⅓ cups sugar
½ teaspoon salt
½ teaspoon cloves
½ teaspoon ginger
1 teaspoon cinnamon
• • •
1⅓ cups seedless raisins
⅓ cup chopped California walnuts
1 tablespoon grated orange peel
2 teaspoons grated lemon peel
⅓ cup lemon juice
¾ cup canned jellied cranberry sauce, crushed
1⅓ cups finely chopped apple
• • •
1 recipe Plain Pastry, page 19

Combine the sugar, salt, and spices. Add raisins, nuts, peels, lemon juice, cranberry sauce, and apple; mix well. Pour into 9-inch pastry-lined pie plate; top with lattice crust. Bake in hot oven (400°) about 35 minutes. Cut in plump wedges; serve warm.

Desserts to top off harvest feasts

Pumpkin Chiffon Tarts

¾ cup brown sugar
1 envelope (1 tablespoon) unflavored gelatin
½ teaspoon salt
1 teaspoon cinnamon
½ teaspoon nutmeg
¼ teaspoon ginger
3 slightly beaten egg yolks
¾ cup milk
1¼ cups canned or mashed cooked pumpkin
3 egg whites
⅓ cup granulated sugar
7 or 8 baked 4-inch tart shells, cooled

In saucepan, combine brown sugar, gelatin, salt, spices. Combine egg yolks and milk; stir into brown-sugar mixture. Cook, stirring constantly, till mixture comes to a boil. Remove from heat; stir in pumpkin. Chill till mixture mounds slightly when spooned (test every now and then). Beat egg whites till soft peaks form; gradually add granulated sugar, beating till stiff peaks form. Fold pumpkin mixture thoroughly into egg whites. Turn into baked tart shells. Chill. Garnish with whipped cream, chopped candied ginger.

Note: Secret of the fluffy filling is not to let gelatin mixture get too stiff before folding it into the egg-white meringue.

Cheesecake Mince Tarts

1¾ cups prepared mincemeat
8 4-inch unbaked pastry tart shells
1 8-ounce package cream cheese, softened
2 well-beaten eggs
1 cup sour cream
½ teaspoon grated lemon peel
½ teaspoon rum flavoring
½ cup sugar
1 tablespoon flour

Reserve ½ cup mincemeat. Spoon remainder into tart shells. Add cheese to eggs; beat till smooth. Blend in sour cream, lemon peel, flavoring. Mix sugar and flour; stir into cheese mixture. Pour over mincemeat in tarts. Bake in moderate oven (375°) 25 to 30 minutes or till lightly browned. Cool. Top with reserved mincemeat.

Date-Orange Dessert

¼ cup shortening
1 cup sifted enriched flour
½ cup sugar
½ teaspoon baking powder
¼ teaspoon soda
¼ teaspoon salt

• • •

⅓ cup buttermilk
1 egg
1 tablespoon grated orange peel
1 cup pitted dates, cut up

• • •

¾ cup orange juice
¼ cup sugar

• • •

1 recipe Orange Hard Sauce

Stir shortening to soften; sift in the flour, ½ cup sugar, baking powder, soda, and salt. Add buttermilk, egg, and orange peel. Beat till smooth, about 1 minute. Add dates. Spoon into 6 greased custard cups.

Bake in moderate oven (350°) 25 to 30 minutes. Combine orange juice and ¼ cup sugar. Pour over hot puddings. Let stand 15 minutes; then remove from cups. Serve warm with Orange Hard Sauce.

Cranberry Steamed Pudding

½ cup shortening
⅔ cup sugar
2 beaten eggs
2½ cups coarsely chopped fresh cranberries
2 tablespoons light molasses

• • •

1⅔ cups sifted enriched flour
¾ teaspoon soda
½ teaspoon cinnamon
¼ teaspoon nutmeg
¼ teaspoon salt

• • •

1 recipe Hard Sauce

Cream the shortening and sugar; add eggs, cranberries, and molasses. Sift together dry ingredients; add to first mixture. Thoroughly grease a 1½-quart mold and dust lightly with flour; pour in batter. Cover tightly; steam about 3½ hours. Makes 10 servings. Serve with Hard Sauce.

Hard Sauce

¼ cup butter or margarine
1 cup sifted confectioners' sugar
½ teaspoon vanilla

Cream butter; gradually add confectioners' sugar, and cream together till light and fluffy; add vanilla and mix well.

Orange Hard Sauce

¼ cup butter or margarine
1 cup sifted confectioners' sugar
¼ teaspoon grated orange peel
1 tablespoon orange juice

Cream butter or margarine; gradually add confectioners' sugar and cream together till light and fluffy. Add grated orange peel and orange juice; mix well.

Pilgrim Hats

Cut rims off 15 ice-cream cones. Cut off cone ends, leaving about 2 inches of cone. Center each 2-inch piece of cone, wide end down, on a 3½-inch round cooky. Heat 4 cups puffed rice cereal at 350° 10 minutes to crisp. Melt 18 vanilla caramels in 4 teaspoons water in top of double boiler over boiling water; stir frequently. Add dash salt.

Place cereal in large bowl and pour caramel sauce over; toss till cereal is well coated. Press cereal mixture over cones to form crown of hats.

For hatbands, cut jelly strings in thin strips; press around base of crowns. For buckles, cut small squares from thin slices of gumdrop; make small hole in center of each; press one against each hatband. Makes 15.

Pumpkin Chiffon Tarts—a flavor bouquet of spice in light airy gelatin

These are perfection! Recipe gives secret for making the filling light as a cloud. Top with whipped cream, candied ginger. Pass nuts, raisins, candy.

Christmas

Add Christmas cheer with easy trims

Give salads a gala look

Ring out good tidings with bells cut from slices of canned jellied cranberry sauce.

More trims: Poinsettias cut from maraschino cherries, or stars from pimiento.

Or chill your favorite cranberry salad in tree mold. Trim with swags of softened cream cheese put through pastry tube.

Popcorn Christmas Trees

Use a whole forest of these in a centerpiece, or as favors for children's party.

Combine 2½ cups sifted confectioners' sugar, 1 unbeaten egg white, and 1 teaspoon water to make smooth icing. Tint a light green with few drops green food coloring. Spread icing over outside of 6 ice-cream cones, covering completely—use about 2 tablespoons icing on each cone.

While icing is still soft, press popped corn (about ½ cup for each cone) all over surface of cones. Dot with red cinnamon candies (second picture). Sprinkle "trees" with green-colored sugar.

Trim your Yule table, too!

This fruit-and-holly tree gives the simplest table setting a Christmas touch, makes your party an occasion.

On plate arrange circle of lush oranges; hold together with toothpicks. Place pretty apples atop; poke toothpicks through apples and into oranges to anchor tower. Fill in between fruit with holly sprigs and California walnuts. Pile crown of holly on ring of apples.

← *Confections and cookies that say "Happy Holiday"*

Fruitcake Ring sparkles with gumdrop "holly"; near by are Divinity and Stuffed Dates. Cooky tray offers Rainbow Wreaths, Gumdrop Cookies, Coconut Balls, Rosettes, and Spritz. Pass mugs of spicy Pineapple Wassail.

Our best yule cookies, candies

Holiday goodies to give to very special neighbors, cousins, aunts and uncles. A nice way to say "just for you" at Santa season!

Springerle

4 eggs
4 cups (1 pound) sifted
  confectioners' sugar
20 drops anise oil
4 cups sifted enriched flour
1 teaspoon soda
• • •
Crushed anise seed

With electric mixer, beat eggs till light. Gradually add sugar and continue beating on high speed for 15 minutes or till like soft meringue. Add anise oil. Sift together flour and soda; blend into egg mixture on low speed. Cover bowl tightly with waxed paper or foil and let stand about 15 minutes (for easier handling).

Divide dough in thirds. On lightly floured surface, roll each piece in an 8-inch square, a little more than 1/4 inch thick. Let stand 1 minute. Dust springerle rolling pin or mold lightly with flour; roll or press hard enough to make clear design. With a sharp knife, cut the cookies apart. Place on lightly floured surface; cover with a towel and let stand overnight.

Grease baking sheets and sprinkle each with 1 1/2 to 2 teaspoons crushed anise seed. Brush excess flour from cookies; with finger, rub underside very lightly with cold water and place on baking sheets. Bake in slow oven (300°) about 20 minutes, till light straw color. Makes 6 dozen. See cookies pictured opposite.

Note: Springerle cookies taste best if you keep them a few days in tightly covered container before eating. (Springerle make excellent gifts if carefully wrapped.)

Cooky Tarts (*Sandbakelser*)

1 cup butter or margarine
1 cup sugar
1 egg
1 teaspoon almond extract
3 cups sifted enriched flour

Thoroughly cream butter and sugar; add egg and beat well. Add almond extract. Stir in flour. Pinch off a small ball of dough and place in center of sandbakelse mold*; with thumb, press dough evenly and as thinly as possible over bottom and sides. Place molds on cooky sheet. Bake at 350° about 12 minutes or till lightly browned. Cool. To remove: Invert molds and tap lightly. (Clean molds with dry cloth only.) Makes 5 dozen.

Eat these cooky tarts as is, or fill with whipped cream, jam, or preserves, as shown.

*They look like tiny fluted tart pans. If you don't have these Swedish molds, you can use the very tiny foilware pans (but cookies won't have fluted edge).

Mailing gift cookies? Pack for a safe journey

Wrap each cooky in waxed paper, foil, or saran wrapping. Line box with waxed paper. Cut waxed paper or newspaper in shreds; spread over bottom of box.

Pack wrapped cookies with sheet of cardboard and several sheets of waxed paper between layers. Top with more paper shreds. Wrap box with heavy cardboard before putting on outside wrapping. Mark box "perishable" and "fragile."

breads

From our house to yours

Tutti-fruitti Tea Ring is hub of basket. Around it are Remarkable Fudge, Bowknots, Swedish Ginger Cookies, Rainbow Wreaths, Cooky Tarts, and Springerle.

Rainbow Wreaths (*Berliner kranser*)

1 cup butter or margarine
½ cup sugar
2 egg yolks
2 hard-cooked egg yolks, sieved
2½ cups sifted enriched flour

Thoroughly cream butter and sugar. Add uncooked egg yolks one at a time, beating well after each. Stir in sieved egg yolks. Add flour, stirring only enough to blend. On lightly floured surface, roll small pieces of dough under your hands to pencil size, about 5 inches long and a little over ¼ inch thick. (If dough gets sticky, flour hands lightly.) Form each in circle, crossing one end over other. Dip in candy decorettes. Bake on ungreased cooky sheet in moderate oven (350°) about 10 to 12 minutes or till set but not brown. Makes about 3½ dozen.

Note: For traditional Berliner kranser, make circle by bringing one end of dough over and through in single knot. Brush with slightly beaten egg white; sprinkle with crushed sugar cubes (omit candy decorettes).

Bowknots (*fattigmann*)

6 egg yolks
¼ cup sugar
1 tablespoon melted butter or margarine
⅓ cup heavy cream, whipped
1 teaspoon ground cardamom
2 cups sifted enriched flour
½ teaspoon salt

Beat egg yolks till thick and lemon-colored; gradually beat in sugar. Gently stir in butter. Fold in whipped cream and cardamom. Sift together flour and salt; gradually fold into yolk mixture just enough to make soft dough. Chill well.

Divide dough in half. On lightly floured surface, roll each piece to ⅛ inch. Cut in 3x¾-inch strips. Cut a slit lengthwise in center of each and pull one end through.

Fry a few at a time in deep, hot oil or fat (375°) about 1 to 1½ minutes, or till a very light golden brown. Drain on paper towels. While warm, sift a little confectioners' sugar over. Makes about 5 dozen.

Note: For fattigmann with points at ends, cut dough in long strips, 2 inches wide, then slash diagonally at 3-inch lengths to make diamonds. Cut slit in center as above. (See picture on page 61.)

Rosette Cookies

2 eggs
1 tablespoon sugar
¼ teaspoon salt
1 cup sifted enriched flour
1 cup milk
1 teaspoon vanilla

Combine eggs, sugar, and salt; beat well. Add remaining ingredients; beat till smooth.

Heat rosette iron in deep, hot oil or fat (375°) 2 minutes. Drain excess oil from iron; dip in batter to ¼ inch from top of iron, then immediately into hot oil (375°). Fry rosette until golden, about ½ minute. Lift out; tip upside down to drain.

With fork, push rosette off iron onto rack placed over paper towels. Reheat iron 1 minute; make next rosette. Sprinkle rosettes with confectioners' sugar. Makes 3½ dozen.

Spritz

Thoroughly cream 1½ cups butter or margarine and 1 cup sugar. Add 1 egg, 1 teaspoon vanilla, and ½ teaspoon almond extract; beat well. Sift together 4 cups sifted enriched flour and 1 teaspoon baking powder; add gradually to creamed mixture, mixing to a smooth dough. Don't chill!

Force dough through cooky press onto ungreased cooky sheet. Decorate with colored sugar, cinnamon candies, jelly strings, or candied pineapple. Bake in hot oven (400°) 8 to 10 minutes. Makes 4 dozen.

Krumkaka

3 eggs
1 cup sugar
¼ teaspoon ground cardamom
1⅓ cups sifted enriched flour
¼ teaspoon salt
1 cup heavy cream

Beat eggs till light; add sugar gradually, beating till thick and lemon-colored. Stir in cardamom. Sift together flour and salt; blend into egg mixture alternately with cream. Bake on moderately hot krumkaka iron: Place 1 tablespoon batter just off center on back half of iron. Bring top of iron down gently, then press firmly (but don't squeeze out much batter); scrape any excess batter from edges. Bake about ½ minute on each side, or till lightly browned. Remove from iron and quickly roll on cone-shaped form (comes with iron). Makes 4 dozen.

Swedish Ginger Cookies
(*Pepparkakor*)

1 cup butter or margarine
1½ cups sugar
1 egg

• • •

1½ tablespoons grated orange peel
2 tablespoons dark corn syrup
1 tablespoon water

• • •

3¼ cups sifted enriched flour
2 teaspoons soda
2 teaspoons cinnamon
1 teaspoon ginger
½ teaspoon cloves

• • •

Blanched almonds

Thoroughly cream the butter and sugar. Add egg and beat till light and fluffy. Add orange peel, corn syrup, and water; mix well. Sift together dry ingredients; stir into creamed mixture. Chill dough thoroughly.

On lightly floured surface, roll to ⅛ inch.* Cut in desired shapes with floured cooky cutter. Place 1 inch apart on ungreased baking sheet. Top each cooky with blanched almond half (see picture, page 61). Bake in moderate oven (375°) 8 to 10 minutes. Cool on rack.

Makes about 8 dozen cookies.

**For sparkly look*, sprinkle rolled dough with sugar, then press it in lightly with a rolling pin.

Fun to give, delicious to eat

In center of this festive tray is Snowball Loaf. Below are Spritz, Toffee Butter Crunch. Between cones of Krumkaka are Sugar Balls; along top—Rosette Cookies and Cooky Tarts.

Bring on the fancy cookies—to herald

Noel Fruit Cookies (*Lebkuchen*)

1 egg
¾ cup brown sugar
½ cup honey
½ cup dark molasses
3 cups sifted enriched flour
1¼ teaspoons cinnamon
1¼ teaspoons nutmeg
½ teaspoon cloves
½ teaspoon allspice
½ teaspoon soda
½ cup chopped mixed candied fruits and peels
½ cup slivered blanched almonds

Beat egg; add brown sugar and beat till fluffy. Stir in honey and molasses. Sift together dry ingredients; add to first mixture; mix well. Stir in fruits, peels, nuts. Chill several hours or overnight. On lightly floured surface, roll to ¼ inch. Cut in rectangles 3½x2 inches. Place on greased cooky sheet. Bake in moderate oven (350°) about 12 minutes. Cool slightly before removing from pan. Makes about 2 dozen.

Gumdrop Cookies

1 cup shortening
1 cup granulated sugar
1 cup brown sugar
2 eggs
2½ cups sifted enriched flour
1 teaspoon salt
½ teaspoon soda
1 teaspoon cinnamon
1 9-ounce package mincemeat
1 cup finely chopped California walnuts
⅔ cup finely cut green and red gumdrops

Thoroughly cream together shortening, sugars, and eggs. Sift together dry ingredients. Dredge mincemeat, nuts, and gumdrops in ½ cup flour mixture; stir remaining dry ingredients into creamed mixture; stir in floured gumdrops. Pack firmly into six 6-ounce frozen-juice-concentrate cans and freeze (slicing will be easier if you do) or chill well. Cut in ⅛-inch slices. Place ¾ inch apart on ungreased cooky sheet; top each with pecan half. Bake at 375° about 6 to 8 minutes. Cool slightly before removing from pan. Makes 7 to 8 dozen.

Sugar Cookies

1 cup butter or margarine
1½ cups sugar
3 eggs
1 teaspoon vanilla
• • •
3½ cups sifted enriched flour
2 teaspoons cream of tartar
1 teaspoon soda
½ teaspoon salt

Cream butter. Add sugar gradually, creaming till light and fluffy. Add eggs, one at a time, beating after each addition. Stir in vanilla. Sift together dry ingredients; add gradually to creamed mixture. Chill *thoroughly* (3 to 4 hours).

On well-floured surface, roll to ⅛ to ¼ inch. Cut in shapes. Bake on ungreased cooky sheets at 375° 6 to 8 minutes. Cool slightly on cooky sheet; remove to rack.

Decorate with red cinnamon candies, candy decorettes, or colored sugar before baking. Or trim with Ornamental Frosting (page 114) or Confectioners' Frosting when cool (see cooky tree, opposite). Makes about 8 dozen cookies rolled thin.

Confectioners' Frosting: Add enough light cream to 2 cups sifted confectioners' sugar to make of spreading consistency (or less cream to make of piping consistency). Add dash salt and 1 teaspoon vanilla.

Coconut Balls

1 cup butter or margarine, softened
¼ cup sifted confectioners' sugar
2 teaspoons vanilla
1 tablespoon water
2 cups sifted enriched flour
1 cup chopped pecans

Thoroughly cream butter, sugar, and vanilla. Stir in water. Add flour and mix well. Stir in nuts. Shape in 1-inch balls. Bake 1 inch apart on ungreased cooky sheet at 300° about 20 minutes, or till firm to touch. Cool thoroughly before removing from pan.

Dip cookies in Confectioners' Frosting and roll in tinted coconut. Makes 4 dozen.

Sugar Balls: Roll unbaked cookies in colored sugar. Omit frosting and coconut.

a merry Christmas

Dessert time? Snip a festive cooky from the cooky tree

Holly Hermits

½ cup shortening
1 cup brown sugar
1 egg
2 tablespoons water
1½ cups sifted enriched flour
½ teaspoon soda
¼ teaspoon salt
½ teaspoon cinnamon
¼ teaspoon nutmeg
¼ teaspoon cloves

• • •

¾ cup chopped mixed candied fruits and peels
½ cup seedless raisins, dark or light
½ cup broken California walnuts

Cream together shortening and brown sugar. Add egg and water; beat well. Sift together dry ingredients; stir into creamed mixture. Stir in fruits and peels, raisins, and nuts. Drop from teaspoon 2 inches apart on lightly greased cooky sheet. Bake in moderate oven (375°) about 10 minutes. Cool slightly before removing from pan. Makes about 3½ dozen.

Sauce your sundae to suit yourself

Holiday callers will be extra glad they came! Let folks spoon cherry sauce, chocolate syrup, or fluffy marshmallow sauce over big dishes of peppermint ice cream. California walnuts go on top. Serve 'round the cooky tree.

Sugarplum surprises–

candies

for family and friends

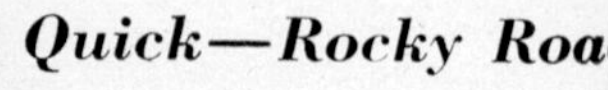

Quick—Rocky Road

No gift is more welcome than candy from your own kitchen. Now, which good recipe will you try first— fudge, toffee, pralines?

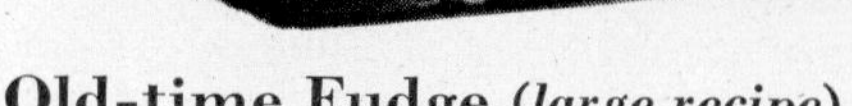

Old-time Fudge

2 cups sugar
¾ cup milk
2 1-ounce squares unsweetened chocolate
Dash salt
1 teaspoon corn syrup, light or dark
2 tablespoons butter or margarine
1 teaspoon vanilla

Butter sides of heavy 2-quart saucepan. In it combine sugar, milk, chocolate, salt, and corn syrup. Heat over medium heat, stirring constantly till sugar dissolves, chocolate melts, and mixture comes to boiling. Then cook to soft-ball stage (234°), stirring only if necessary. Immediately remove from heat; add butter and cool to lukewarm (110°) without stirring. Add vanilla. Beat vigorously until fudge becomes very thick and starts to lose its gloss. Quickly spread in buttered shallow pan or small platter. Score in squares while warm and, if desired, top each with a walnut half; cut when firm.

Note: If you like, quickly stir in ½ cup broken nuts at end of beating time when fudge begins to lose its gloss.

Old-time Fudge (*large recipe*)

Even experienced home candy makers are wary of batches larger than this—they take longer to beat, are more likely to go wrong—

3 cups sugar
1 cup milk
3 1-ounce squares unsweetened chocolate
Dash salt
2 teaspoons corn syrup, light or dark
3 tablespoons butter or margarine
1½ teaspoons vanilla

Follow the method given in Old-time Fudge, but use 3-quart saucepan.

Rocky Road

4 4½-ounce milk-chocolate bars
3 cups tiny marshmallows
¾ cup coarsely broken California walnuts

Partially melt chocolate over hot water; remove from heat and beat till smooth. Stir in marshmallows and nuts. Spread in buttered 8x8x2-inch pan. Chill firm. Cut in squares.

Old-fashioned Panocha

Remarkable Fudge—well named, you'll see

Remarkable Fudge

Just velvety—wonderful! And so foolproof, you can make a big batch like this.

4 cups sugar
1 14½-ounce can (1⅔ cups) evaporated milk
1 cup butter or margarine

• • •

1 12-ounce package (2 cups) semisweet chocolate pieces
1 pint marshmallow creme
1 teaspoon vanilla
1 cup broken California walnuts

Butter sides of heavy 3-quart saucepan. In it combine sugar, milk, and butter. Cook over medium heat to soft-ball stage (236°), stirring frequently.

Remove from heat and add chocolate, marshmallow creme, vanilla, and nuts. Beat till chocolate is melted and blended. Pour into a buttered 9x9x2-inch pan.* Score in squares, while warm; cut when firm. Makes 3 dozen 1½-inch pieces.

*For thinner pieces, pour fudge into 13x 9½x2-inch pan.

Panocha

Rich and creamy brown-sugar fudge—one of Grandma's favorites—

1½ cups granulated sugar
1 cup brown sugar
⅓ cup light cream
⅓ cup milk
2 tablespoons butter or margarine

• • •

1 teaspoon vanilla

• • •

½ cup broken pecans

Butter sides of heavy 2-quart saucepan. In it combine sugars, cream, milk, and butter. Heat over medium heat, stirring constantly till sugars dissolve and mixture comes to boiling. Then cook to soft-ball stage (238°), stirring only if necessary. Immediately remove from heat and cool to lukewarm (110°) without stirring. Add vanilla.

Beat vigorously till fudge becomes very thick and starts to lose its gloss. Quickly stir in nuts and spread in buttered shallow pan or small platter. Score in squares while warm; cut when firm.

Toffee Butter Crunch

Toffee's coated with chocolate, then with nuts. *See picture, page 63—*

1 cup butter
1⅓ cups sugar
1 tablespoon light corn syrup
3 tablespoons water
• • •
1 cup *coarsely* chopped blanched almonds, toasted
• • •
4 4½-ounce bars milk chocolate, melted
1 cup *finely* chopped blanched almonds, toasted

Melt butter in large saucepan. Add sugar, corn syrup, and water. Cook over medium heat, stirring now and then, to hard-crack stage (300°)—watch carefully after temperature reaches 280°. Quickly stir in coarsely chopped nuts; spread in well-greased 13x 9½x2-inch pan. Cool thoroughly.

Turn out on waxed paper; spread top with *half* the chocolate; sprinkle with *half* the finely chopped nuts. Cover with waxed paper; invert; spread again with chocolate. Sprinkle top with remaining nuts. If necessary, chill to firm chocolate. Break in pieces.

So-good Southern pralines

Success secret—Double-check for soft-ball stage, using a candy thermometer *and* the cold-water test. You'll need both to assure good results each time.

Stuffed Dates

4½ cups sifted confectioners' sugar
⅔ cup sweetened condensed milk
¼ teaspoon salt
1½ teaspoons vanilla
¼ teaspoon almond extract
1½ pounds whole pitted dates

Gradually add *4 cups* of the sugar to milk, blending well. Mix in salt and extracts. Sprinkle remaining ½ cup sugar on board and knead fondant till smooth and creamy, working in the sugar. Wrap in foil and let ripen 24 hours in refrigerator. Stuff dates and top with walnut halves. Makes enough fondant to fill 9 to 10 dozen dates.

Divinity

2½ cups sugar
½ cup light corn syrup
½ cup hot water
¼ teaspoon salt
2 stiff-beaten egg whites
1 teaspoon vanilla
Candied cherries, quartered

Combine sugar, corn syrup, water, and salt. Cook to very hard-ball stage (260°). Slowly pour syrup in a thin stream over beaten egg whites, beating constantly. Beat till mixture holds shape (about 4 to 5 minutes). Stir in vanilla and cherries. Drop by heaping tablespoons on waxed paper, lifting and twirling spoon to form a peak. If divinity becomes too stiff for twirling, add a few drops hot water. Makes about 1½ dozen.

Creole Pralines

1½ cups medium-brown sugar
1½ cups granulated sugar
1 cup water
1 teaspoon vinegar
1 tablespoon butter or margarine
2 cups pecan halves

Combine the sugars, water, and vinegar. Cook to soft-ball stage (236°). Add butter, nuts, and few drops red food coloring.

Remove from heat. Immediately beat till mixture starts to thicken and become cloudy. Quickly drop by heaping tablespoons onto buttered waxed paper or foil. Cool. Makes fourteen 3- to 3½-inch pralines.

Note: Pralines should be granular, so don't cool syrup before beating.

Gala fruitcakes for the holidays

Noel Brazil Loaves

1 1-pound package (3 cups) pitted dates
4 ounces red candied pineapple
4 ounces green candied pineapple
4 ounces red candied cherries
4 ounces green candied cherries
1 pound shelled Brazil nuts (3 cups) or pecan halves (4 cups)

• • •

1 cup sifted enriched flour
1 cup sugar
1 teaspoon baking powder
¼ teaspoon salt
4 well-beaten eggs

• • •

1 teaspoon vanilla or rum extract

Halve dates and cut pineapple in chunks. Combine with the whole cherries and nuts. Sift together dry ingredients; add to fruits and nuts, coating well. Stir in eggs and vanilla. Line two 8½x4½x2½-inch loaf pans* with heavy paper; grease paper and pour in batter. Bake in slow oven (325°) 1 hour or till done. Cool. Top with Gumdrop Rose. *Or, two 10x3½x2½-inch loaf pans.

Gumdrop Rose: Between sugared sheets of waxed paper, roll 3 or 4 big pink gumdrops into flat ovals. Cut each in half crosswise. Fold corner of one piece at an angle and wind to make rose center; place atop cake. Now tuck and press other half-ovals around center to make petals. Roll out green jelly string for stem, green gumdrops for leaves; cut out, arrange atop Noel Brazil Loaves.

Fruitcake-ettes

Prepare fruitcake batter from your favorite recipe. Add fruits and nuts according to recipe directions. Place plain paper nut cups, about 1¾ inches in diameter and 1¼ inches deep, on cooky sheet. Spoon batter into cups, filling almost full.

Bake in slow oven (300°) 40 minutes or till done. Cool. For a Christmas glow, use pastry tube to pipe on green confectioners' icing in cluster of holly leaves atop each cupcake; insert tiny red birthday candle in center of each.

Note: You can eat these right away, but they'll taste even better a few days later.

Fruitcake Balls

Prepare fruitcake batter from your favorite recipe. Fill well-greased custard cups ¾ full. Bake in slow oven (300°) 1½ hours or till toothpick inserted in cake comes out clean. Cool thoroughly. To make ball: Turn a cake out of its custard cup and invert over a cake still in cup. Wrap each ball tightly with saran wrapping. Tie with ribbon; attach tiny tree ornaments to bow.

Pineapple Glaze for Fruitcake

Combine ¼ cup canned unsweetened pineapple juice and ½ cup light corn syrup. Bring quickly to a rolling boil. Remove from heat. Immediately brush over cooled fruitcakes with pastry brush. Decorate top of cakes with blanched almonds, candied fruit, or candies. When set, brush on second coat of glaze. (Reheat glaze to boiling each time you use it.) Let glaze dry thoroughly before wrapping or storing cakes. Makes enough to double-coat 6 pounds fruitcake.

Fruitcake pointers

- Cool fruitcake in pan, then turn out. If baked in a foilware pan or a pan that is part of the gift, leave as is and wrap gaily.

- Store fruitcake in foil, saran wrapping, or airtight container. Keep in a cool place.

- Keep fruitcake at least a week before eating—flavors will blend and become mellow. Make fruitcakes for the holidays 3 or 4 weeks ahead. They'll be at their best and you'll avoid Christmas rush.

- Chill fruitcake before slicing—it's easier to cut thin, perfect slices.

White Fruitcake

4 cups (1¾ pounds) mixed diced fruits and peels for fruitcake
½ cup pitted dates, cut up
½ cup dried apricots, cut up
½ cup dried figs, cut up
1¼ cups (8 ounces) light seedless raisins
2 cups (8 ounces) blanched almonds, slivered
2 cups flaked coconut
• • •
2 cups sifted enriched flour
1½ teaspoons baking powder
1 teaspoon salt
• • •
1 cup shortening
1 cup sugar
1 teaspoon rum flavoring
5 eggs
½ cup unsweetened pineapple juice

Mix fruits and peels, dates, apricots, figs, raisins, almonds, and coconut. Sift together flour, baking powder, and salt; sprinkle ½ *cup* over fruit mixture, mixing well. Thoroughly cream shortening, sugar, and flavoring; add eggs, one at a time, beating well after each. Add dry ingredients to creamed mixture alternately with pineapple juice, beating well after each addition. Add fruit mixture, stirring until well mixed. Line two 8½x4½x2½-inch loaf pans* with paper, allowing ½ inch to extend above all sides of pan. (Or bake in smaller pans.)

Pour batter into pans, filling ¾ full. Bake in very slow oven (275°) 2½ hours or till done. (Place pan containing 2 cups water on bottom shelf of oven to get cake of greater volume, moist texture, shiny glaze.) Makes about 5 pounds.

*To match picture, see recipe for Ring Fruitcake. Trim top with wreath of tiny marzipan fruits.

Note: You can mix your own candied fruits and peels if you prefer. We like 4 ounces each candied citron, orange peel, lemon peel, and cherries; and 12 ounces of candied pineapple. Buy already-chopped fruits, or dice them yourself.

Key to our fruitcake "window"

← Tray, top row, offers Fruitcake-ettes (sporting candles), Holly Hermits. On second row—Noel Brazil Loaf, gaily wrapped Fruitcake Ball, miniature Dark Fruitcakes. Bottom row displays plum pudding, gala White Fruitcake.

Dark Fruitcake

3½ cups (1½ pounds) mixed diced fruits and peels for fruitcake
1¼ cups (8 ounces) dark seedless raisins
1¼ cups (8 ounces) light seedless raisins
1 cup (4 ounces) chopped California walnuts
1 cup (4 ounces) chopped pecans
• • •
3 cups sifted enriched flour
1 teaspoon baking powder
1 teaspoon salt
1 teaspoon cinnamon
1 teaspoon allspice
½ teaspoon nutmeg
½ teaspoon cloves
• • •
1 cup shortening
2 cups brown sugar
4 large eggs (1 cup)
¾ cup grape juice

Mix fruits and peels, raisins, and nuts. Sift together flour, baking powder, salt, and spices; sprinkle ¼ cup over fruit mixture, mixing well. Thoroughly cream shortening and sugar; add eggs, one at a time, beating well after each. Add sifted dry ingredients to creamed mixture alternately with grape juice, beating smooth after each addition. Pour batter over fruits and mix well.

Line two 8½x4½x2½-inch loaf pans* with paper, allowing ½ inch to extend above all sides. Pour batter into pans, filling ¾ full; do not flatten. Bake in very slow oven (275°) 3 to 3½ hours or till done. (Have pan of water on bottom shelf of oven while baking.) Makes about 6 pounds.

*Or for smaller cakes, use five 5½x3x2¼-inch loaf pans. Bake in slow oven (300°) for 2 to 2½ hours or till fruitcakes are done.

Ring Fruitcake

Prepare batter from either Dark Fruitcake or White Fruitcake recipe. Line the bottom and sides of a 10-inch tube pan with paper and pour in the batter.

Bake in very slow oven (275°) 2½ hours or till toothpick inserted in cake comes out clean. Cool in pan. Trim with holly leaves cut from flattened green gumdrops; use red cinnamon candies for berries, to match picture, page 58. (In using ring molds and other shapes, grease well and fill ¾ full.)

Yuletide **breads**—full of fruit

Tutti-frutti Ring

1 package active dry yeast
¼ cup water
¾ cup milk, scalded
⅓ cup sugar
1 teaspoon salt
⅓ cup shortening
4 to 4½ cups sifted enriched flour
2 eggs

Soften yeast in ¼ cup *warm* water. Combine milk, sugar, salt, and shortening; cool to lukewarm. Stir in 2 cups of the flour. Add eggs; mix well. Stir in softened yeast. Add remaining flour or enough to make soft dough. Turn onto lightly floured surface; cover; let rest 10 minutes. Knead till smooth and elastic 5 to 8 minutes. Place in lightly greased bowl, turning once to grease surface.

Cover and let rise in warm place till double (about 1½ hours). Punch down; let rise again till double (about 1 hour). Round dough into ball; cover and let rest 10 minutes. On lightly floured surface, roll in 18x9-inch rectangle, ¼ inch thick.

For *Candied-fruit Filling:* Spread dough with 2 tablespoons soft butter. Combine ½ cup sugar and 2 teaspoons cinnamon; add ½ cup chopped mixed candied fruits and peels. Sprinkle over dough. Roll as for jelly roll beginning at long end. Seal long edge.

Shape in ring, sealed side down, on greased baking sheet; seal ends of ring. Snip ⅔ of the way to center at 1½-inch intervals. Turn each section slightly to one side. Cover; let double (about 45 minutes). Bake at 375° about 25 minutes.

German Stollen

1 package active dry yeast *or* 1 cake compressed yeast
¼ cup water
½ cup butter or margarine
1 cup milk, scalded
¼ cup sugar
1 teaspoon salt
¼ teaspoon ground cardamom
4¾ to 5 cups sifted enriched flour
1 egg
1 cup seedless raisins
½ cup currants
¼ cup chopped mixed candied fruits
2 tablespoons grated orange peel
1 tablespoon grated lemon peel
¼ cup chopped blanched almonds

Soften active dry yeast in ¼ cup *warm* water *or* compressed yeast in ¼ cup *lukewarm* water. Melt butter in hot milk; add sugar, salt, and cardamom; cool to lukewarm. Stir in 2 cups of the flour. Add egg and beat well. Stir in softened yeast, fruits, peels, and nuts. Add remaining flour to make soft dough. Turn out on lightly floured surface.

Cover and let rest 10 minutes. Knead 5 to 8 minutes or till smooth and satiny. Place in lightly greased bowl, turning once to grease surface. Cover; let rise in warm place till double, about 1½ hours. Punch down; turn out on lightly floured surface and divide in 3 equal parts. Cover; let rest 10 minutes.

Roll each part into a 12x7-inch rectangle. Without stretching dough, fold long side over to within 1 inch of opposite side to make typical stollen shape; seal edges. Place on greased baking sheets. Cover, and let rise till almost double, about 30 to 45 minutes. Bake in moderate oven (375°) 20 to 25 minutes, or till golden brown.

While warm, brush with butter; sift confectioners' sugar over; or glaze as below. Makes 3 loaves.

German Stollen—glazed, oven-warm

Chock-full of fruits and nuts—so good you'll make it a Christmas tradition! You may want to glaze warm stollen: To 2 cups sifted confectioners' sugar, add ¼ cup hot water and 1 teaspoon butter.

French Raisin Bread

1 package active dry yeast *or* 1 cake compressed yeast
¼ cup water
1¼ cups milk, scalded
¾ cup butter or margarine
½ cup sugar
1 teaspoon salt
4 cups sifted enriched flour
2 eggs
Blanched whole almonds
½ cup light seedless raisins

Soften 1 package active dry yeast in *warm* water, or compressed yeast in *lukewarm* water. Combine milk, butter, sugar, and salt; stir till butter melts. Cool to lukewarm. Add *1 cup* of the flour. Add eggs, one at a time, and beat well after each. Stir in softened yeast. Add remaining flour to make a batter; beat *hard* 5 to 7 minutes (this is important because this bread isn't kneaded). Cover; let dough rise in warm place till double, about 1½ hours.

Place circle of almonds in bottom of well-greased 3-quart crown mold (see note below for baking in other types of pans). Stir batter down; stir in raisins. Spoon batter into mold. Cover and let rise till almost double, about 1 hour.

Bake in moderate oven at 350° till done and top is well browned, about 50 minutes. Cool 5 minutes. Remove from mold, almond side up, and sprinkle with sugar.

Note: Or bake in well-greased 10-inch tube pan about 50 minutes. Or use 2 well-greased 6-cup ring or plain molds and bake 30 to 40 minutes or till done.

Orange Bubble Loaf

1 package hot-roll mix
¾ cup sugar
2 teaspoons grated orange peel
¼ cup butter or margarine, melted
Mixed candied fruits
California walnut or almond halves

Prepare roll mix and let rise according to package directions. Form dough in 1-inch balls. Mix sugar and orange peel. Dip balls in butter, then roll in sugar mixture.

Grease a ring mold, tube pan, or loaf pan. *Loosely* fill pan ½ full with layers of balls. (If extra dough, shape as rolls.) Let double. Bake in moderate oven (375°) 15 to 25 minutes or till done. Invert on rack. Trim with candied fruits and nuts.

Snowball Loaf

2 packages active dry yeast *or* 2 cakes compressed yeast
¼ cup water
1 cup milk, scalded
½ cup sugar
¼ cup shortening
1½ teaspoons salt
4 to 4½ cups sifted enriched flour
1 teaspoon grated lemon peel
2 beaten eggs
1 cup mixed diced candied fruits, peels

Soften active dry yeast in *warm* water, or compressed yeast in *lukewarm* water. Combine milk, sugar, shortening, and salt. Cool to lukewarm. Add about 2 cups flour and the lemon peel; beat till smooth. Add eggs; beat well. Stir in softened yeast. Add fruits and peels. Stir in remaining flour to make soft dough. Cover; let rest 10 minutes. Knead on lightly floured surface till smooth and elastic (6 to 8 minutes). Place in lightly greased bowl, turning once to grease surface. Cover; let rise in warm place till double (about 2 hours). Punch down. Divide dough in half. Cover; let rest 10 minutes. Shape in 2 balls. Place on greased cooky sheet; pat tops to flatten slightly. Cover; let rise till almost double (about 2 hours). Bake in moderate oven (350°) 25 to 30 minutes. While warm, frost with Confectioners' Frosting, trim with candied fruit. Makes 2 loaves.

Almonds top French Raisin Bread

Pretty as a cake—and just right for holiday hostessing. For handsome shape, bake this luscious bread in a crown mold or angel-cake pan.

Wonderful food with a holiday flair— come to our Christmas dinner

Here are ideas for the Big Dinner, from hot soup starter to pie. Now pick the star—Holiday Duckling or Merrie Roast of Beef

Six hungry people? Roast a pair of ducklings. Trim with fresh-kumquat posies. Tangy accompaniment is Cranberry Sauce (recipe, page 52).

Holiday Duckling

Select a duckling, weighing 3½ to 5 pounds ready-to-cook weight, or 5 to 7 pounds dressed weight. Clean duckling; remove wing joints and tips, leaving only the meaty second joints.

Rub inside with salt and stuff lightly with Orange Stuffing. Do not truss or prick the skin. Close opening with skewers and lace with cord. Place, breast side up, on rack in shallow roasting pan. Do not add water.

Roast uncovered in slow oven (325°) 1½ to 2 hours for moderately done, 2 to 2½ hours for well done. Meaty part of leg should feel tender (use paper towel), and it should be easy to move leg up and down.

For a pretty shine, 30 minutes before duckling is done, brush with *Honey Glaze:* Combine 2 tablespoons honey and 1 teaspoon kitchen bouquet. Makes 3 or 4 servings.

Trim duckling with Kumquat Posies.

Orange Stuffing for Duck

3 cups toasted bread cubes
2 cups finely diced celery
1 tablespoon grated orange peel
⅔ cup diced orange sections
¾ teaspoon salt
½ teaspoon poultry seasoning
Dash pepper
1 beaten egg
¼ cup melted butter or margarine

Toss together bread, celery, orange peel, diced orange sections, and seasonings. Combine egg and butter; add to bread mixture, tossing lightly. Makes enough stuffing for a 5-pound duckling.

Party Sweet Potatoes

4 medium sweet potatoes
1 teaspoon salt
3 tablespoons butter or margarine
¼ cup honey
½ teaspoon grated lemon peel
1 tablespoon lemon juice
¼ teaspoon salt
4 maraschino cherries, halved

Pare sweet potatoes and cut in ½-inch slices. Sprinkle with salt. Brown slices on both sides in butter. Cover and cook 8 to 10 minutes or till potatoes are tender. Combine honey, lemon peel and juice, and salt; pour over potatoes. Simmer, covered, 5 minutes. Add cherries. Makes 4 to 5 servings.

DUCKLING DINNER

French Onion Soup
Holiday Duckling
With Orange Stuffing
Cranberry Sauce
Mushroom Wild Rice
Almond Green Beans
Gala Fruit Wreath
Parkerhouse Rolls Butter
Assorted Cheese and Crackers
Hot Coffee

Kumquat Posies

Leave kumquat whole. Make 4 petals by cutting peel in fourths from blossom end, going *almost* to stem end. Peel the petals about ¾ way back. (Leave the fruit portion as is—it makes the center of the flower.) Place in ice water about 1 hour or till petals open as much as you like. Use as platter trim.

French Onion Soup

2½ cups thinly sliced onions
2½ tablespoons butter or margarine
3 cans condensed beef broth*
1 teaspoon Worchestershire sauce
2 French or hard rolls, sliced and toasted
Grated Parmesan cheese

Cook onions in butter till lightly browned. Add broth and Worcestershire. Bring to boil; season with salt and pepper. Sprinkle toast with Parmesan cheese. Pour soup into bowls; float toast. For a gourmet touch, place in preheated broiler a few seconds till cheese is lightly browned. Makes 4 to 6 servings.

*Or, use 6 bouillon cubes or 6 teaspoons instant bouillon dissolved in 4 cups hot water, instead of the broth.

Almond Green Beans

1 10-ounce package frozen French-style green beans
2 tablespoons butter or margarine
¼ cup slivered blanched almonds, toasted
Salt and pepper

Cook beans in boiling salted water till tender; drain. Add butter and almonds; toss till butter melts. Season to taste. Serves 3 to 4.

More good ideas for Christmas dinner

RIB-ROAST SPLURGE

Merrie Roast of Beef
Roast Potatoes
French-fried Onion Rings
Broccoli with Easy Hollandaise
Salad Apple Ring
Brown-and-serve Fantans
Candle Cake
Hot Coffee Mugs of Milk

Merrie Roast of Beef

Select a 4- to 6-pound standing rib roast. Place fat side up in shallow pan—bones make the rack. Sprinkle with salt and pepper. Insert a meat thermometer into the center of roast—do not let tip touch bone or fat. Do not add water. Roast *uncovered* in moderate oven (325°) to desired doneness. Your meat thermometer will read 140° for rare, 160° for medium, and 170° for well done. Allow 2¼ to 2¾ hours for rare, 2¾ to 3¼ hours for medium, and 3¼ to 3½ hours for well done. Let roast stand out of oven about 15 minutes to firm before carving. Count on 2 to 3 servings per pound.

For roast beef *au jus*, skim fat from pan drippings and serve the hot, natural meat juices (do not thicken) with the roast.

Onion Mums

First peel a large white onion for each. *Cutting only to ½ inch from bottom*, slice through center of onion. Again, *without cutting through*, cut in quarters; then cut each quarter in eighths. Petals should be about ⅛ to ¼ inch wide.

Add food coloring (red or green) to warm water, in bowl large enough for petals to spread. Place onion in deeply colored water to cover; let come to room temperature. Place in refrigerator several hours or till petals curl. Drain thoroughly before using.

Roast Potatoes

Pare medium potatoes; cook in boiling salted water 15 minutes; drain. About 45 minutes before roast is done (oven temperature, 325°) place hot potatoes in the meat drippings around the roast, turning potatoes to coat. Roast till potatoes are done, turning occasionally to baste. Sprinkle lightly with salt before serving.

French-fried Onion Rings

6 medium Bermuda or mild white onions, sliced ¼ inch thick
2 cups milk
3 eggs
Enriched flour

Separate onion slices into rings. Combine milk and eggs; beat thoroughly and pour into shallow pan. Drop onion rings into pan. With your fingers, swish rings around till well coated. Lift onions out; shake over pan to drain. Then drop in pan of flour, a few rings at a time, coating each well. Place in wire French-frying basket (don't fill more than one-fourth full). Shake off excess flour. Fry in deep hot oil or fat (375°), stirring once with fork to separate rings while frying. When onions are golden, drain on paper towels. Just before serving, sprinkle with salt. Serve hot. Makes 8 servings.

Easy Hollandaise

½ cup butter or margarine
¼ teaspoon salt
Dash cayenne
1 tablespoon lemon juice
2 egg yolks

Beat butter in top of double boiler (*not* over heat or hot water) till creamy. Add salt and cayenne. Add lemon juice a few drops at a time, beating constantly. Add the yolks, one at a time, beating till mixture is light and fluffy. Set over *hot, not boiling*, water a few minutes, or until glossy, stirring constantly. (Water should not touch top pan, and sauce shouldn't stay over hot water too long.) Serve warm with hot drained broccoli. Makes about ¾ cup.

1 *To carve rib roast:* Place on platter, cut side up. Insert fork between top ribs. Cut from outside to rib.

2 Cut slice ⅜ inch thick. To loosen slice, cut along bone with tip of carving knife at a vertical angle.

3 Lift the slice with carving knife, steadying it with fork. Place slice on side of the platter or on plate.

An all-time favorite—

Holiday or anytime—nothing's better than rib roast of beef! Serve with natural meat juices, Roast Potatoes. Trim—Onion Mums.

Merrie Roast of Beef

Now for the light touch—salads

Pink-grapefruit Refresher

- 4 pink grapefruit, pared and cut in sections, drained
- Lettuce or romaine
- 1½ cups fresh cranberries, halved
- 3 to 4 tablespoons sugar
- Parsley
- Honey Dressing

Arrange grapefruit sections on bed of lettuce. Sweeten cranberries with sugar; mound in center of grapefruit. Garnish with fluffs of parsley. Makes 8 servings. Serve with bowl of Honey Dressing.

Note: Another time omit cranberries and sugar and use 1 cup pomegranate seeds.

Honey Dressing

- ⅔ cup sugar
- 1 teaspoon dry mustard
- 1 teaspoon paprika
- 1 teaspoon celery seed
- ¼ teaspoon salt
- ⅓ cup honey
- ⅓ cup vinegar
- 1 tablespoon lemon juice
- 1 teaspoon grated onion
- 1 cup salad oil

Combine dry ingredients. Stir in honey, vinegar, lemon juice, onion. Very slowly pour salad oil into mixture, beating constantly with rotary or electric beater. Makes 2 cups.

Gala Fruit Wreath

Cinnamon Apple Cups
Canned pear halves
(for Cheese-stuffed Pears)
Canned peach halves
Canned pineapple slices
Canned whole peeled apricots
Red Tokay or Emperor grapes
(for Frosted Grapes)
Green grapes
Fresh kumquats

• • •

Cream cheese
Candied ginger
California walnut halves

• • •

Fluffy Mayonnaise
Lettuce
Holly leaves

Prepare Cinnamon Apple Cups and chill till set. Drain canned fruits and chill. Frost red grapes.

Fix *Cheese-stuffed Pears:* Dry drained chilled canned pears well on paper towels. To tint, add a few drops of water to red food coloring; daub on pears with bit of paper towel or paper napkin to give pink blush. Fill hollows with softened cream cheese mixed with a little finely chopped candied ginger. Seal two pear halves together with cream cheese; pipe on cream-cheese ruffle with pastry tube.

To assemble: Center a large round platter with bowl of Fluffy Mayonnaise. Arrange Cinnamon Apple Cups in groups of 3 on lettuce ruffles. Fill in with the various chilled fruits—see picture.

When arranging peach halves on pineapple rings, fill each peach hollow with a cream-cheese ball pressed between 2 walnut halves. Tuck in a few holly leaves and some extra walnut-cream cheese "sandwiches".

Frosted Grapes

Brush clusters of grapes with slightly beaten egg white (or use fruit juice). Sprinkle grapes with sugar. Let dry before arranging on plate or platter.

←Salad and dessert all in one

Perfect for a buffet is Gala Fruit Wreath—clusters of red and green grapes with lush canned fruits and Cinnamon Apple Cups. Makes a couldn't-be-prettier centerpiece, too.

Cinnamon Apple Cups

2 packages lemon-flavored gelatin
½ cup red cinnamon candies
2 cups boiling water
2 cups unsweetened applesauce or
1 1-pound can
1 tablespoon lemon juice
Dash salt

• • •

1 3-ounce package cream cheese
½ cup broken California walnuts

Dissolve gelatin and candy in boiling water. Stir in applesauce, lemon juice, and salt. Chill till partially set. Form cream cheese in tiny balls. Stir cheese balls and nuts into gelatin mixture. Spoon into small molds* and chill till firm. Serve on fruit-salad tray. Makes fifteen ⅓-cup molds.

*Or pour in 10x6x1½-inch baking dish.

Tomato-aspic Ring

4 cups tomato juice
⅓ cup chopped onion
¼ cup chopped celery leaves
2 tablespoons brown sugar
1 teaspoon salt
2 small bay leaves
4 whole cloves

• • •

2 envelopes (2 tablespoons) unflavored
gelatin
3 tablespoons lemon juice

• • •

1 cup finely chopped celery (optional)

Combine 2 *cups* of the tomato juice, the onion, celery leaves, sugar, salt, bay leaves, and cloves. Simmer uncovered 5 minutes; strain. Meanwhile, soften gelatin in 1 *cup* of the remaining *cold* tomato juice; dissolve in *hot* tomato mixture. Add remaining tomato juice and the lemon juice. Chill till partially set. Add celery. Pour into 5-cup ring mold. Chill till firm. Makes 8 to 10 servings.

Fluffy Mayonnaise

Whip ½ cup heavy cream; fold in 1 cup mayonnaise till blended.

Italian Mix Dressing

Prepare 1 envelope Italian or garlic salad-dressing mix according to package directions. Add a few thinly sliced stuffed green olives. Toss with salad of juicy orange slices, onion rings, and curly endive.

Waldorf Salad

4 tart red medium apples, diced
1 tablespoon lemon juice

• • •

1 cup diced celery
1 cup halved, seeded Emperor grapes
1 cup tiny marshmallows (optional)
¼ cup mayonnaise or salad dressing
¼ cup heavy cream, whipped

• • •

½ cup coarsely broken
California walnuts

Sprinkle diced apple with lemon juice. Combine with celery, grapes, marshmallows, and mayonnaise. Fold in whipped cream. Chill. Just before serving, add nuts. Serve in lettuce-lined bowl. Garnish with apple wedges and perfect walnut halves. Makes 6 servings.

Salad Apple Ring

1 package apple-flavored gelatin
2 tablespoons lemon juice
1 7-ounce bottle lemon-lime carbonated beverage, well chilled
1 unpared tart red apple
½ cup halved seedless green grapes

Dissolve gelatin and dash salt in 1 cup hot water; cool to room temperature and add lemon juice. Carefully pour lemon-lime carbonated beverage down side of bowl; stir *gently with up and down motion.* Chill till partially set. Meanwhile core apple and slice *very thin.* Add apples and grapes to gelatin mixture, stirring *gently with up and down motion.* Pour into 1-quart ring mold. Chill till firm. Unmold. Makes 6 servings.

Crown luscious Waldorf Salad with an apple poinsettia for Christmas

An old-time favorite, this! It's full of apple, grapes, marshmallows, and California walnuts. For the flower, poke in lemon-brushed apple wedges and center with perfect walnut halves.

Red-cabbage Toss

- 3 cups finely shredded red cabbage
- 1 cup sliced cauliflowerets
- ½ cup chopped green pepper
- ¼ cup finely chopped onion
- 2 to 3 tablespoons sugar
- 3 tablespoons vinegar
- 2 tablespoons salad oil
- 1 teaspoon salt

In bowl, combine chilled vegetables. Mix together remaining ingredients for dressing, stirring to dissolve sugar. Pour over vegetables; toss lightly. Trim with green-pepper rings. Makes 4 to 5 servings.

Rosy Fruit-cocktail Slices

- 2 3-ounce packages cream cheese
- 1 cup mayonnaise or salad dressing
- 1 cup heavy cream, whipped
- 1 No. 2½ can (3½ cups) fruit cocktail, well drained
- ½ cup drained maraschino cherries, quartered
- 2½ cups tiny marshmallows

Soften cream cheese; blend with mayonnaise. Fold in next four ingredients. Add few drops red food coloring to tint pink.

Pour salad mixture into two 1-quart round freezer containers. Freeze firm, about 6 hours or overnight. To serve, let stand out a few minutes; remove from container, slice, and place on crisp lettuce. Serves 10 to 12.

Cranberry-relish Mold

- 1 No. 2 can (2½ cups) crushed pineapple
- 2 packages cherry-flavored gelatin
- ¾ cup sugar
- 2 cups hot water
- ½ cup cold water
- 1 to 2 tablespoons lemon juice
- 1½ cups ground raw cranberries (1 pound)
- 1 small orange, ground (½ cup)
- 1 cup chopped celery
- ½ cup broken California walnuts

Drain pineapple, reserving syrup. Combine gelatin and sugar; dissolve in hot water. Add cold water, lemon juice, and reserved pineapple syrup. Chill till partially set.

Add pineapple and remaining ingredients. Turn into 2-quart mold. Chill till firm. Unmold. Makes 12 servings.

Yuletide Mold

- 1½ envelopes (1½ tablespoons) unflavored gelatin
- ½ cup cold water
- ¾ cup boiling water
- 2 tablespoons lemon juice
- 1¼ teaspoons salt
- 1 teaspoon grated onion
- 2 dashes Tabasco sauce
- 2½ cups sieved or mashed ripe avocado
- 1 cup dairy sour cream
- 1 cup salad dressing or mayonnaise

Soften gelatin in cold water; dissolve in boiling water. Add lemon juice, salt, onion, and Tabasco. Cool to room temperature; stir in avocado, sour cream, and salad dressing. Turn into 6-cup mold; chill till firm, 5 to 6 hours or overnight. Unmold on greens; trim platter with orange sections. Makes 8 to 10 servings.

Stuffed Cinnamon Apples

- 6 tart medium apples
- ¾ cup red cinnamon candies
- 2 cups water
- 1 3-ounce package cream cheese
- 2 tablespoons milk
- 1 teaspoon lemon juice
- ⅓ cup chopped pitted dates
- 1 9-ounce can (1 cup) pineapple tidbits, drained
- 2 tablespoons chopped California walnuts

Pare and core apples. Cook candies in water till dissolved. Add apples and cook slowly, uncovered, till just tender, about 15 to 20 minutes. Turn once during cooking. Chill apples in syrup several hours; turn once while chilling.

Blend cream cheese, milk, and lemon juice. Add dates, pineapple, and nuts. Drain apples, place on greens. Stuff centers with cream-cheese mixture. Makes 6 servings.

Sour-cream Dressing

Refreshingly tart with sweet fruits—

- ½ cup salad dressing
- ½ cup sour cream
- 1 tablespoon lemon juice
- 1 tablespoon orange juice
- 2 teaspoons sugar

Combine salad dressing and sour cream. Stir in remaining ingredients. Makes 1 cup.

All tinseled up—delicious desserts that

Noel Eggnog Pie

1 package lemon-flavored gelatin
1 cup hot water
1 pint vanilla ice cream
¼ teaspoon nutmeg
¾ teaspoon rum flavoring
2 well-beaten egg yolks
2 stiff-beaten egg whites
Golden Coconut Shell

Dissolve gelatin in hot water. Cut ice cream in 6 chunks; add to gelatin and stir till melted. Chill till partially set. Add nutmeg and flavoring; stir in egg yolks; fold in the egg whites. Pour into cooled Golden Coconut Shell and chill till set. Top with fluffs of whipped cream; dust with nutmeg.

Golden Coconut Shell

Combine 3 tablespoons soft butter or margarine and two 3½-ounce cans (2½ cups) flaked coconut. Press evenly into lightly buttered pie plate, building up sides. Bake in slow oven (300°) 20 to 25 minutes, or till crust is golden. Cool.

Frozen Christmas Pudding

1 9-ounce can (1 cup) crushed pineapple
1 4-ounce jar (½ cup) maraschino cherries
½ cup light raisins
2 cups tiny marshmallows
⅓ cup chopped blanched almonds, toasted
1 tablespoon grated lemon peel
2 tablespoons lemon juice
2 teaspoons rum flavoring
2 egg whites
¼ teaspoon salt
⅓ cup sugar
1 cup heavy cream, whipped

Drain pineapple and cherries, reserving syrups. Chop cherries. Combine syrups and raisins; heat to boiling. Add marshmallows; stir till dissolved. Cool; add pineapple, cherries, nuts, lemon peel and juice, rum flavoring. Beat egg whites and salt till foamy; gradually add sugar, beating to stiff peaks. Fold into mixture. Fold in cream. Freeze firm in refrigerator tray. Makes 8 servings.

Cherry Candle Cake

1 package cherry angel-cake mix
1 No. 2 can (2½ cups) crushed pineapple
1 package lime-flavored gelatin
1 cup heavy cream
Few drops green food coloring
1½ cups heavy cream
Few drops red food coloring
Gumdrop Bows
1 sturdy 10-inch red candle

Prepare batter from cake mix and bake in an ungreased 10-inch tube pan according to package directions. Cool. Meanwhile prepare *Pineapple Filling:* Drain pineapple and add enough water to the syrup to make 1¾ cups. Heat syrup mixture to boiling; add gelatin and stir until dissolved. Chill till partially set; beat with rotary or electric beater till light and fluffy. Fold in drained pineapple. Whip 1 cup heavy cream; fold into gelatin mixture. Tint pale green with food coloring. Chill, stirring occasionally, until the mixture will *mound* when spooned.

To assemble cake: Cut cake crosswise in 3 equal layers. Place bottom layer on serving plate; spread with *half* the gelatin mixture; add second layer of cake and spread with remaining gelatin; top with third cake layer. Chill till filling is firm, 2 to 3 hours. Just before serving, whip 1½ cups heavy cream and tint pale pink with red food coloring; spread on top and sides of cake. Trim cake with Gumdrop Bows. Secure candle in center. Makes 12 to 16 servings.

Mincemeat Ice-cream Cake

Rub brown crumbs off 1 sponge-, angel-, or pound-cake loaf (about 10x4x2 inches). Cut cake lengthwise in 3 even layers.

Stir 1 quart vanilla ice cream just to soften. Fold in 1 cup prepared mincemeat, ½ cup slivered blanched almonds, toasted, and 1 teaspoon grated orange peel. Spread between cake layers. Freeze firm.

Before serving, frost top and sides with 1 cup heavy cream, whipped. Trim with almonds, maraschino cherries. Serves 10.

you can make ahead of time

Christmas on a platter—tuck in a holly sprig, light the candle, whisk this beauty to the table!

Christmas Candle Cake gets trim of *Gumdrop Bows:* Between sugared sheets of waxed paper, roll green jelly strings in flat strips.

Trim to make 4-inch strips, ½ inch wide. Use two strips for each bow. To make loop, bend one end of strip away from you, turning end so its outer side faces inner side of strip one-third of way down; press to hold.

Place two loops together at an angle to form bow; press together. Cut a 1¼-inch strip of rolled jelly string; wrap it around the center of bow to finish.

Jack Frost Dessert

1 recipe Date Bars
3 medium oranges
About 1 cup green grapes
1 ripe pear
2 fully ripe flecked-with-brown bananas
1 9-ounce can pineapple tidbits, drained
¼ cup quartered maraschino cherries
1½ cups tiny marshmallows
1 tablespoon brandy flavoring
1 9-ounce can (1 cup) crushed pineapple
1 cup heavy cream, whipped
1 3½-ounce can (1¼ cups) flaked coconut

Break Date Bars in bite-size pieces and spread out on pan; set aside. Prepare fresh fruits: Pare and section oranges, removing white membranes; cut sections in half (1 cup). Halve and seed grapes (1 cup). Pare, core, and cube the pear (1 cup). Peel bananas, cut lengthwise in half; slice (1½ cups).

Combine fresh fruits, drained pineapple tidbits, cherries, marshmallows, and flavoring; toss lightly. Chill at least 1 hour. Then arrange *half* of date-bar pieces in an 8-inch circle on large plate. Mound fruit mixture on top, shaping like igloo. Cover with remaining date-bar pieces. Over this, carefully spoon undrained crushed pineapple. Chill about 1 hour.

Before serving, frost all with whipped cream; sprinkle with coconut, covering completely. Stud with Gumdrop Stars (opposite page). Top dessert with Sugar Bells. Makes 6 to 8 servings.

Date Bars

2 eggs
1 teaspoon vanilla
½ cup sugar
¼ cup *unsifted* enriched flour
½ teaspoon baking powder
¼ teaspoon salt
1 8-ounce package (1½ cups) pitted dates, cut up
½ cup broken California walnuts

Beat eggs well and add vanilla; gradually beat in sugar. Sift together flour, baking powder, and salt; mix with dates and nuts. Fold into egg mixture. Spread in greased 11x7x1½-inch pan. Bake in moderate oven (350°) 20 to 22 minutes or till done. Cool thoroughly.

To-each-his-own Alaskas

1 pint vanilla ice cream
½ cup crushed peppermint candy or chopped walnuts
1 packet (½ package) meringue mix
4 cake dessert cups (1 package)

Scoop ice cream into 4 balls; roll in crushed candy or chopped nuts. Return to freezer. Meanwhile, prepare meringue mix according to package directions. Put dessert cups on ungreased baking sheet; place ice-cream ball in each. *Quickly* swirl meringue over top and sides, sealing to cake. Freeze several hours or overnight. Bake in extremely hot oven (500°) 3 minutes or till meringue is lightly browned. Serve immediately.

Ring in the holidays with Sugar Bells—a sweet trim for desserts

To 3 cups sugar, add 1 unbeaten egg white, and about 20 drops red food coloring. Blend till color is even. Squeeze mixture in hand; if it holds print of fingers, it's moist enough. If too dry, add few drops water. Pack into bell mold.

Stand filled mold on waxed paper. Tap bell gently; lift off mold. (If mixture sticks to mold, it's too wet—add more sugar. If bell won't hold its shape, sugar is too dry.) Let bell harden about 1 hour—longer for large bells.

Carefully scrape moist sugar from inside bell, leaving wall ⅛ to ¼ inch thick. (If first bell crumbles, let others dry longer.) Poke small hole in top of bell. String small Christmas tree ball on ribbon; draw through hole.

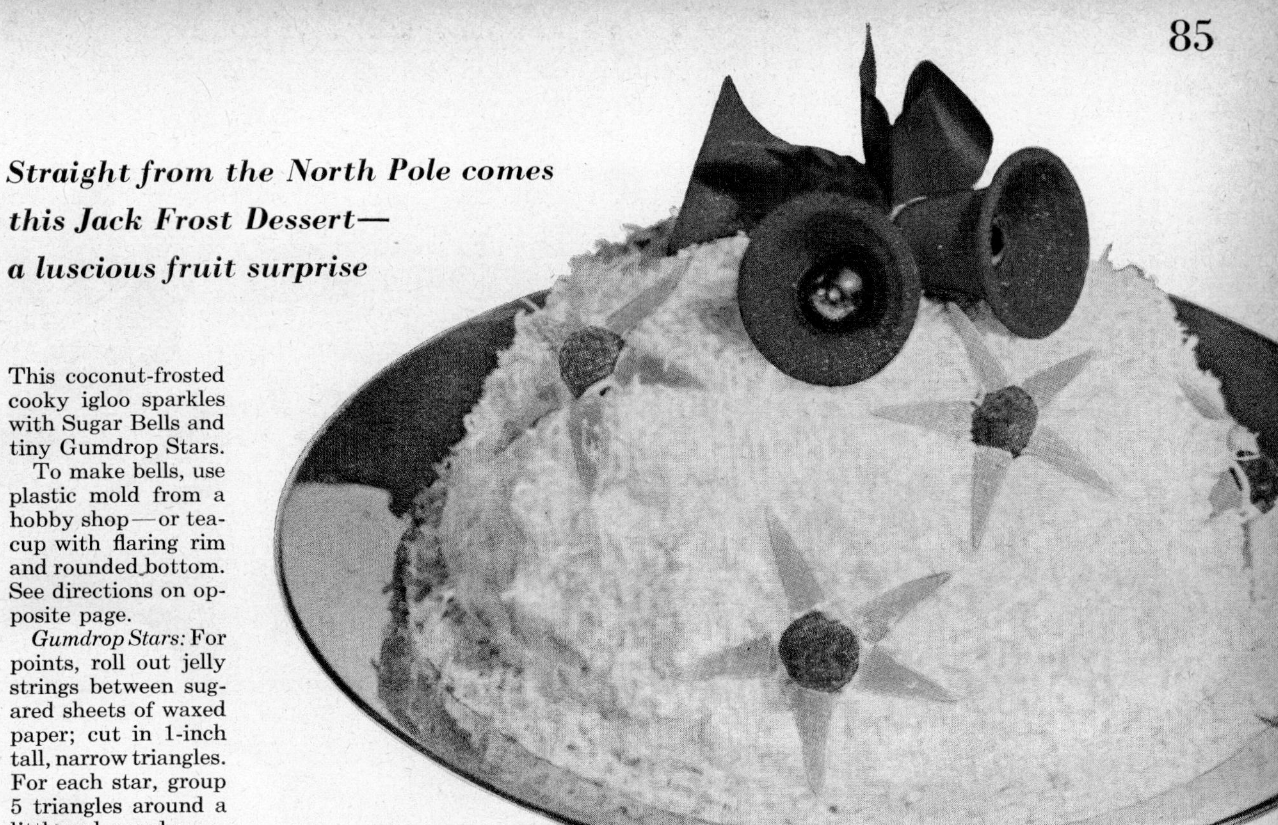

Straight from the North Pole comes this Jack Frost Dessert— a luscious fruit surprise

This coconut-frosted cooky igloo sparkles with Sugar Bells and tiny Gumdrop Stars.

To make bells, use plastic mold from a hobby shop—or teacup with flaring rim and rounded bottom. See directions on opposite page.

Gumdrop Stars: For points, roll out jelly strings between sugared sheets of waxed paper; cut in 1-inch tall, narrow triangles. For each star, group 5 triangles around a little red gumdrop.

Chocolate Torte Royale

2 egg whites
¼ teaspoon salt
½ teaspoon vinegar

• • •

½ cup sugar
¼ teaspoon cinnamon
1 recipe Twin Cream Fillings

Cover a cooky sheet with piece of heavy paper; draw an 8-inch circle in center.

To make meringue shell, beat egg whites, salt, and vinegar till soft peaks form. Blend sugar and cinnamon; gradually add to egg whites, beating till very stiff peaks form and all sugar has dissolved. Spread within circle, making the bottom of the shell ½ inch thick and mounding around edge, making it 1¾ inches high. For trim, form ridges on outside with back of teaspoon. Bake in very slow oven (275°) 1 hour; turn off heat and let dry in oven (door closed) about 2 hours. Peel off paper.

Meanwhile, prepare Twin Cream Fillings. Spoon into cooled meringue shell as directed in filling recipe. Chill several hours or overnight. Trim with a fluff of whipped cream and sprinkle with pecans.

Makes 8 to 10 servings.

Twin Cream Fillings

Melt one 6-ounce package (1 cup) semisweet chocolate pieces over *hot, not boiling,* water. Cool slightly, then spread 2 tablespoons of the chocolate over bottom of cooled meringue shell. To remaining chocolate add 2 beaten egg yolks and ¼ cup water; blend. Chill till mixture is thick.

Combine 1 cup heavy cream, ¼ cup sugar, ¼ teaspoon cinnamon; whip stiff. Spread *half* over chocolate in shell; fold remainder into chocolate mixture, spread on top.

Cocktail Pie

Vanilla wafers (about 32)

• • •

2 cups dairy sour cream
½ cup sugar
1 teaspoon vanilla
1 No. 2½ can (3½ cups) fruit cocktail, well drained

Line 9-inch pie plate with vanilla wafers. Combine sour cream, sugar, and vanilla; fold in drained fruit. Pour into cooky-lined pie plate. Bake in moderate oven (350°) about 25 minutes or till set. Cool, then chill thoroughly. Makes 6 to 8 servings.

Foreign fare

Around the world in 60 good recipes

Coconut Chips—simple to make!

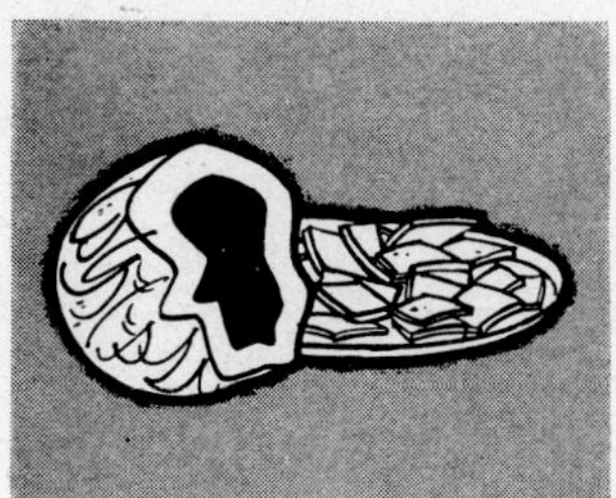

Good with Polynesian foods, or for nibbling. Poke holes in coconut "eyes;" drain milk. Heat coconut in oven at 350° to crack shell. Use hammer to remove shell. Cut meat in pieces. With potato parer, slice coconut in strips. Spread out in jelly-roll pan; lightly salt. Toast at 350° 8 minutes or till golden; stir now and then.

Mold rice for a pretty shape

Glamorous rice molds are nice for Indian or Oriental meals. You make them in a minute! Spoon hot rice into small custard cup, packing slightly. Immediately turn out on plate.

Tip: If rice is to be eaten with chopsticks, hold ends almost together and use as a scoop. Rice will pile up in bite-size mound.

Keep spaghetti hot till served

Late guests? The spaghetti will wait! Drain in colander over pan containing small amount boiling water. Coat spaghetti with 3 or 4 tablespoons butter or margarine (for 6 servings) to keep strands from sticking together. Cover.

For a short time, return drained spaghetti to empty cooking pan, add butter, then cover.

Asparagus Oriental—delicious

Heat large skillet; add 2 tablespoons salad oil; when hot, add 3 cups asparagus cut on the bias in thin 1½-inch pieces. Sprinkle with ½ teaspoon salt, ½ teaspoon monosodium glutamate.

Quickly heat through, stirring constantly. Cover; cook over high heat till just tender, about 5 minutes, shaking skillet often. Serves 6.

← *Oriental supper, delicious, fast—has a packaged start*

Appetizers are Egg Rolls and Fried Shrimp, lower left—you just heat them in oven, serve with Red Mustard Sauce and Sweet-sour Shrimp Sauce. Hub of meal is Speedy Chicken Chow Mein, top. (It's packaged—you add the plus.) Serve with Chinese Fried Rice. Fun to use—Oriental spoons, chopsticks, lacquered dishes.

From cherry-blossom land–an Oriental

QUICK ORIENTAL DINNER

Egg Rolls — Fried Shrimp
Sweet-sour Shrimp Sauce
Red Mustard Sauce
Speedy Chicken Chow Mein
Chinese Fried Rice — Soy Sauce
Preserved Kumquats
Oriental Salad
Mandarin Orange Dessert
Coconut Macaroons
Green Tea

Egg Rolls and Fried Shrimp

They're the starter for this Cantonese-American feast. Just heat frozen ones (they are already cooked) in the oven, according to package directions. Serve hot with Sweet-sour Shrimp Sauce and Red Mustard Sauce.

Sweet-sour Shrimp Sauce

1 9-ounce can (1 cup) pineapple tidbits
½ cup brown sugar
1½ tablespoons cornstarch
Dash salt

. . .

¾ cup water
½ cup vinegar
½ cup green-pepper strips

Drain pineapple, reserving syrup. Combine brown sugar, cornstarch, and salt. Slowly stir in water, vinegar, and reserved pineapple syrup. Bring to boiling; simmer about 5 to 7 minutes or till thick, stirring constantly. Add pineapple and green pepper, simmer a few minutes longer.

Makes 2⅓ cups.

Red Mustard Sauce

Combine ¾ cup catsup, ¼ cup water, 1 to 1½ tablespoons dry mustard, 1 teaspoon salt; mix thoroughly. Chill. Makes 1 cup.

Speedy Chicken Chow Mein

Grease large skillet lightly; add two 20-ounce packages frozen chicken chow mein. Cover and heat over low heat, stirring occasionally, till mixture comes to boiling.

Add one 6-ounce can (1⅓ cups) broiled sliced mushrooms, drained, one 5- or 6-ounce can water chestnuts, sliced and drained, and ¼ cup toasted slivered blanched almonds. Heat to boiling. Makes 5 servings.

Chinese Fried Rice

1 4⅝-ounce package precooked rice
2 tablespoons salad or peanut oil
1 6-ounce can (1⅓ cups) broiled sliced mushrooms, drained
¼ cup chopped green onions
2 tablespoons soy sauce
8 slices cooked bacon, crumbled
1 beaten egg

Prepare rice according to directions. Chill. Heat oil in skillet; add rice, mushrooms, onions, and soy sauce. Cook over low heat 10 minutes; stir occasionally. Add bacon and egg. Cook and stir 5 minutes. Serves 5.

Chopsticks—fun for a party

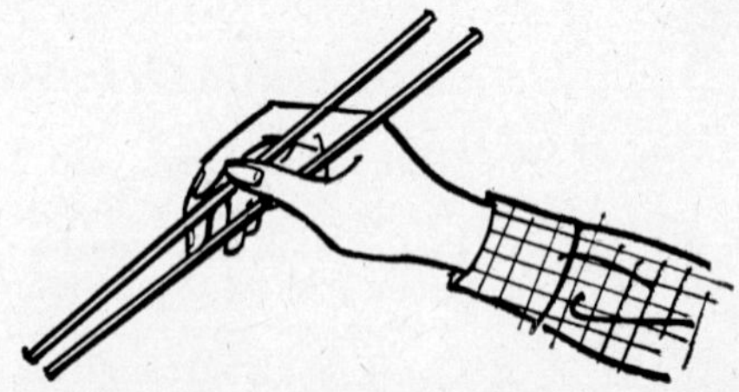

How to use: Hold top stick like a pencil, a little above the middle, small end down. Grip *loosely* between *tips* of index and middle finger; anchor *gently* with the thumb—whole hand must be relaxed. Now practice moving stick a few times till you get the feel of it.

Next slip lower stick into position. Rest it *lightly* in the V formed by your thumb and index finger and on the first joint of the ring finger. (Resist temptation to touch lower stick with middle finger.) Lower stick never moves.

style supper

You make the sauces, salad, and desserts early. Last—add your own "monogram" to packaged main dishes

Set an Oriental party mood! Hang paper lanterns; set each place with a bamboo mat or open paper fan, chopsticks, a moist Oriental napkin.

For napkin, dip cloth once in hot water scented with 2 or 3 drops white ginger perfume. Twist napkin in the middle. While hot and damp, place in individual basket or on plate.

Oriental Salad

This salad will keep several days in the refrigerator—just cover; leave in dressing—

- 2 teaspoons salt
- 2 medium cucumbers, sliced paper thin (2 cups)
- 2 cups shredded carrots
- ¼ teaspoon salt
- ½ cup sugar
- ½ cup white vinegar

Sprinkle 2 teaspoons salt over cucumbers. Chill thoroughly, 1 hour or longer. Drain in sieve, pressing with paper towels to remove as much moisture as possible.

Sprinkle carrots with ¼ teaspoon salt. Combine sugar and vinegar, stirring to dissolve sugar. Place cucumbers in one side of bowl and carrots in other side; pour vinegar mixture over. Chill at least 1 hour.

To serve, drain, reserving liquid to pass as dressing; arrange carrots in center of cucumber ring. Trim with radish roses, if desired. Makes 5 servings.

Mandarin Orange Dessert

- 1 package instant vanilla pudding
- 3 cups milk
- 2 11-ounce cans (2½ cups) mandarin orange sections, drained

Combine instant pudding and milk following label directions. Pour in serving bowl; let stand till set, about 10 minutes. Serve over orange sections. Makes 5 to 6 servings.

Coconut Macaroons

- 1 8-ounce package shredded coconut
- ⅔ cup sweetened condensed milk (½ 15-ounce can)
- 1 teaspoon vanilla

Thoroughly combine coconut and condensed milk; add vanilla. Drop from teaspoon on *well-greased* baking sheet about 1 inch apart. Bake at 350° 8 to 10 minutes, or till lightly browned. Let cool slightly; remove from baking sheet. Cool on rack. Makes about 2 dozen.

From Japan—wonderful sukiyaki

Sukiyaki

2 to 4 ounces dry bean threads (optional)

• • •

Few small pieces beef suet
1 pound beef tenderloin, sliced paper-thin (across the grain)

• • •

2 tablespoons sugar
1 teaspoon monosodium glutamate
½ cup soy sauce
½ cup beef stock *or* canned condensed beef broth *or* ½ beef bouillon cube dissolved in ½ cup hot water

• • •

2 cups 2-inch lengths bias-cut green onions
1 cup 2-inch bias-cut celery slices
½ cup thinly sliced fresh mushrooms

• • •

1 5-ounce can (⅔ cup) water chestnuts, drained and thinly sliced
1 5-ounce can (⅔ cup) bamboo shoots, slivered or diced, drained
5 cups small spinach leaves or 2-inch lengths (stems removed)
1 1-pound can (2 cups) bean sprouts, drained

Prepare bean threads ahead by soaking 2 hours in cold water; drain.

Just before cooking time, arrange meat and vegetables attractively on large platter. Have small containers of sugar, monosodium glutamate, soy sauce, and beef stock handy. For "toss-stirring" you'll want to use two tools at once—big spoon and fork.

Preheat large (12-inch) skillet (or Oriental saucepan); add suet; rub over bottom and sides to grease; when you have about 2 tablespoons melted fat, remove suet. Add beef; cook briskly, turning it over and over, 1 or 2 minutes or just till browned. Now sprinkle meat with sugar and monosodium glutamate; pour soy sauce and beef stock over. Push the meat to one side and let the soy mixture bubble.

Keeping in separate groups, add onions, celery, and mushrooms. Continue cooking and toss-stirring *each group* over high heat about 1 minute; push to one side. Keeping in separate groups, add bean threads and remaining vegetables. Cook and toss-stir each food just until heated through. Let guests help themselves to some of everything, including sauce. Serve with hot cooked rice. Pass cruet of soy sauce. Makes 4 servings.

For more batches, leave remaining sauce in pan and add soy sauce, beef stock, and seasonings by guess and by golly. This is very informal—guests may even cook their own. Sukiyaki may "keep going" all evening.

Note: To prepare fresh mushrooms: Wash in small amount water—don't peel. Cut off tip of stem. Slice through crown and stem.

Chawan-Mushi *(Custard Soup)*

8 raw shrimp, peeled and deveined
8 spinach leaves, cut in 1½-inch pieces
½ cup sliced mushrooms
8 water chestnuts, sliced
2 slightly beaten eggs
2 cups chicken broth
½ teaspoon salt

Make small slit in each shrimp; pull tail through. Wilt spinach in hot water, drain. Line up 8 Chawan-Mushi cups or 5-ounce custard cups. In each, place shrimp, spinach, mushrooms, and water chestnuts. Combine eggs, chicken broth, and salt; pour into cups; cover with lids or foil. Set cups on rack in Dutch oven; pour hot water around cups 1 inch deep; cover to steam. Over medium heat, bring water *slowly* to simmering; reduce heat and cook about 7 minutes more or till knife inserted off center comes out clean. Top each custard with ¼ teaspoon soy sauce and a thin twist of lemon peel.

SUKIYAKI SUPPER

Chawan-Mushi (Hot Custard Soup)
Sukiyaki
Fluffy Rice
Chilled Peach Slices in Orange Juice
Fortune Cookies
Hot Tea

← Delicious blend of East, West

It's our American version of Sukiyaki (pronounced "skiyaki")—thin strips of beef tenderloin, crisp-cooked vegetables.

This is friendly, cook-at-the-table entertaining! Use an hibachi or other grill—fix no more than 4 servings at a time.

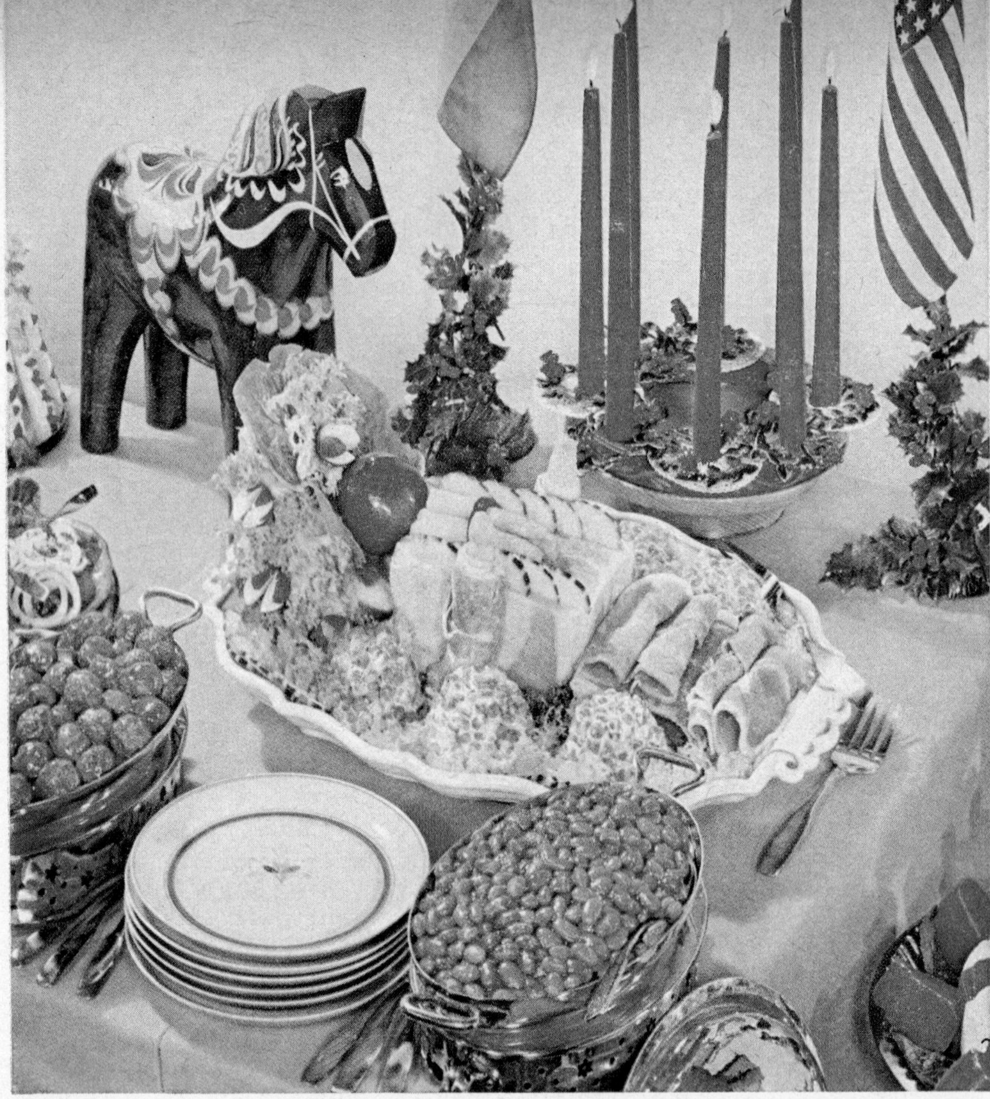

Choose main course from meats, Brown Beans, salads (or try all!)

Swedish Meat Balls and Brown Beans keep *hot* on warmers. For contrast—Chilled Decorated Ham with Vegetable Cups (peas, carrots, asparagus in mayonnaise), and Red-and-white Salad.

Swedish smorgasbord

SMORGASBORD

Swedish Relishes and Breads
Swedish Meat Balls Brown Beans
Decorated Chilled Ham Dill Potatoes
Vegetable Cups Red-and-white Salad
Swedish Pancakes With
Lingonberry Sauce
Caraway Seed Cheese Toasted Wafers
Swedish Coffee

Smorgasbord is for folks who *enjoy* eating! Offer fresh plates three times—first for appetizers, then meats, last desserts. This is an ideal "several-hostess" meal—plan jointly, make foods at home, and carry to party.

Swedish Relishes

Bed appetizer dishes on ice. Fill with Herring Salad, pickled herring, anchovies, smoked salmon, sardines, pickled beets.

Other choices: Anchovy-stuffed eggs, pickled shrimp, liver pate, Stuffed Celery.

Herring Salad (*Sillsallad*)

1½ pounds salt herring
2 pared medium potatoes, cooked and finely cubed
4 medium beets, cooked, peeled, and finely cubed or cut julienne
1 medium apple, pared, finely cubed
1 tablespoon finely chopped onion
2 medium sweet pickles, finely cubed
1 tablespoon sugar
2 tablespoons vinegar
¼ teaspoon white pepper
½ cup heavy cream, whipped (optional)

Soak herring overnight in water to cover. Bone; skin, and cut in small cubes. Lightly mix all ingredients except cream. Chill. Fold in cream. Trim with sieved egg yolks and finely chopped whites. Makes about 6 cups.

Stuffed Celery

Beat together cream cheese and crumbled blue cheese (to suit taste) till fluffy. Fill celery. Dot with capers, pimiento diamonds.

Delicious beginning—appetizers

Choose from Swedish Relishes, potatoes with dill, breads. For penguins, toothpick olives, olive slices, to eggs; add carrot feet, bills.

Swedish Meat Balls (*Kottbullar*)

¾ pound ground beef round
½ pound ground veal
¼ pound ground pork
1½ cups soft bread crumbs (3 slices)
¼ cup milk
½ cup chopped onion
1¾ cups half-and-half
¼ cup finely chopped parsley
1 teaspoon salt
1 teaspoon monosodium glutamate
¼ teaspoon ginger
½ to 1 teaspoon instant coffee
½ teaspoon concentrated meat extract

Have meats ground together twice. Soak bread in milk 5 minutes. Cook onion in 2 tablespoons butter till tender but not brown. Combine ground meats, crumbs, onion, *1 cup* of the half-and-half, parsley, and seasonings. Beat vigorously till fluffy (about 5 minutes at medium speed on electric mixer). Mixture will be soft. Form in 1-inch balls (for easier shaping, wet hands when necessary).

Brown lightly in 2 tablespoons butter, shaking skillet to keep balls round. (Don't try to brown too many at a time.) Remove meat balls. Stir 1 tablespoon flour into drippings; add remaining half-and-half, coffee, meat extract, and dash monosodium glutamate; heat and stir till gravy thickens.

Return meat balls to gravy; simmer uncovered about 10 minutes. Add more half-and-half if needed. Makes 5 dozen balls.

Brown Beans (*Bruna Bonor*)

Wash 2 cups Swedish brown beans; drain. Add 5 cups water; cover, let stand overnight. (Or bring water and beans slowly to boiling; simmer 2 minutes; cover, let stand 1 hour.)

Add 3-inch cinnamon stick and 1½ teaspoons salt; cover and simmer 2 hours or till tender. (Add more water if needed.) Stir in ½ cup brown sugar or light molasses and ¼ cup vinegar. Cook, uncovered, 15 minutes longer, stirring occasionally. Serves 6.

Decorated Chilled Ham

Place chilled canned ham on large platter. Run tines of fork down unpared cucumber; cut in ¼-inch slices; halve slices. Stand half-slices on edge atop ham, overlapping them in two rows. In center place bundle of chilled canned asparagus, "tied" with pimiento strip. Wrap asparagus spear in ham slice, stand on end; toothpick to ham; repeat on other side.

For dramatic backdrop, stand big wedge unsliced bread on end. Cover with lettuce and curly endive, tacking with toothpicks; dot with radish roses on toothpicks. Add red apple. Trim platter with individual salads.

Red-and-white Salad

Red Tomato Mold:

4 cups tomato juice
⅓ cup chopped onion
¼ cup chopped celery leaves
2 tablespoons brown sugar
1 teaspoon salt
2 small bay leaves
4 whole cloves
2 envelopes unflavored gelatin
3 tablespoons lemon juice

Combine *2 cups* of the tomato juice, onion, celery leaves, sugar, salt, bay leaves, and cloves. Simmer uncovered 5 minutes. Strain.

Meanwhile, soften gelatin in *1 cup* of remaining *cold* tomato juice; dissolve in *hot* mixture. Add rest of tomato juice, lemon juice. Chill firm in 5-cup ring mold.

Snowy Cheese Mold:

1 12-ounce carton (1½ cups) cream-style cottage cheese
2 3-ounce packages cream cheese, softened
½ cup finely chopped celery
2 tablespoons finely chopped chives
¼ teaspoon salt
1 envelope unflavored gelatin
1 cup mayonnaise

With electric or rotary beater, beat together cottage cheese and cream cheese till fluffy. Stir in celery, chives, and salt. Soften gelatin in ¼ cup cold water; dissolve over hot water. Stir into cheese mixture. Stir in mayonnaise. Chill firm in 5-cup ring mold.

Unmold both salads; cut in wide slices, alternate slices, red and white, reassembling 2 identical salads. Makes 12 servings.

Swedish Pancakes

Beat 3 eggs till thick and lemon-colored. Stir in 1¼ cups milk. Sift together ¾ cup sifted enriched flour, 1 tablespoon sugar, and ½ teaspoon salt. Add; mix till smooth.

Drop small amount batter (1 tablespoon for 3-inch cake) onto moderately hot, buttered griddle (or bake on special Swedish griddle). Spread batter evenly to make thin cakes. Turn when underside is delicately browned.

(To keep first pancakes warm, place on towel-covered baking sheet in 250° oven.) Spoon melted butter over; sprinkle with sugar. Stack in chafing dish. Makes 3½ dozen.

Lingonberry Sauce

Drain 4 cups lingonberries; wash. Place in saucepan. Add ½ cup water; bring to boiling. Add 1 cup sugar; stir to dissolve. Simmer 10 minutes. Place pan in cold water; stir sauce a minute or two. Makes 3 cups.

To make your party craft—

Staple sides of ship together along outside edge; paint ship black. Insert brass paper fasteners for dragon eyes. Carefully bend sides of ship apart to curve outward.

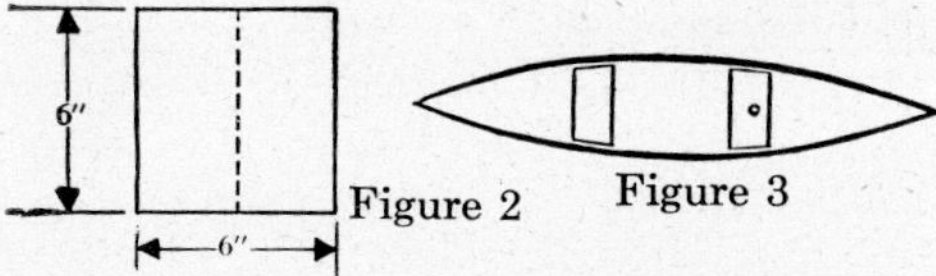

To make braces—With sharp knife, score 6-inch square of Bristol board down center (figure 2); fold. Fold ends to make narrow tabs. Staple tabs forward in ship so brace is seat-style, holding sides apart (figure 3).

Make rear brace from 5½x4-inch piece; fold long way. *Shields*—Cut 14 2-inch disks red cardboard; secure with paper fasteners.

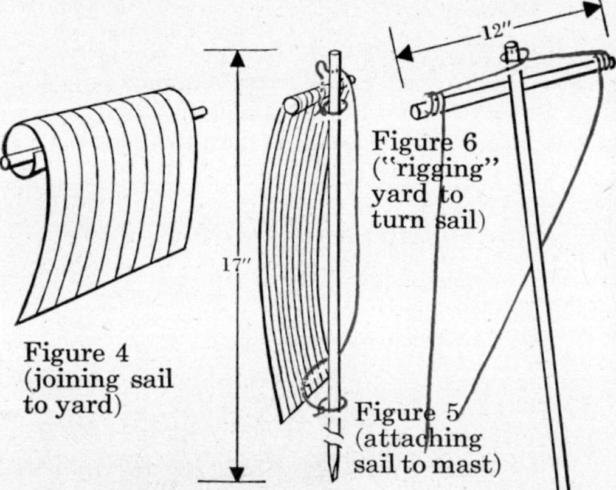

For mast, use a 17-inch piece of ¼-inch doweling. Whittle point at bottom; drill tiny holes ½ and 1½ inches from top. Use a 12-inch piece of doweling for yard.

For sail, cut a 24x11-inch piece of gift-wrapping paper; fold in half crosswise. Fold and glue "raw" edges around yard (figure 4). Make hole in center of yard, going through sail; run string through it, then through lower hole in mast (figure 5); tie lower end to mast. Poke hole in bottom center of sail; pull free string end through; tie to mast high enough so sail will billow.

Tie long string to one end of yard (figure 6); leave one end (24 inches long) dangling; pull other end through hole at top of mast and tie to other end of yard; leave 24-inch end. Poke sharp end of mast through center of forward brace; anchor in seam.

Poke holes in sides of ship near back; pull string ends from yard through holes toward inside of ship. Pull one string to turn sail slightly; tie ends together.

To make stand—Cut two 12x1½-inch strips, two 6x2½-inch pieces of Bristol board.

Scallop top edges of long strips. Cut V's 1½ inches deep in short crosspieces to hold ship. Round off ends of all strips. Paint blue. Cut slits near ends of each; fit together.

Launch a paper Viking ship on smorgasbord table—it's a striking centerpiece; bread basket too!

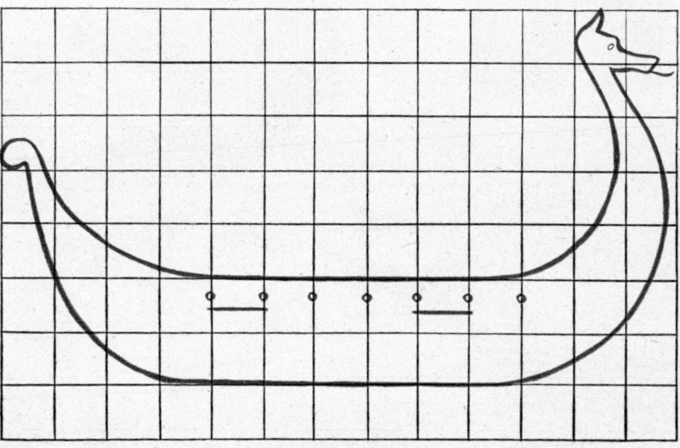

Figure 1—Rule paper in 2-inch squares. Draw pattern for side of Viking ship. Cut two sides from light Bristol board.

Tempting buffets from India and Mexico

MEXICAN FIESTA

Mexican Relish Tray
Turkey-stuffed Tamales
Cheese Enchiladas
Mexican Fried Rice
Chiles Rellenos Tomato Sauce
Fried Tortillas
Caramel Custard
Hot Coffee

No need to go south-of-the-border to enjoy this Mexican-style meal!

Your hostess is serving jumbo turkey-stuffed tamales. Appetizers on Mexican Relish Tray are Guacamole in tomato holders, chopped red onions and radishes in green-pepper cups, corn chips, and tiny tamales. Help yourself to Mexican Fried Rice and ripe-olive-topped Cheese Enchiladas. Ladle extra Tomato Sauce over an airy Chile Relleno. Now for a crisp, fried tortilla from the sombrero. Dessert is caramel custard.

From India—an exotic curry

Guests ladle spicy Shrimp Curry over Yellow Rice served in individual bowls. Golden duck holds preserved kumquats; little bowls offer curry condiments.

Mexican Fried Rice

1 cup long-grain rice
1½ cups hot water

• • •

6 slices bacon, chopped
1 can condensed consomme
1 8-ounce can (1 cup) seasoned tomato sauce
¼ cup chopped green pepper
¼ cup chopped onion
1 clove garlic, minced
½ teaspoon cumin seed

Soak rice in hot water 25 minutes; drain; let stand to dry, about 1 hour. Cook bacon till crisp; remove bacon. Add rice to drippings and cook till rice is lightly browned. Add bacon and remaining ingredients. Cover, and cook over low heat, stirring occasionally, till rice is done and liquid absorbed, about 30 minutes. (Add water during cooking if needed.) Makes 4 to 6 servings.

CASUAL CURRY BUFFET

Shrimp Curry
Yellow Rice
Curry Condiments
Romaine Salad
Chilled Orange Sections
Coconut Chips
Hot Tea

Cheese Enchiladas

Sprinkle enchiladas (from can or frozen package) with shredded sharp process American cheese. Heat according to label directions. Trim with olives speared on toothpicks.

Guacamole

2 medium ripe avocados, mashed (2 cups)
1 tablespoon minced onion
1 clove garlic, minced
¼ teaspoon chili powder
¼ teaspoon salt
⅓ cup mayonnaise or salad dressing
6 slices crisp-cooked bacon, crumbled

Combine mashed avocado, onion, garlic, seasonings in small bowl. Spread top with mayonnaise, sealing to edges of bowl; chill. At serving time, stir in mayonnaise, bacon; spoon into tomato cups. Makes 2 cups.

Chiles Rellenos

2 large green peppers
¼ pound sharp Cheddar cheese
4 egg whites
2 tablespoons water
½ teaspoon salt
2 tablespoons enriched flour
4 egg yolks

Remove tops and seeds from peppers. Cut peppers in quarters lengthwise; cook in simmering water 8 to 10 minutes or till tender. Drain, cool, and peel.

Cut cheese in four ¼-inch slices and sandwich each between green-pepper pieces. Beat egg whites till frothy; add water and salt; beat till stiff but not dry. Add flour and dash pepper to yolks; beat till thick and lemon-colored; fold into whites.

Pour 4 mounds (½ cup each) on hot, greased griddle or skillet. Brown lightly on bottom, then gently top each with cheese-stuffed pepper. Divide remaining egg mixture over peppers, making sure the peppers are covered. Continue cooking till underside is nicely browned. Turn carefully and cook till second side is browned. Serve with Tomato Sauce. Makes 4 servings.

Tomato Sauce

⅓ cup chopped onion
1 clove garlic, minced
1 tablespoon salad oil
1 8-ounce can seasoned tomato sauce
¾ teaspoon salt
½ teaspoon chili powder
½ teaspoon oregano

Cook onion and garlic in hot salad oil till tender but not brown. Add remaining ingredients. Simmer 5 minutes. Makes 1 cup.

Quick Chili Supper

¼ cup chopped onion
¼ cup chopped green pepper
1 11-ounce can tamales
1 1-pound can (2 cups) chili con carne with beans
½ cup shredded sharp American cheese

Cook onion and green pepper in hot fat till tender. Add chili. Remove shucks from tamales; arrange spoke-fashion on top. Cover; heat 10 to 15 minutes. Sprinkle with cheese and serve. Makes 4 or 5 servings.

Shrimp Curry

⅓ cup butter or margarine
½ cup chopped onion
¼ to ½ cup chopped green pepper
2 cloves garlic, minced
2 cups dairy sour cream
2 teaspoons lemon juice
2 teaspoons curry powder
¾ teaspoon salt
½ teaspoon ginger
Dash chili powder
3 cups cleaned cooked or canned shrimp, split lengthwise in half (about 2 pounds in shell)

Melt butter in chafing dish or skillet. Add onion, green pepper, and garlic; cook till tender but not brown, about 3 minutes. Stir in sour cream, lemon juice, and seasonings; add shrimp. Cook over *low* heat, stirring constantly, just till thoroughly heated.

Serve over Yellow Rice. Offer flaked coconut, peanut halves, chutney, chopped chives, and chopped hard-cooked egg. Serves 6.

Yellow Rice

2 cups boiling water
1 teaspoon salt
15 grains saffron
1 cup uncooked long-grain rice

To boiling water add the salt and saffron. Stir in rice; return to boiling, then lower heat. Cover and cook over *low* heat till tender and water is absorbed, about 25 minutes. Serve hot. Makes 3 cups.

Jiffy Yellow Rice: Prepare one 4⅝-ounce package (1⅓ cups) precooked rice according to package directions, but add 4 to 6 drops of yellow food coloring.

Italian Lasagne is a natural for buffets—it can be fixed ahead and stored in the refrigerator until baking time. To carry out the Latin theme—peppers, pottery, and raffia-trimmed glasses.

For hearty appetites, hot Italian supper specialities

Snappy pizzas and pastas—complemented by expertly seasoned salads and crusty Italian breads—are tops for casual entertaining. Start from scratch or use speedy cans and mixes.

"Little Italy" table touches are easy—a checkered cloth, candles in pretty bottles.

ITALIAN SUPPER

Antipasto Tray
Lasagne, Pizza, or Spaghetti
Italian Green Salad
Italian Long Loaf or Bread Sticks
Spumone or Cherry Ice Cream
Coffee

Lasagne

1 pound Italian sausage, bulk pork sausage, or ground beef
1 clove garlic, minced
1 tablespoon chopped parsley
1 tablespoon basil
1½ teaspoons salt
1 1-pound can (2 cups) tomatoes
2 6-ounce cans (1⅓ cups) tomato paste
1 10-ounce package lasagne noodles
2 12-ounce cartons (3 cups) large-curd cream-style cottage cheese
2 beaten eggs
1 teaspoon salt
½ teaspoon pepper
2 tablespoons chopped parsley
½ cup grated Parmesan cheese
1 pound Mozzarella cheese, sliced *thin*

Brown meat slowly; spoon off excess fat. Add next 6 ingredients to meat. Simmer, uncovered, till thick, about 30 minutes, stirring occasionally.

Cook noodles in boiling salted water till tender; drain; rinse in cold water. Combine cottage cheese with next 5 ingredients.

Place *half* the noodles in 13x9x2-inch baking dish; spread *half* the cottage-cheese mixture over; add *half* the Mozzarella cheese and *half* the meat mixture. Repeat layers.

Bake in moderate oven (375°) 30 minutes. Let stand 10 to 15 minutes before cutting in squares. Makes 12 servings.

Antipasto Tray

Here's a relish dish with zingo! It's extra easy—every item comes ready to eat.

On a large serving dish, arrange spiced hearts of artichoke, Italian-style mild Tuscan salad peppers, pickled peppers (very hot!), sweet red-pepper halves, ripe and stuffed green olives, paper-thin slices of pepperoni, and roll-ups of salami.

Italian Green Salad

1 head romaine
1 bunch leaf lettuce

• • •

2 tomatoes, cut in wedges
½ cup celery slices
½ cup diced green pepper
½ cup radish slices
¼ cup sliced green onions
1 2-ounce can anchovies, chopped

• • •

3 tablespoons olive or salad oil
2 tablespoons tarragon vinegar
2 tablespoons chopped parsley
¾ teaspoon salt
Dash freshly ground pepper
½ teaspoon whole basil

Tear greens in bite-size pieces in a bowl; arrange vegetables and anchovies over lettuce. Sprinkle with remaining ingredients. Toss lightly. Makes 6 to 8 servings.

Italian Spaghetti and Meat Balls

1½ pounds ground beef
½ cup fine dry bread crumbs
1 slightly beaten egg
¼ cup grated Parmesan cheese
¼ cup warm water
1½ teaspoons salt
½ teaspoon basil
¼ teaspoon pepper

• • •

1 No. 2½ can (3½ cups) tomatoes
1 6-ounce can (⅔ cup) tomato paste
¼ cup chopped onion
2 cloves garlic, minced
2 tablespoons chopped parsley
1 teaspoon salt
1 teaspoon crushed oregano
¼ teaspoon anise seed

• • •

1 8-ounce package long spaghetti

Combine meat with next 7 ingredients; form in about 36 one-inch balls. In large skillet, brown meat slowly in small amount of hot fat. Add remaining ingredients except spaghetti. Simmer uncovered (*don't boil*), stirring occasionally, 1½ to 2 hours or till thick.

Cook spaghetti in boiling salted water (about 1 tablespoon salt to 3 quarts water) till tender but still firm. Drain.

Serve meat balls and sauce over spaghetti. Pass Parmesan cheese. Makes 6 servings.

Long-time favorite—Spaghetti and Meat Balls

Tomato sauce, chock-full of chunky meat balls, simmers long and lazily, develops rich full flavor. Serve over spaghetti cooked *al dente* (just tender, but firm) and pass the Parmesan. Leave spaghetti "long"—then folks can eat it wrapped around the fork, Italian style.

Other times, serve this sauce over a different pasta—*mezzani, ziti, iolanda* (yolanda), and *elena* are distinctive stand-ins for spaghetti.

Pane Italiano is famous for its wonderful crustiness and airy inside. Serve husky slices of Italian bread with salami, lots of butter!

Pizza

1 package hot roll mix
1 pound Italian or bulk pork sausage
2 cloves garlic, minced
1 tablespoon crushed sweet basil
1½ tablespoons crushed oregano
2 6-ounce cans (1⅓ cups) tomato paste
1 6-ounce can (1⅓ cups) broiled sliced mushrooms, drained
2 6-ounce packages sliced Mozzarella cheese, cut in pieces
⅔ cup grated Romano cheese

Prepare dough from roll mix following label directions, but omit rising. Divide in half. Roll in two 13-inch circles. Place on ungreased cooky sheet; turn up edges.

In skillet, break up sausage; fry slowly till evenly browned; drain. Add garlic; seasonings. Spread 1 can tomato paste over each dough circle; cover with sausage, mushrooms.

Bake at 425° 10 minutes; remove from oven; top with Mozzarella; bake 10 minutes more or till crust is done. Sprinkle with Romano.

Speedy Pizza

For in-a-hurry pizza, buy the frozen kind or a box of pizza mix. Make it "yours" with peppy garnishes: anchovy fillets, pepperoni "wreath," Mozzarella cheese triangles dotted with antipasto, or Italian-style Bologna.

Italian Long Loaf

2 packages active dry yeast *or* 2 cakes compressed yeast
2½ cups water
1 tablespoon salt
7¼ to 7¾ cups sifted enriched flour

• • •

Yellow corn meal

• • •

1 slightly beaten egg white

In large mixing bowl, soften active dry yeast in *warm* water or compressed yeast in *lukewarm* water. Stir in *2 cups* of the flour; beat well. Add salt. Then stir in *about 4½ cups* of remaining flour. (Dough should be stiffer than for ordinary bread.)

Turn out on lightly floured surface. Cover; let rest 10 minutes. Knead *15 to 25 minutes* or till very elastic, kneading in remaining *¾ to 1¼ cups* flour. (The longer kneading time develops gluten more, makes a more typical Italian bread.) Place dough in lightly greased bowl, turning once to grease surface. Cover; let rise in warm place till double (about 1½ hours). Punch down; let rise again till double (about 1 hour).

Turn out on lightly floured surface. Divide in half and form each part in a ball. Cover; let rest 10 minutes.

Shaping long loaves: Roll each half of dough in 15x12-inch rectangle, about ¼ inch thick. Beginning at long side, roll up tightly, sealing well as you roll. Taper ends. Place each loaf diagonally, seam side down, on greased baking sheet sprinkled with corn meal (gives crunchy bottom crust). With a *sharp* knife, slash down center (⅛ to ¼ inch deep).

Add 1 tablespoon water to egg white; brush over top and sides of loaves. Cover with damp cloth, but don't let it touch dough. (Make tent by placing cloth over tall tumblers.) Let rise in warm place till double (1 to 1½ hours).

(When ready to bake, place large shallow pan on lower rack of oven; fill with boiling water. This makes the crust crisper.)

Bake in moderate oven (375°) till light brown, about 20 minutes; brush again with egg-white mixture. Continue baking about 20 minutes longer or till nicely browned.

For crackled top crust, cool in a draft—you can hear the crust crackle!

Eat Italian breads while fresh. Because they are made with water and have little or no fat, they dry out fast.

Polynesian hospitality–the luau

Gaiety reigns at an easy-going Polynesian luau. Traditionally everyone samples the exotic foods with his fingers (though chopsticks or forks are permissible) and ti leaves substitute for cloths on table *or* ground. (No ti leaves? Use ferns or matting instead.)

Your luau can include any number of these dishes from "Trader Vic's" of Oakland and San Francisco. (Co-hostesses might plan a choice of main dishes, island style.)

Mass flowers everywhere—exotic blooms, or garden flowers that don't wilt too quickly—daisies, mums, carnations. In the centerpiece, group tropical fruits with flowers.

ISLAND FEAST

Water Chestnuts with Chicken Livers
Kona Chicken — Steamed Rice
Batter-fried Shrimp with Sauces
Chinese Peas with Water Chestnuts
Waikiki Salad
Raspberry Sherbet with Coconut
Beach Boy Punch

Luau, Trader Vic's style

← Up front are Barbecued Shrimp, Baked Bananas, broiled chicken, sweet potatoes. Serving shells hold Island Spareribs and Batter-fried Shrimp. Coconut husks offer Kona Chicken.

The Outrigger is a salad boat of hollowed-out cucumber carrying seasoned shrimp and crab over a sea of cottage cheese. Fresh asparagus spears make her outrigger. Dolls are Chinese.

Waikiki Salad—lush tropical fruits heaped high in a pineapple shell. Keep it cool on a bed of crushed ice and tuck in a flower for the exotic touch. Serve with Oahu Spice Dressing.

Water Chestnuts With Chicken Livers

Wash fresh water chestnuts thoroughly and slice each in thirds. Or use canned ones.

Cut chicken livers in slices slightly larger than chestnut slices; dip in soy sauce.

Using two slices of chicken liver and one of chestnut, make a sandwich. Wrap in thin slice of bacon, skewer with toothpick, and fry in deep hot fat (375°) 2 or 3 minutes.

Chinese Peas With Water Chestnuts

Heat 1 tablespoon salad oil in skillet; fry ⅓ cup finely chopped raw pork. Add 2 cups Chinese green peas, ½ cup finely sliced water chestnuts, and 1 teaspoon monosodium glutamate. Add 1 cup chicken broth.

Steam, covered, over high heat about 3 minutes. Combine 1 tablespoon cornstarch with 2 tablespoons cold water. Push vegetables to one side; add cornstarch mixture to broth. Cook and stir till slightly thick. Salt to taste. Makes 3 to 4 servings.

Beach Boy Punch

Mix 1 quart cranberry juice, juice of two lemons, and 1 pint orange juice; pour into punch bowl over cake of ice. Add 2 quarts chilled ginger ale. Makes about 4 quarts.

Oahu Spice Dressing

In jar, combine ¼ cup lemon juice, ¼ cup mixed fruit juices or pineapple juice, ½ cup salad oil, 1 teaspoon each brown sugar and paprika, and ¼ teaspoon each salt and celery seed. Shake thoroughly.

Island Spareribs

½ cup soy sauce
½ cup catsup
3 tablespoons brown sugar
1 egg-size ginger root, grated
1 teaspoon monosodium glutamate
3 sides (about 3 pounds) small, meaty pork spareribs
¼ cup sugar
1 teaspoon salt

Mix first five ingredients for Island Barbecue Sauce. Let stand overnight.

Rub spareribs on both sides with sugar and salt; let stand 2 hours. Brush with Island Barbecue Sauce; let stand at least an hour.

Barbecue or hang in Chinese barbecue oven about an hour. Or, barbecue in range oven: Place meat side up, on rack in shallow pan; bake in very hot oven (450°) 15 minutes; pour off fat. Continue baking in moderate oven (350°) 1 hour or till done, turning ribs and brushing with barbecue sauce a few times. Cut in pieces. Makes 6 servings.

Kona Chicken in a Coconut

1 teaspoon each chopped tomato, bell pepper, and pineapple, well mixed
2 cups Trader Vic's Susu Curry Sauce
1 cup cubed cooked chicken meat
Dash bottled meat sauce
Salt to taste
Seasoned mashed potatoes
Hollandaise sauce

Mix all ingredients except potatoes and Hollandaise; heat. Fill coconut shell (or 1-quart casserole) with this mixture. Decorate sawed-off section of husk with hot mashed potato squeezed through a pastry tube. Cover curry mixture with a tablespoon or so of Hollandaise sauce. Bake in very hot oven (450°) 10 to 12 minutes. Serve with fluffy steamed rice. Makes 2 to 3 large servings.

Trader Vic's Susu Curry Sauce

1 tablespoon curry powder
1 tablespoon butter
1 onion, minced
2 stalks celery, diced
½ cup sliced mushrooms
1 cup diced apple
½ cup soup stock
1 cup light cream
1 cup milk
2 tablespoons cornstarch
2 tablespoons cold water
Monosodium glutamate to taste
Salt to taste

Saute curry powder in butter until nicely browned; stir in vegetables and apple. Add stock and bring to a boil, then stir in cream and milk; bring to boil again.

Combine cornstarch and cold water; add to hot mixture. Cook and stir constantly till thick. Season. Makes 3½ cups. Use sauce in Kona Chicken, or heat cubed chicken or seafood in it and serve over fluffy rice.

Baked Bananas

In Tahiti, bananas are baked in underground ovens, then split and eaten from the skins as a vegetable.

Mainland method is to bake firm green-tipped bananas, skins on, in a slow oven (300° to 325°) about 30 minutes or until a fork will pierce them easily.

Serve with skins on. Let guests peel their own, sprinkle sparingly with salt.

Batter-fried Shrimp

2 cups sifted enriched flour
½ cup cornstarch
¼ cup white corn meal
½ teaspoon baking powder
1 egg, slightly beaten
3 cups water
½ cup milk
5 pounds large, shucked raw shrimp

Combine all ingredients except shrimp, but *don't stir too much*—that's part of the secret of the crisp almost-lacy jackets on these shrimp. Use a small amount of batter at a time, in a small bowl; mix in plenty of shrimp, so each one is only *lightly coated*.

Fry in deep hot fat (about 400°) 3 or 4 minutes. Serve with Sweet and Sour Sauce, Red Sauce, and/or Chinese Mustard for dipping.

Barbecued Shrimp

Let large unpeeled shrimp stand in soy sauce a few minutes. String on skewers. Barbecue over glowing coals about 10 minutes or till done, turning a few times. Let guests remove shells, dip in Chinese Mustard, Red Sauce, and/or Sweet and Sour Sauce.

Chinese Mustard

Stir ¼ cup boiling water into ¼ cup dry English mustard. Add ½ teaspoon salt and 2 teaspoons salad oil. If sauce is not yellow enough, add turmeric. Makes ⅓ cup.

Red Sauce

Combine 3 tablespoons each catsup, chili sauce, and horseradish, 1 teaspoon lemon juice, dash Tabasco sauce, and salt and pepper to taste. Makes about ½ cup.

Sweet and Sour Sauce

Mix 1 cup sugar, ½ cup each distilled vinegar and water, 1 tablespoon each chopped green pepper and chopped pimiento, and ½ teaspoon salt. Simmer 5 minutes.

Combine 2 teaspoons cornstarch with 1 tablespoon cold water and add to hot mixture. Cook and stir until thick.

Let cool. Before serving, strain out the pepper and pimiento. Add 1 teaspoon paprika, a few bits of pimiento, and a little finely chopped parsley. Makes about 1 cup.

Shrimp Pinwheel Casserole stars in supper for six. Tender biscuit topper bakes on mixture of pink shrimp and new peas in tomato sauce. Next time serve chilled Fruit-soup Dessert hot, as a spicy appetizer.

SHRIMP MAKES IT SPECIAL

Shrimp Pinwheel Casserole
Tossed Green Salad   Stuffed Olives
Pinwheel Biscuits
Fruit-soup Dessert   Hot Coffee

Timesavers: Day before, make Fruit-soup Dessert; chill. Morning of party, combine casserole ingredients; chill. (Before baking, heat through; pour into casserole; top with biscuits; bake.)

Also fix salad greens early; chill. Toss salad at table; call on your favorite bottled dressing or salad-dressing mix.

Fruit-soup Dessert

1 11-ounce package mixed dried fruits
½ cup golden seedless raisins
3 to 4 inches stick cinnamon
4 cups water
1 orange, unpared, cut in ¼-inch slices
1 No. 2 can (2¼ cups) unsweetened pineapple juice
½ cup currant jelly
¼ cup sugar
2 tablespoons quick-cooking tapioca
¼ teaspoon salt

Combine mixed fruits, raisins, cinnamon, and water. Bring to boiling, reduce heat; simmer uncovered till fruits are tender, about 30 minutes. Add remaining ingredients. Bring to boiling; cover, cook over low heat 15 minutes longer, stirring occasionally. Serve warm or chilled. Makes 8 to 10 servings.

Casual buffets, American style

Shrimp Pinwheel Casserole

⅓ cup chopped green pepper
¼ cup chopped onion
¼ cup butter or margarine
2 tablespoons enriched flour
½ teaspoon salt
1 1-pound can (2 cups) tomatoes
1½ cups shredded process American cheese
1½ cups cooked cleaned shrimp
¾ cup drained cooked or canned peas
1 recipe Pinwheel Biscuits

Cook green pepper and onion in butter till tender but not brown. Blend in flour, salt. Add tomatoes and cook, stirring constantly, till thick. Add cheese; stir till melted. Add shrimp and peas.

Pour into greased 2-quart casserole. Top with Pinwheel Biscuits; bake at 450° 15 to 20 minutes or till biscuits are done and golden brown. Makes 6 servings.

Pinwheel Biscuits

⅔ cup milk
2 cups packaged biscuit mix
1½ cups shredded American cheese
¼ cup chopped pimiento
1 tablespoon butter, melted

Add milk to biscuit mix all at once; mix and knead according to package directions.

Roll in rectangle ½ inch thick. Sprinkle with cheese and pimiento; roll as for jelly roll. Cut in 1-inch slices. Place 5 or 6 biscuits, cut side down, atop *hot* casserole mixture; brush tops with melted butter; bake as above. (Bake remaining biscuits on greased baking sheet.)

Tossed Green Salad

For 6 servings, break ½ head lettuce into bowl; tear ¼ bunch curly endive and ½ bunch water cress in small pieces; add.

Take your pick of extras—tomato wedges, sliced avocado, croutons, artichoke hearts, radish or celery slices, green-pepper strips, or snipped chives. Sprinkle with salt and freshly ground pepper. Pour your favorite clear French dressing over; toss lightly.

SKILLET CHICKEN SUPPER

Chicken in Jiffy Tomato Sauce
Buttered Broccoli
Fruit Platter — Hot French Bread
Refrigerator Cheese Pie — Hot Coffee

Timesavers: Day ahead, make dessert; chill. Morning of party, arrange assorted fruit on platter; chill. Cook chicken in electric skillet—serve from it at the table (no platter to wash).

Chicken in Jiffy Tomato Sauce

Cut up one 2½- to 3-pound ready-to-cook frying chicken; salt. Brown *slowly* in small amount hot salad oil; spoon off excess fat.

Combine one 1½-ounce envelope spaghetti-sauce mix, one 8-ounce can (1 cup) seasoned tomato sauce, and 1 cup water*; pour over chicken. Cover; simmer 20 to 30 minutes or till chicken is done. Serves 4.

**Or*, use two 10¾-ounce cans spaghetti sauce with mushrooms, omitting spaghetti-sauce mix, tomato sauce, water. Cook as above.

Refrigerator Cheese Pie

1½ cups fine vanilla-wafer crumbs
⅓ cup butter or margarine, melted
1 8-ounce package cream cheese, softened
⅔ cup sweetened condensed milk
1 teaspoon grated lemon peel
3 tablespoons lemon juice
½ cup heavy cream, whipped

Mix together crumbs and butter; press into buttered 9-inch pie plate. Chill till firm, about 45 minutes. Blend cream cheese, sweetened condensed milk, lemon peel, and juice. Fold in whipped cream; pour into crumb crust. Chill till firm, about 4 hours.

See tips on buffet service, pages 154-155.

How much to buy for 25

Beef, veal, or pork roasts. 10 pounds
Ham (to bake) . . . . 10 pounds
Ground beef (for burgers) . 6 pounds
Poultry (to roast) . . . . . . 15 pounds

• • •

Baked beans . . . . . . 6 1-pound cans
Cabbage (to shred) . . . . . . 4 pounds
Carrots . . . . 6 pounds
Corn, canned . . . . . 6 1-pound cans
Corn, frozen . . 6 10-ounce packages
Green beans, canned
. . . . 6 1-pound cans
Green beans, fresh . . . . . 5-6 pounds
Green beans, frozen
. . . . 6 10-ounce packages
Peas, canned . . . . . . 6 1-pound cans
Peas, frozen . . 6 10-ounce packages
Potatoes . . . . 6½-7½ pounds
Tomato juice . . . . . 2 46-ounce cans

Saturday Supper for the crowd!

Turn your electric roaster into a jumbo bean pot—our baked-bean recipe cooks enough for 30 guests. Set out Tossed Green Salad, page 107. Offer Parsleyed French Slices or Boston brown bread (from a can). Crisp apples, mugs of hot coffee are dessert.

Baked Beans for the Crowd

16 1-pound cans pork and beans in tomato sauce
1½ cups brown sugar
2 tablespoons dry mustard
2 14-ounce bottles (2½ cups) catsup
1 pound (26 slices) bacon, cut in pieces

Preheat electric roaster to 300°. Into inset pan in roaster, empty *8 cans* of the beans.

Combine brown sugar and mustard; sprinkle *half* of mixture over beans. Drizzle with *one bottle* of catsup.

Top with remaining beans, brown sugar mixture, catsup. Sprinkle bacon pieces over. Top with bacon strips if desired. Cook covered at 300° for 3½ to 4 hours. Keep hot at 150°. Makes 30 one-cup servings.

Parsleyed French Slices

1 loaf French bread (about 15 inches)
½ to ⅔ cup soft butter or margarine
2 tablespoons chopped onion
1 tablespoon chopped parsley
1 tablespoon whole basil
1 teaspoon lemon juice

Cut loaf in ¾-inch slices, almost to bottom crust. Combine remaining ingredients and spread on each slice. Heat uncovered on cooky sheet in oven at 250° 25 minutes. Separate slices to serve.

Easy Chocolate Eclairs

½ 8½-ounce package (1 stick) cream-puff mix
1 recipe Chocolate Icing
1 recipe Creamy Pudding

Prepare and bake eclairs according to package directions, making 8 to 10 eclairs. To dry out shells, remove from oven when baked and split in half lengthwise; return to oven with *heat off*, *door open* 15 to 20 minutes. Cool. Frost tops with Chocolate Icing. At serving time, fill with Creamy Pudding.

Chocolate Icing: Melt one 1-ounce square unsweetened chocolate, 2 teaspoons butter or margarine in double boiler. Remove from heat; stir in ⅓ cup sifted confectioners' sugar, 1 tablespoon milk; blend till smooth.

Creamy Pudding: Prepare 1 package vanilla pudding according to package directions, but *using only 1¾ cups milk;* chill. Beat pudding smooth; fold in 1 cup of heavy cream, whipped, and ½ teaspoon vanilla.

Beef Stroganoff

1 pound trimmed beef tenderloin, sliced ¼ inch thick
6 ounces mushrooms, sliced (about 2 cups)
½ cup chopped onion
1 can condensed beef broth
1 cup dairy sour cream
2½ tablespoons enriched flour

Cut meat in strips, ¼ inch wide. Brown quickly in ¼ cup butter. Push meat to one side; add mushrooms and onion; cook just till tender. Add broth; heat just to boiling. Blend sour cream and flour; stir into broth. Cook and stir till mixture thickens (sauce will be thin). Season to taste. Serve over hot Yellow Rice, page 98, or buttered noodles. Makes 4 or 5 servings.

Ambrosia Molds

Dissolve 1 package cherry-flavored gelatin in 1 cup hot water; add 1 cup cold water. Pour into 10 to 12 individual molds, filling ½ full. Chill till just set.

Meanwhile dissolve 1 package lemon-flavored gelatin in 1 cup hot water; add ¾ cup orange juice. Chill till partially set; stir in 1½ cups diced orange sections (white membranes removed), drained, 1 cup banana slices, and ¼ cup flaked coconut; spoon over cherry layer; chill firm. Unmold on pineapple rings. Trim with orange sections, curly endive.

PARTY-BEST BUFFET

Tomato Refresher, page 22
Beef Stroganoff
Yellow Rice
Ambrosia Molds — Crisp Relishes
Brown-and-serve Hard Rolls
Pink Confetti Pie *or*
Easy Chocolate Eclairs
Coffee

Timesavers: Day before, make salad. If you're serving Pink Confetti Pie, also make it and freeze. Morning of party, make Tomato Refresher, and fix relishes; chill. Beef Stroganoff cooks at table in chafing dish—takes only 10 minutes.

Party-best Buffet—elegant fare! Beef Stroganoff is the star—stir it up in chafing dish or electric skillet. Dessert? Pink Confetti Pie or Easy Chocolate Eclairs. (Florist will make carnation trees.)

Pink Confetti Pie

3 egg whites
¼ cup granulated sugar

• • •

¾ cup coarsely chopped blanched almonds, toasted
⅓ cup maraschino cherries, cut in fourths
2 tablespoons maraschino-cherry syrup

• • •

1 teaspoon vanilla
⅓ cup sifted confectioners' sugar
1½ cups heavy cream, whipped

• • •

Graham-cracker Crust

Beat the egg whites till foamy; add the granulated sugar gradually and beat till stiff. Fold in the almonds, cherries, cherry syrup, and vanilla. Fold confectioners' sugar into whipped cream; fold into the first mixture. Pour into chilled Graham-cracker Crust; dot top with additional cherry cuts and slivered almonds. Freeze firm.

Graham-cracker Crust: Combine 1½ cups fine graham-cracker crumbs, ¼ cup sugar, and ½ cup melted butter or margarine. Press into buttered 9-inch pie plate; chill till firm, about 45 minutes.

Birthdays and anniversaries

Easy cake trims for a red-letter day

Speedy cake decorating

You won't wait for a birthday to try this simple trick, it's so pretty!

Start with a creamy confectioners'-sugar frosting—here it's chocolate. Spread smoothly over the cake.

Cover top with parallel lines made by drawing tines of fork through frosting. Now, at right angles, draw fork through frosting again, leaving a ½-inch space between strokes, to make pattern.

Party-going cupcakes

Try these quick cupcake toppers, or dream up a finishing touch of your own.

Swirl frosting over cupcakes; polka-dot with red cinnamon candies or semi-sweet chocolate pieces. Then smack in the middle, poke a stick of peppermint candy or a red birthday candle.

Another time, stud frosted cakes with whole almonds, blanched and toasted. Or crown each cake with a walnut half.

Blossoms from Brazils—

Count on this cake to steal the show—it's dolled up with Brazil-nut daisies.

Cover *unshelled* Brazils with cold water; simmer 3 minutes; drain. Let stand in cold water 1 minute; drain and shell. Cover nuts with cold water; simmer 3 minutes; drain.

Cut paper-thin, lengthwise slices with vegetable parer. Place petals around centers of candied cherries.

←Gay gumdrop tulips to give cake a celebration look

To "grow" tulips: With rolling pin, flatten big red gumdrops between sugared sheets of waxed paper; cut with tulip cutter; press in toothpicks. Roll out green jelly strings; with scissors, snip "leaves."

Delightful cakes that say "happy

A memorable birthday cake usually calls for an all-out decorating job. But try these easy-do trims, and cake decorating's a snap!

Start with the "favorite" cake, made from mix or your best recipe. Swirl on the frosting. Then say, "happy birthday!" with one of our fun finishes—or create your own!

Candyland Cake

Bake two 8- or 9-inch layers from chocolate- or fudge-cake mix, according to package directions. Frost with Snowy 7-minute Frosting tinted pink. Decorate top with flower mints in a variety of pastel colors.

Border cake with candles in Coconut-Mallow Holders: Dip marshmallows in milk, roll in pink-tinted coconut. (See how to tint coconut on page 124.) Top with birthday candles in pink candleholders.

Enchant children with an exciting fortune cake

"Fortune charms" discovered in a birthday cake are almost like buried treasure to the children.

The charms might be small toys —airplanes to foretell travel, doll-size dark glasses for a movie career, rocket for first man to the moon.

Remember time-honored charms, too—ring for marriage, thimble for old maid, button for seamstress, penny for wealth. Tip off guests to expect a surprise, then ask birthday child to read the fortunes.

Insert foil-wrapped charms in cake after it's baked. Mark top as it will be cut, then make a slit in each piece. Poke charms into slits. Frost and decorate to conceal all.

Snowy 7-minute Frosting

- 2 egg whites
- 1½ cups sugar
- 1½ teaspoons light corn syrup *or* ¼ teaspoon cream of tartar
- ⅓ cup cold water
- Dash salt
- 1 teaspoon vanilla

Combine all ingredients except vanilla in top of double boiler. Beat 1 minute with electric mixer or rotary beater. Place over boiling water; beat constantly until frosting forms peaks, *about* 7 minutes (*don't overcook*). Remove from boiling water. Pour into mixing bowl. Add vanilla (for tinted frosting, add few drops food coloring, too).

Beat until of spreading consistency, about 2 minutes. Frosts two 8- or 9-inch layers.

Candy-peanut Rocket Cake

Bake two 8-inch layers, using peanut cake mix, cool. Frost with Chocolate Frosting.

Swirl chocolate-mint wafers atop cake. Deck edge of cake with candy peanuts. To stand them up rocket-fashion, "drill" hole in one end of each with metal skewer; insert one end of toothpick in candy, other in cake.

Circle platter with Candy-mint Candleholders: Put flat sides of two mints together with frosting, then stack two of these double candies with frosting between. Melt candle wax to hold candles to candy.

Chocolate Frosting

- 2 3-ounce packages cream cheese
- 1 egg
- 1 teaspoon vanilla
- Dash salt
- 5 cups sifted confectioners' sugar
- 3 1-ounce squares unsweetened chocolate, melted

Soften cream cheese; blend in egg, vanilla, and salt; gradually beat in sugar. Blend in slightly cooled chocolate. Frosts top and sides of two 8- or 9-inch layers.

birthday"

Quick candy trims

A Candy-peanut Rocket Cake, with "rockets" poised to take off in swirls of chocolate frosting, is sure to please young missile men.

Girls from 8 to 80 will love a dainty pink-and-white Gumdrop-rose Cake (recipe on page 117).

For quick mix-cakes—

Off-to-the-moon Cake

Bake two 8-inch layers using chocolate malt cake mix. Cool. Prepare 1 package milk chocolate frosting mix and frost cake.

Poke a 6-inch peppermint stick into cake for base of rocket; pipe Ornamental Frosting around it as shown below; add toy rocket.

Tint remaining frosting yellow and pipe birthday greeting on cake. Add candles.

Ornamental Frosting: Cut 2 tablespoons butter into $2\frac{1}{2}$ cups sifted confectioners' sugar until mixture resembles corn meal. Add 1 unbeaten egg white, $\frac{1}{2}$ teaspoon vanilla, and $\frac{1}{8}$ teaspoon cream of tartar. Beat until stiff.

Make frosting "blast-off" for rocket

Using pastry tube, pipe Ornamental Frosting around a peppermint stick in shape of cone, leaving top 1 inch of candy unfrosted.

Cut or snip a hole in base of small plastic toy rocket; push down over unfrosted part of peppermint stick.

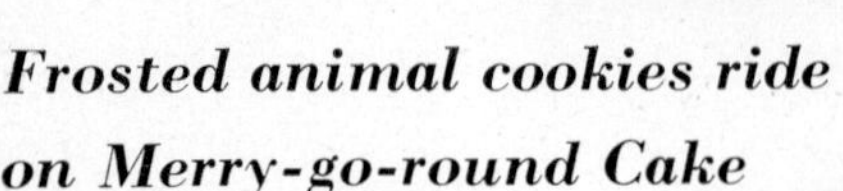

Frosted animal cookies ride on Merry-go-round Cake

Get out your pretty pedestal cake plate or Lazy Susan to display this colorful cake.

Prepare three-layer cake from mixes; use mix for frosting, too. See page 116 for recipe.

Timesaving tip: No need to wash a pastry tube—pipe the "poles" around cake using paper-envelope tubes.

Snip a tiny corner from envelope, fill with frosting; squeeze. Use a new envelope for each color frosting.

party trims

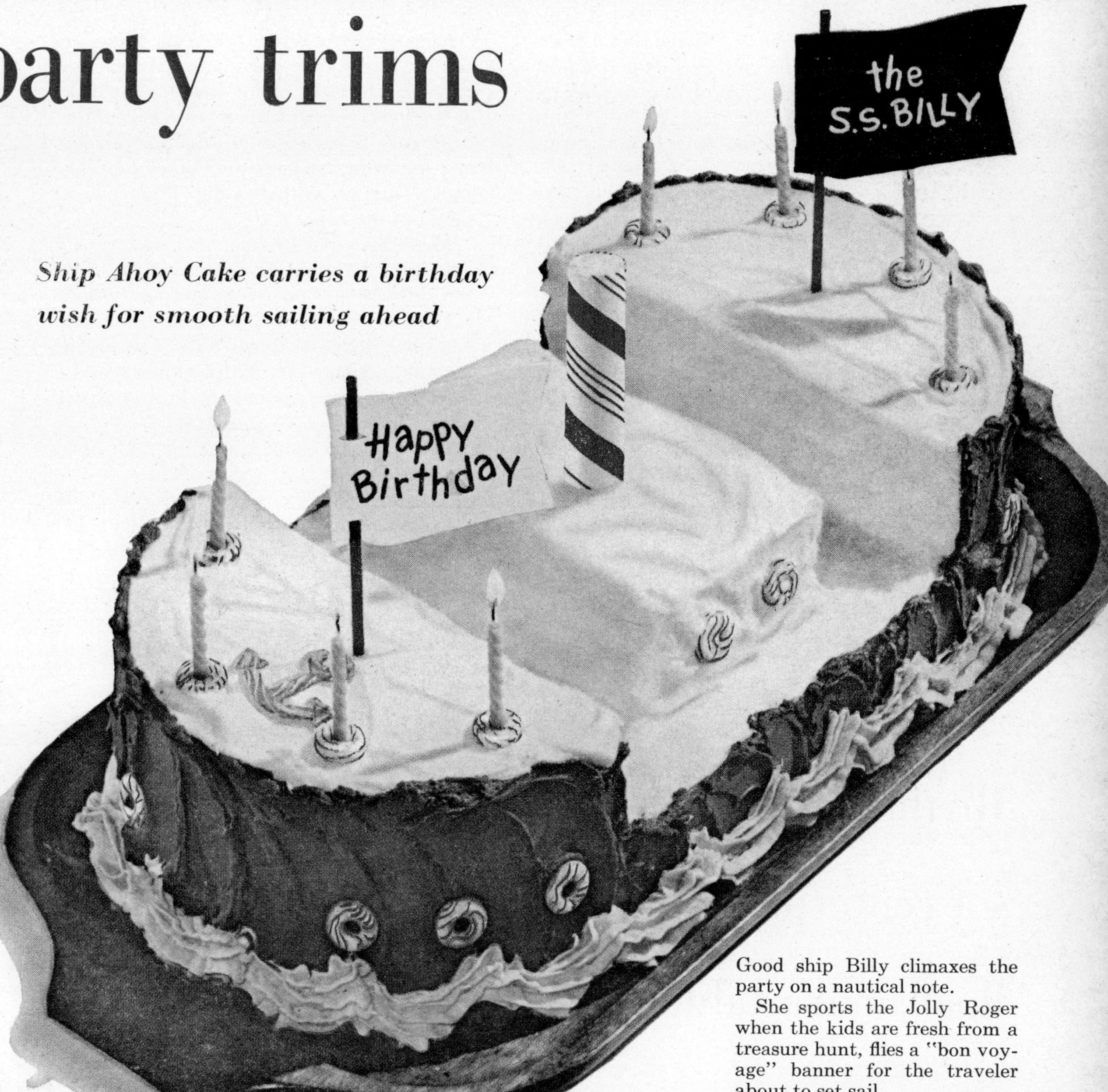

Ship Ahoy Cake carries a birthday wish for smooth sailing ahead

Good ship Billy climaxes the party on a nautical note.

She sports the Jolly Roger when the kids are fresh from a treasure hunt, flies a "bon voyage" banner for the traveler about to set sail.

See recipe for Ship Ahoy Cake on page 116 and directions below for arranging pieces of cake.

"Shipshape" cake is quick to fix, delights the back-yard pirate crew

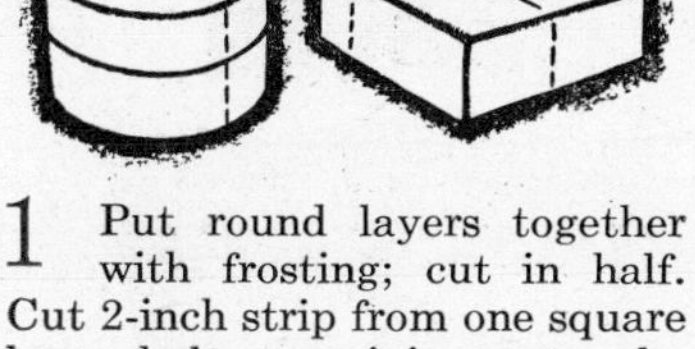

1 Put round layers together with frosting; cut in half. Cut 2-inch strip from one square layer; halve remaining rectangle.

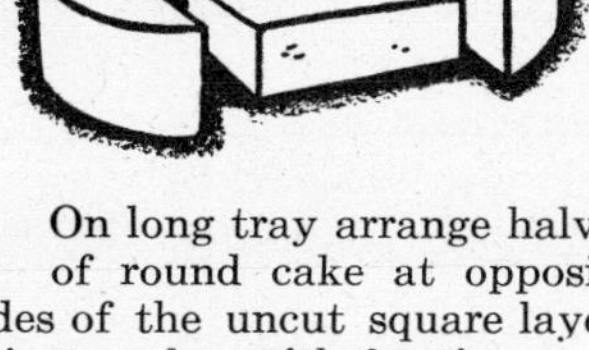

2 On long tray arrange halves of round cake at opposite sides of the uncut square layer. Join together with frosting.

3 In center of "ship," stack two same-size pieces from square layer—frost between. Follow recipe to complete.

Ship Ahoy Cake

Using mixes, bake two 8-inch round layers of devil's food cake and two 8-inch square layers of white cake, according to package directions. Prepare one package fluffy white frosting mix and one package fudge frosting mix, according to package directions.

Put round chocolate layers together with white frosting. Following directions on page 115, cut cakes and arrange pieces on tray to make "ship."

Reserve 1 cup white frosting for "waves." With remainder, frost ship's "upper deck." Spread sides with the fudge frosting. Make Speedy Ornamental Frosting with reserved white frosting. Tint green. Pipe waves around base of cake, and a frosting anchor on "deck," if desired.

Use peppermint stick candy for smokestack. Press striped hard-candy circles on sides for portholes, on deck for candleholders. Hoist paper flags.

Merry-go-round Cake

Prepare two 2-layer white cake mixes according to package directions. (Mix both at once and increase mixing time by ½.) Bake in three 9x1½-inch cake pans. Cool.

Prepare 2 packages fluffy white frosting mix following package directions. Put cake layers together with frosting. Frost *sides* of cake but not top.

Make Speedy Ornamental Frosting with remaining frosting. Divide in thirds. Tint one third pink, one green, and one yellow.

With toothpicks, mark center top of cake and divide edge in thirds. Frost top of cake as shown on page 114. With spoon or spatula, swirl scallops at edge of frosting. Use pastry tube to pipe "poles" around sides.

Place animal cookies (one for each pole) on rack over waxed paper. Add water to each frosting till of consistency to pour; add more food coloring. Pour over cookies. Let dry, then fasten a cooky to each "pole."

Birthday party fun —a centerpiece to float above table

What could be more fun than a birthday party bursting with balloons? You might serve Mint-balloon Cake, give every child balloon favors, *and* float this "round-the-world" balloon above table.

To make balloon, follow directions at right, then glue into circular shape. Fit small plastic bowl inside basket of balloon and a large balloon into collar. Trim with swags, pleats, and pinked circles of colored paper. Place dolls in basket. Suspend from ceiling fixture with threads.

Make balloon nut cups to match: Use ⅓-size pattern pieces with matchsticks from place mats.

Passenger balloon carries dolls

Speedy Ornamental Frosting

For each cup of fluffy white frosting (from mix), measure about $1\frac{1}{2}$ cups sifted confectioners' sugar and 1 tablespoon butter. Add sugar to frosting until of piping consistency. Blend in butter. (If frosting becomes too thick, add a few drops of water; if too thin, add more sugar.) Use for frosting trims.

Mint-balloon Cake

Prepare confetti angel cake mix according to package directions. Bake and cool.

Prepare one package fluffy white frosting mix following directions on package. Tint pink with red food coloring.

Frost cake, reserving small amount of frosting for trim. To make "balloons," press pink, yellow, and green candy mints on sides of cake. (See picture, page 2.) Tint reserved frosting deep pink. Using pastry tube, pipe curved "strings" on balloons.

For Gumdrop-rose Cake, shape roses as directed below and add leaves snipped from green gumdrops. Twist leaves for "3rd-dimension" effect.

Gumdrop-rose Cake

Prepare two 8- or 9-inch layers from white cake mix, according to package directions. Frost cooled cake with Snowy 7-minute Frosting or fluffy white frosting mix. Circle base of cake with tiny gumdrops, gumdrop leaves.

Top with Gumdrop-rose Candleholders: For each rose, roll 3 or 4 big pink gumdrops into ovals—sprinkle sugar on board and over candy. Cut ovals in half crosswise.

Fold one corner of a half-oval at an angle, then wind to form rose center. Press on additional half-ovals, shaping outer edges to resemble petals. Trim base. Insert wire candleholder in center. Add gumdrop leaves.

Round up a big balloon, some heavy paper, and tiny doweling—then try your hand at this airborne centerpiece

Small balloon holds nuts, candy

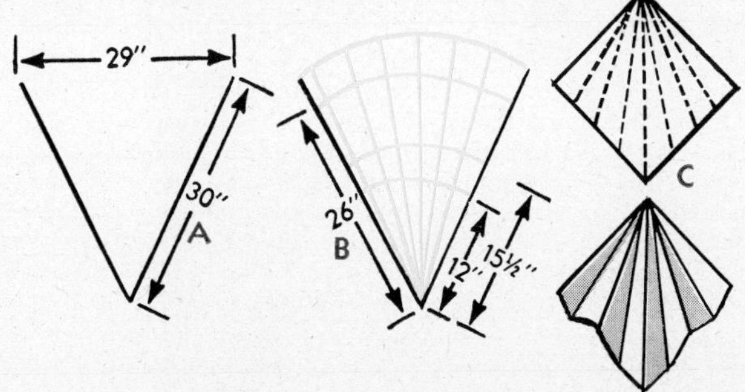

Make patterns for collar and basket of balloon on wrapping paper: Draw two 30-inch sides of a triangle, 29 inches apart at base (sketch A). Tie long string to pencil; use as compass to draw 4 arcs between lines (sketch B).

Pieces between two top and two bottom arcs are the patterns. Cut pieces from colored paper; glue to opposite ends of 6 painted ⅛-inch dowels or sticks from place mat.

For decorative pleats, fold paper squares in half diagonally, then in-and-out in eighths, according to sketch C. Complete balloon following direction on opposite page.

Fabulous for summertime parties-

Easy—Strawberry Swizzle; elegant—Rainbow Meringue Torte, iced tea

Tower Parfait

In tall glass, place 2 tablespoons crushed pineapple. Next comes a scoop of cherry ice cream, then a layer of chopped maraschino cherries. Mound up lime or mint ice cream to rim of glass. Top with a dollop of whipped cream, a small scoop of cherry ice cream, and a stem-on maraschino cherry.

Serve with small sandwiches or cookies.

Rainbow Meringue Torte

1 package (2 packets) meringue mix

• • •

1 pint chocolate ice cream
1 pint pistachio or green mint ice cream
1 pint strawberry ice cream
½ cup heavy cream, whipped

• • •

Toasted slivered blanched almonds

Meringue layers: Preheat oven to 400°. Meanwhile prepare meringue mix according to package directions for meringue shells. Cover 2 large or 4 small cooky sheets with foil or brown paper. Draw four 8½-inch circles on foil (use cake pan as a guide).

Spoon equal amounts of meringue on the 4 circles; spread evenly. Place in hot oven (400°). Close door quickly and *turn off* oven heat. Leave in oven 3 hours or overnight without opening door. When done, remove meringues from foil and cool.

To fill torte: Let ice cream soften *slightly*. Place a meringue layer on serving plate; spoon chocolate ice cream atop and spread evenly (work quickly); place in freezer.

Spread second meringue with pistachio ice cream; set atop first layer in freezer.

Spread third meringue with strawberry ice cream; set atop other layers. Frost remaining meringue with whipped cream, and add to stack. Freeze till ice cream is firm, about 5 hours or overnight.

Ten or 15 minutes before serving, remove from freezer; sprinkle with toasted almonds. With sharp knife, cut in 16 servings.

ce-cream coolers

Strawberry Swizzle

2 packages strawberry-flavored gelatin
2 cups hot water
1 cup cold water
1 large bottle (3½ to 4 cups) ginger ale, chilled
1 quart vanilla ice cream

Dissolve gelatin in hot water. Add cold water; chill till syrupy (about 1 hour).

Into each of 6 chilled 16-ounce glasses, pour ½ *cup* of gelatin. Add *half* of ginger ale to the six glasses; stir. (It's important to add part of ginger ale before ice cream, so gelatin won't harden in flecks.)

Divide ice cream among glasses; fill with ginger ale. Trim with whole strawberries.

Chocolate Soda

For each serving, mix ¼ cup chocolate syrup and 2 tablespoons milk in a 14- or 16-ounce glass. Add chilled carbonated water to fill glass ¾ full (about ½ small bottle or ½ cup). Stir. Then add 1 to 2 scoops vanilla ice cream. Fill with carbonated water. Serve with straws, long-handled spoons.

Dazzler in a tall glass—

Tower Parfait stars trio of fruit flavors—pineapple, cherry, and lime. Topknot is whipped cream, pink ice cream, and bright red cherry. Delicious with tiny sandwiches.

Go bold with flavors—team the unusual

Arrange *Chocolate-Orange Delight* on a long dessert plate. Stack two scoops of chocolate ice cream. Spoon over marshmallow sauce and pineapple sundae topping. Add two scoops of orange sherbet rolled in coconut.

Spectacula

Like your sundaes extravagant? This is your dish! It's Banana Split with a choice of sauces —spoon on some of each, top with nuts, and start in!

;undaes and ice-cream pickups

Banana Splits

For each serving, slice a banana in half lengthwise and turn cut side up. Top with large scoop of vanilla ice cream, in center, then a scoop of strawberry ice cream on one side, and mint-chocolate-chip on the other.

Top vanilla ice cream with marshmallow sauce and broken walnuts. Serve with a line-up of Minted Pineapple Sauce, Chocolate Marble Sauce, sugared sliced strawberries, and Jiffy Caramel Sauce. Each guest sauces his own sundae, then tops all with whole walnut halves!

Minted Pineapple Sauce

1 9-ounce can (1 cup) pineapple tidbits
½ cup light corn syrup
¼ teaspoon mint extract
2 drops green food coloring

Combine ingredients; blend well. Chill. Makes 1½ cups of sauce.

Chocolate Marble Sauce

1 cup sugar
½ cup light corn syrup
1 cup water
3 1-ounce squares unsweetened chocolate
1 teaspoon vanilla
1 cup evaporated milk
• • •
1 cup marshmallow creme
1 tablespoon water

Combine sugar, syrup, and 1 cup water; cook to soft-ball stage (236°). Remove from heat; add chocolate, stirring until melted. Add vanilla. Slowly stir in evaporated milk. Cool slightly. Blend marshmallow creme and 1 tablespoon water; stir into chocolate sauce just until marbled. Makes 3 cups.

Jiffy Caramel Sauce

Heat ½ pound (28) caramels with ½ cup hot water in top of double boiler, stirring occasionally, till caramels are melted and sauce is smooth. Makes about 1 cup.

Neiman-Marcus Fresh Flowerpot

This is a speciality of N-M's Zodiac Room —each dessert sprouts real flowers!

Line bottoms of real red-clay flowerpots with rounds of sponge cake. Top with several kinds of ice cream, then high meringue; brown a few minutes in a very hot oven. Poke two soda straws in each, as channels for flower stems. Insert flower in each straw.

Big-top Strawberry Sundae

Build up an ice-cream mound by alternating layers of vanilla and strawberry ice cream. Use a large kitchen spoon or ice-cream dipper to scoop out ice cream. Top with sugared strawberries. Or add light corn syrup to strawberry jam for quick sauce.

Ice-cream Clown

Pleat a small lace paper doily for each plate. Center it with a large scoop of strawberry or vanilla ice cream. For eyes, poke in semisweet chocolate pieces. For mouth, use red cinnamon candy.* Top each clown with a colored ice-cream-cone hat.

*To fix clowns ahead, prepare faces, then store in freezer till nearly serving time.

Ice-cream Lollipops

4 wooden spoons
1 pint vanilla brick ice cream
1 5-ounce bar milk chocolate
¼ cup melted shortening
½ cup chopped California walnuts

Write names of guests on spoon handles. Mark ice cream in fourths. Insert bowl of wooden spoon in each section. Cut ice cream in 4 servings. Freeze hard.

Melt milk chocolate and shortening over hot water; mix well. Cool till just warm. Spread one side of ice-cream square with chocolate; dip lower half of that side in chopped nuts immediately. Repeat with remaining sides and bottom. Makes 4 servings.

On 25th anniversary table, pink brings a rosy glow to gleaming silver, enhances the traditional wedding cake

An elegant anniversary buffet

Anniversaries are as sentimental as the scent of old lavender. Early ones are celebrated with in-the-family gifts, or casual suppers like a paper-plate luncheon for the first year, a tin-pan picnic for ten.

But the "extra-specials"—the 25th, 50th, and 75th anniversaries—are candlelight-and-roses occasions. Friends plan a buffet or tea honoring the couple—everyone's invited to drop in and offer congratulations. (Guests may also bring gifts.) Silver, gold, or white table trims and/or serving pieces are in order.

Wedding Anniversary Themes, Gifts

1	Paper	13	Lace
2	Cotton	14	Ivory
3	Leather	15	Crystal
4	Fruit and flowers	20	China
5	Wood	25	Silver
6	Sugar and candy	30	Pearl
7	Wool or copper	35	Coral
8	Bronze or pottery	40	Ruby
9	Willow or pottery	45	Sapphire
10	Tin or aluminum	50	Gold
11	Steel	55	Emerald
12	Silk or linen	60, 75	Diamond

"Silver buffet" for 25th anniversary

Star high and handsome Anniversary Cake as a lovely centerpiece. Let guests choose hot Tea or Pink Punch.

Offer tempting Coconut Ice-cream Balls, assorted dainty sandwiches (Water-cress Roll-ups, Nut-bread Crescents, and Wedding Bells), and nuts and candies.

ANNIVERSARY BUFFET

Anniversary Cake
Coconut Ice-cream Balls
Party Sandwiches
Mixed Nuts   Mints
Pink Punch or Frosty Golden Punch
Tea

Anniversary Cake

3 packages white cake mix
3 packages fluffy white frosting mix
2½ to 3 cups sifted confectioners' sugar
2 tablespoons softened butter
Few drops red food coloring

In bowl, prepare two cake mixes, according to package directions, but increasing mixing time by one-half. Fill paper-lined 10x2- and 6x2-inch round pans half full. Prepare remaining cake mix and pour into 8x2-inch pan (buy all three pans in set). Bake in moderate oven (350°) until done, about 45 minutes for 6-inch layer, 50 minutes for 8-inch layer, and 55 minutes for 10-inch layer. Cool.

Prepare frosting mix according to package directions. Reserve 2 cups prepared frosting for trim. Put layers together with frosting, then frost sides smoothly. Allow to set.

Blend the confectioners' sugar gradually into reserved frosting until of piping consistency. Blend in butter and food coloring.

With pastry tube, pipe swags and rosettes around cake—see finished cake, page 122. Top cake with anniversary decoration.

When ready to serve, set aside top tier for honored couple. Cut about 12 slices from center tier, about 20 from bottom tier.

Water-cress Roll-ups

Remove crusts from sandwich loaf; slice thin. Spread with pimento-cheese spread, then mayonnaise. Sprinkle with chopped water cress. Roll; anchor with toothpick. To serve, remove picks; tuck sprigs of water cress in ends of sandwiches.

Nut-bread Crescents

Whip together softened cream cheese and orange marmalade; spread generously between thin crescents of nut bread.

Wedding Bells

1 8-ounce package cream cheese, softened
Maraschino cherry juice
Unsliced sandwich loaf

Thoroughly blend cream cheese with enough maraschino cherry juice to make it of spreading consistency.

Slice sandwich loaf thin. With cooky cutter, cut bell shapes from bread slices. Spread filling on cut-outs. Trim with maraschino-cherry slices, if desired.

This amount of filling will spread about 32 medium-size bell sandwiches.

Golden Wedding Rings

1 3-ounce package cream cheese, softened
3 tablespoons salad dressing
½ cup chopped pecans
½ cup drained crushed pineapple

Blend cream cheese and salad dressing. Add chopped nuts and pineapple. Makes 1½ cups of filling.

Bake your favorite nut bread in 1-pound cans, filling each can ⅔ full. When cool, remove from cans and slice thin*. Remove center from each slice with center of doughnut cutter. Spread generously with filling.

*Or slice square loaf and cut rings with doughnut cutter.

Coconut Ice-cream Balls

2 quarts vanilla ice cream
3 3-ounce cans (3¾ cups) flaked coconut, tinted*

Make balls of ice cream, using medium (No. 20) scoop. Roll each ball in tinted coconut, coating generously. Place on a foil-lined tray and freeze. Makes 24 to 28 balls.

**To tint coconut:* Add food coloring to 1 tablespoon water till you get the color you want. Put coconut in jar; add colored water, cap jar, and shake until uniformly tinted. Dry on a paper towel.

Pink Punch

½ cup sugar
1 cup fresh mint leaves *or* ¼ cup dried mint
2 cups boiling water

• • •

2 10-ounce packages frozen raspberries
2 6-ounce cans frozen pink-lemonade concentrate
5 cups water*

• • •

Raspberry sherbet*

Combine sugar, mint leaves, and boiling water; let stand 5 minutes.

Add raspberries and concentrate; stir until thawed. Strain. Pour into punch bowl. Add water. Chill thoroughly.

Float with scoops of raspberry sherbet to match picture on page 122. Makes 2½ quarts or 20 one-half-cup servings.

*Or, reduce water to 4 cups and serve chilled punch over crushed ice. For trim, freeze part of punch mixture in ring mold and float atop punch. Deck ring with twists of lemon and sprigs of mint.

Frosty Golden Punch

2 cups sugar
1½ cups fresh mint leaves *or* ⅓ cup dried mint
2 cups boiling water

• • •

¾ cup lemon juice
1 12-ounce can (1½ cups) apricot nectar, chilled
1 6-ounce can frozen limeade concentrate
1 6-ounce can frozen orange-juice concentrate
1 6-ounce can frozen pineapple-juice concentrate
2 large bottles (7 to 8 cups) ginger ale, chilled

• • •

1 quart lemon sherbet

Combine sugar, mint leaves, and boiling water; stir to dissolve sugar. Cool. Chill. Strain into chilled punch bowl.

Add lemon juice, apricot nectar, the concentrates, and ginger ale. Top with scoops of lemon sherbet.

Garnish with mint leaves, or float thin slices of lemon or orange atop, if desired. Makes 20 to 25 servings.

How to cut wedding, anniversary cake

Traditionally, the couple's wedding and anniversary cakes are made, and cut, alike. (One difference—at wedding-reception picture-taking time, the bride may cut a first slice from the center tier.) First, lift off top tier and set aside for the honored couple.

Mark center tier of cake lightly in fourths with cake breaker or knife. Cut first fourth as shown, or start from outside and work toward center. Turn cake breaker and cut second fourth at right angles to first. Turn cake and cut remaining fourths the same way.

Mark bottom tier of cake in fourths. (If large, cut in eighths, as shown.) Cut as you did the second tier. It's a good idea to have a damp napkin at hand, but out of sight, to wipe frosting off cake breaker or knife. For pretty touch, tie satin bows on the handles.

For fancy-dress coffees—

Pick a spectacular dessert—a real dazzler! We show handsome Candy-confetti Torte, luscious with whipped cream and almond-brittle topping.

Just make the coffee—you're all set for a party, simple and elegant.

Coffee, tea, and punch parties

Entertaining? Try these hostess helpers

Give your punch a pretty setting

No punch service? Use what you have. Here, jumbo salad bowl on dinner plate, plus matching teacups, makes smart punch set. For trim, twist orange slice, float on block of ice with sprig of mint.

More punch bowls—use a big stainless steel or glass mixing bowl; ice bucket; or scooped-out watermelon half. Or start from scratch—disguise a large can or wood keg. Conceal sides with leaves and flowers anchored with ribbon.

Refreshing iced tea in seconds

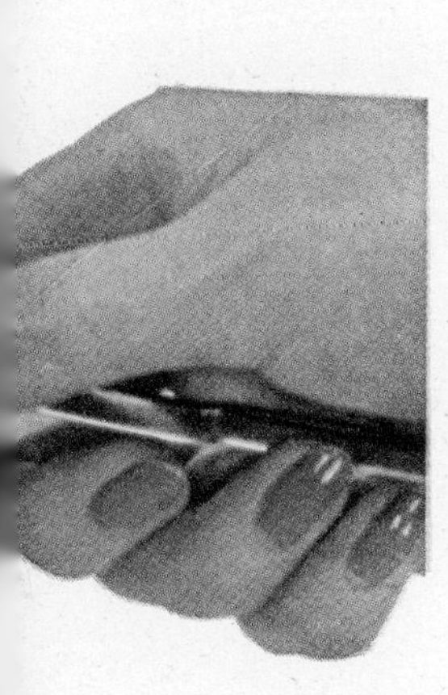

Here's a speedy way to beat summer heat. To each glass cold water, add 1 rounded teaspoon instant tea—more or less to suit your taste. Stir to dissolve. Add the ice and serve. Like lots of tea? Make a pitcherful at a time. Pass sugar and juicy lemon wedges. Now for a cool sip—delicious!

Instant tea makes a quick base when you're stirring up punch for the crowd. Concoct your own recipe by adding fruit juices and sugar.

Jigsaw sandwiches with party flair

Cut breads in 2-inch rounds—half white, half whole wheat. For bottoms, spread *half* the rounds of each color with cheese spread. Make toppers.

Double Rounds: With hole of a doughnut cutter, cut circles from center of rounds. Fit tiny whole-wheat circles in white rings and vice versa.

Striped and Checked Rounds: Cut rounds in 3 strips, making center strip widest. Or cut rounds in quarters. Arrange, alternating colors as shown.

Butter with a touch of glamour

Butter Curls—a perfect partner for coffee-time breads! You'll need a butter curler (shown in picture). Dip curler in hot water; pull lightly over stick or pound of butter, making curls ⅛ inch thick. Repeat hot-water dip each time. Have butter firmer than from butter keeper, yet not hard.

Whipped Butter adds an easy dress-up note. Cream butter with electric mixer or wooden spoon till fluffy; heap in serving dish and swirl top.

Coffee Brazilian

1 cup instant-cocoa mix
⅓ cup instant coffee
4 cups boiling water
Whipped cream or light cream

Combine cocoa mix and instant coffee. Gradually add boiling water, stirring constantly. Pour into cups, then top with dollops of whipped cream, or pass a pitcher of cream. Makes 6 servings.

Cardamom Coffee

Wonderful spicy aroma makes it doubly good!

Place two crushed cardamom seeds in each demitasse cup. Fill cups with hot double-strength coffee (3 tablespoons instant coffee in 2 cups boiling water serves six).

Cafe-au-lait

1 cup milk
1 cup light cream
3 tablespoons instant coffee
2 cups boiling water

Heat milk and cream over low heat or hot water. Dissolve coffee in water. Beat milk mixture till foamy and pour into one warmed pitcher; pour coffee into another.

To serve: Fill cups from both pitchers at the same time, making the streams meet before reaching cup. Makes 6 servings.

Turkish Coffee

Add water to powdered, Turkish-type coffee mix (from specialty food store); bring to boil. Pour into demitasse cups. Dash in few drops cold water to settle grounds.

Time out to relax

When you pass steaming cups of coffee, you're inviting folks to sit back and enjoy easy conversation, good company, warm hospitality.

Easygoing entertaining—"coffee"

There's no more cheery invitation than, "Come on in for coffee!" And if "coffee" includes a wedge of rich dessert or freshly made doughnuts, it's an occasion!

Coffee is a magic "perk-up" morning, noon, or night, whether you're taking 10 minutes out from dusting, chatting between rubbers of bridge, or admiring shower gifts of the bride or mother-to-be.

When coffee time is fancy, it's fun to go gourmet. If coffee's in the morning, borrow Cafe-au-lait from the French and pass hot brioche or sweet rolls. After an evening out, serve spicy Rio Mocha or cocoa-spiked Coffee Brazilian with oven-hot wedges of coffeecake. Folks will sip and say, "Umm, this is *good!*"

Demitasse Coffee and Petits Four— elegance in miniature

This double-strength coffee (or stronger) gives you a wonderful excuse for bringing out your demitasse-cup collection.

Arrange the coffee tray in the kitchen—tiny sugar bowl filled with half-size cubes, sugar tongs, demitasse cups and saucers, spoons. (Have cup and spoon already on saucer.) After dinner, add the pot of hot demitasse and pitcher of cream.

Pour at your coffee table and ask Dad or the children to pass filled cups and cream and sugar.

Demitasse Coffee: To make six ⅓-cup servings, measure 3 tablespoons instant coffee (more or less, to suit your taste) into your coffee server. Stir in 2 cups boiling water. Serve in tiny cups. Pass cream and sugar. Or, if you like, serve with dabs of whipped cream.

Fruited Demitasse: Add one teaspoon orange juice per cup of hot water. Or offer twists of orange or lemon peel.

For a dainty accompaniment, serve Petits Fours, flaky Napoleons, or beautifully frosted French Pastries.

Make the most of coffee—

- Always start with a coffee maker that's thoroughly clean—one that has been scrubbed faithfully after each use to get rid of the fats and oils that form on the sides of the coffee maker.

  Use scouring pad to remove stains, then sudsy hot water; rinse well. Scald with boiling water before using.
- The fresher, the better—that's the secret of delicious coffee. Help coffee stay at its best by storing it in an airtight container in a cool place. Also, buy coffee in small quantities or enough for just one week's supply.
- Choose coffee of the proper grind for your coffee maker—saves you money and gives you top flavor.
- Always draw fresh, cold water for making coffee. Water from the hot tap may rob your coffee of flavor.
- No cheating in measuring! Be sure to measure accurately each time. Allow 2 tablespoons of coffee for each 3/4 measuring cup of water.
- The water should come to a full, rolling boil before it mixes with the ground coffee.
- Never boil coffee. If you do, the flavor floats away in escaping steam.
- Find the best timing for your flavor preference and coffee maker, then stick to it.

  Instant Coffee for the Crowd is fast: Empty 2-ounce jar instant coffee into large kettle; add about 5 1/2 quarts boiling water. Stir, then cover several minutes. Do not boil. Makes 32 servings.
- Sweeten iced coffee with *Sugar Syrup:* Simmer 1 cup water with 1 cup sugar 3 to 5 minutes. Store in refrigerator—it keeps several weeks. Pass pitcher of syrup instead of confectioners' sugar.

Try spicy chocolate-coffee from south of the border—

Here's a drink for a cold night, when you ask friends in to chat by the fire. Or, stir it up for dessert bridge or a Sunday brunch.

Rio Mocha: In top of double boiler, combine two 1-ounce squares unsweetened chocolate, 1/4 cup sugar, 4 teaspoons instant coffee, 3/4 teaspoon cinnamon, 1/4 teaspoon nutmeg, dash salt, and 1 cup water.

Cook over low heat, stirring till chocolate is melted and blended. Bring to boiling and cook 4 minutes, stirring constantly. Now place over boiling water; stir in 3 cups milk, and heat thoroughly.

To serve: Beat with rotary beater till foamy. Pour into cups. Top with fluff of whipped cream. Use cinnamon sticks as stirrers. Makes 6 servings.

Serve sugary candied orange peel for guests to munch, with this delightful hot-chocolate-and-spiced-coffee combination.

Iced Coffee

Make coffee double-strength, using 4 level tablespoons for each measuring cup water. Pour ¾ cup coffee immediately into each ice-filled glass.

Serve with confectioners' sugar and plain or maple-flavored whipped cream. Dust with cinnamon, if desired.

Black-bottom Cooler

¾ cup chocolate syrup

• • •

1 quart vanilla ice cream
1½ cups milk
1 tablespoon instant coffee

• • •

Shaved unsweetened chocolate

Into each of 4 chilled 8- or 10-ounce glasses, spoon 3 tablespoons of the chocolate syrup. Stir ice cream to soften slightly; quickly blend in milk and coffee. Pour mixture over syrup in glasses. Garnish with shaved chocolate. Guests stir, then sip.

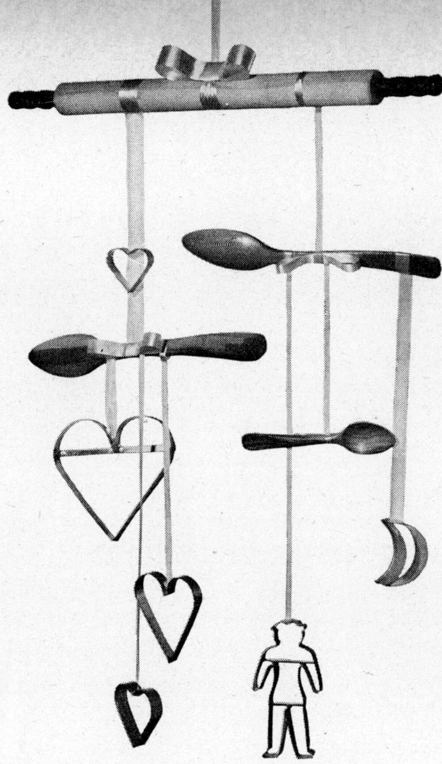

For shower, make a mobile

Hang wooden spoons and appropriate cooky cutters on ribbons from narrow rolling pin—pretty for coffee-time shower *and* useful later! Tips: Balance each small unit first; hang heavy items near centers of crossbars.

Whipped-cream fluffs underscore the rich flavor of hot Rio Mocha

Coffee Angel Torte

4 egg whites
½ teaspoon salt
1 cup brown sugar
1 cup blanched almonds, finely chopped and toasted
2 tablespoons blanched almonds, halved and toasted
1 recipe Coffee Cream "Frosting"

Beat egg whites and salt till soft peaks form. Gradually beat in brown sugar. When stiff peaks form, fold in *chopped* almonds. Cut out six 7-inch rounds of brown paper; grease paper, then spread with egg-white mixture. Top one with almond *halves*. Place rounds on ungreased cooky sheets.

Bake in slow oven (300°) about 35 minutes, or till lightly browned. Cool slightly. While still warm, peel off paper. Cool. Reserving almond-topped round for top, put layers together with Coffee Cream "Frosting." Swirl frosting over top and sides.

Chill 3 to 4 hours. Trim with walnut halves. Cut in 10 to 12 wedges.

Coffee Cream "Frosting": Beat 2 cups heavy cream until it begins to thicken. Slowly add ½ cup brown sugar, 2 tablespoons instant coffee. Beat till ready to spread.

Sweet treats that go with coffee

Company Cheese Cake

Graham-Nut Crust:

1¾ cups fine graham-cracker crumbs
¼ cup finely chopped walnuts
½ teaspoon cinnamon
½ cup butter or margarine, melted

Combine ingredients. Reserve 3 tablespoons mixture; press remainder on bottom and 2½ inches up on sides of 9-inch spring-form pan.

Rich filling:

3 well-beaten eggs
2 8-ounce packages cream cheese, softened
1 cup sugar
¼ teaspoon salt
2 teaspoons vanilla
½ teaspoon almond extract
3 cups dairy sour cream

Combine all ingredients except sour cream; beat smooth. Blend in sour cream; pour into Graham-Nut Crust. Trim with reserved crumbs. Bake in moderate oven (375°) 35 minutes or till just set. Cool. Chill well, about 4 or 5 hours. (Filling will be soft.) Makes about 10 servings.

Glitter Torte

Crumb liner:

1½ cups fine graham-cracker crumbs
⅓ cup sugar
½ cup butter or margarine, melted

Mix crumbs, sugar, and butter; press in bottom and 2½ inches high on sides of buttered 9-inch spring-form pan. Chill.

"Glitter":

1 package orange-flavored gelatin
1 package lime-flavored gelatin

Dissolve each kind of gelatin separately in 1 cup hot water. Add ½ cup cold water to each. Pour each into an 8-inch square pan. Chill till firm. Cut in ½-inch cubes.

Pineapple-Cream Base:

1 package lemon-flavored gelatin
¼ cup sugar
1 cup hot water
1 9-ounce can (1 cup) crushed pineapple
½ cup cold water
3 tablespoons lemon juice
Dash salt
1½ cups heavy cream, whipped
¼ cup chopped walnuts

Dissolve gelatin and sugar in hot water. Add pineapple, cold water, lemon juice, and salt; chill till partially set. Whip till fluffy. Reserve some of the "Glitter" for trim; fold remainder into pineapple mixture; fold in whipped cream.

Pour into crumb-lined pan. Sprinkle top with walnuts and reserved "Glitter." Chill till set. Cut in wedges. Makes 12 servings.

Luscious—Glitter Torte

Bright-colored cubes of gelatin give jewel sparkle and delicious fruit flavor to this rich whipped-cream "cake." Glitter Torte pairs perfectly with coffee, serves three tables of bridge. *And* it's a refrigerator make-ahead.

Warm up after the game with coffee, doughnuts

While the coffee perks, set out a basket of shiny apples and start the corn popping. Fry golden doughnuts (*or* bismarcks) at table—fast when made from refrigerated biscuits!

Jiffy Doughnuts: Open refrigerated biscuits. With finger, punch hole in center of each and stretch to doughnut shape. Fry in deep hot fat (375°) about 2 minutes. (Automatic saucepan or electric skillet can double as deep-fat fryer.) Drain on paper towels. Coat with confectioners' sugar. One package makes 10.

Bismarck Quickies: Open refrigerated biscuits. Flatten each to ¼ inch. Place 1 teaspoon jelly on half the biscuits; cover with remaining biscuits; seal edges. Fry in deep hot fat (375°) 3 minutes on each side. Drain. Dust with cinnamon sugar.

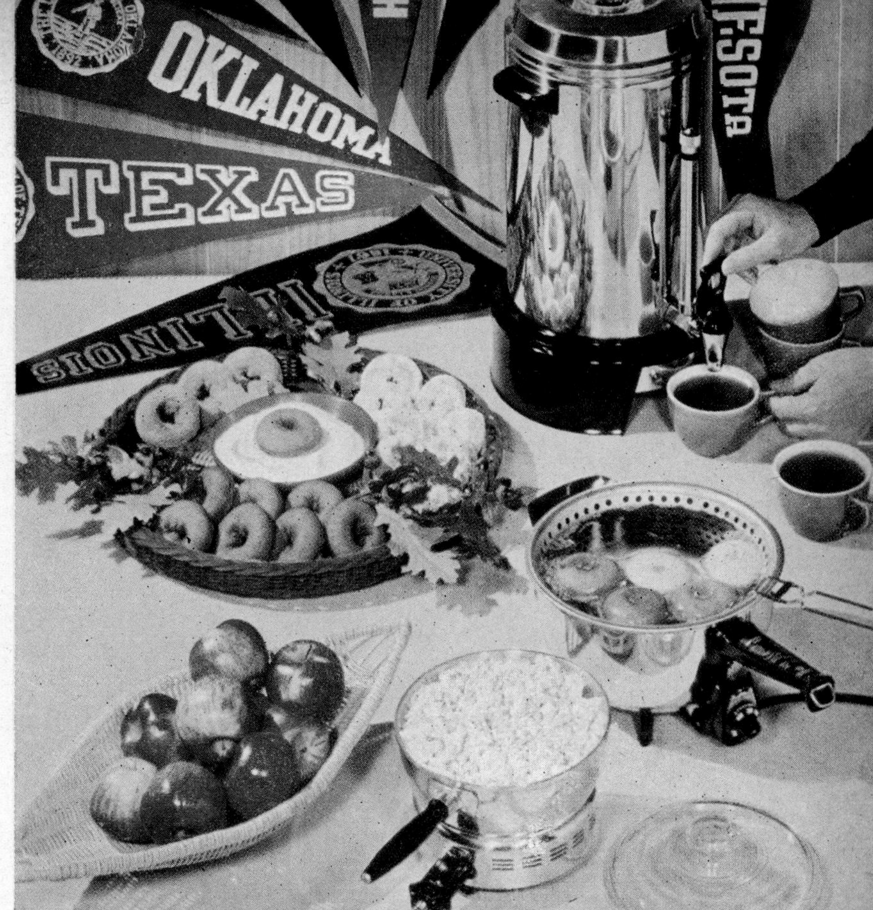

Candy-confetti Torte

1½ cups sifted enriched flour
¾ cup sugar
½ cup (8) egg yolks
¼ cup cold water
1 tablespoon lemon juice
1 teaspoon vanilla
1 cup (8) egg whites
1 teaspoon cream of tartar
1 teaspoon salt
¾ cup sugar
1 recipe Almond-brittle Topping

Sift flour and ¾ cup sugar into bowl. Make well in center; add next 4 ingredients. Beat till smooth. Beat egg whites with cream of tartar and salt till *very* soft peaks form; add remaining sugar gradually, 2 tablespoons at a time. Beat till stiff peaks form.

Fold first mixture gently into meringue. Pour batter into ungreased 10-inch tube pan. Carefully cut through batter, going around tube 5 or 6 times with knife to break large air bubbles. Bake in moderate oven (350°) 50 to 55 minutes. Invert pan to cool.

Remove cake from pan; split crosswise in 4 equal layers. Follow recipe for Almond-brittle Topping to complete torte.

Almond-brittle Topping

1½ cups sugar
¼ teaspoon instant coffee
¼ cup light corn syrup
¼ cup hot water
1 tablespoon *sifted* soda
2 cups heavy cream
2 tablespoons sugar
2 teaspoons vanilla
Almonds, blanched, halved, and toasted

While cake bakes, fix candy-brittle part of topping: In saucepan, combine first 4 ingredients; stir well. Cook to hard-crack stage (290°). Remove from heat; immediately add soda. Stir vigorously, *but only till mixture blends and pulls away from sides of pan.* Then quickly pour *foamy* mixture into ungreased shallow metal pan (9 inches square). Do not spread or stir; let stand till cool. Knock out of pan; with rolling pin, crush candy into coarse crumbs between waxed paper.

When cake is thoroughly cool, whip cream and fold in sugar and vanilla. Spread half of cream between layers and remainder over top and sides. Cover cake with the candy crumbs, and trim with almond halves inserted porcupine-style (see page 126).

Black-bottom Pie

½ cup sugar
1 tablespoon cornstarch
2 cups milk, scalded
4 beaten egg yolks
1 teaspoon vanilla

• • •

1 6-ounce package (1 cup) semisweet chocolate pieces
1 cooled baked 9-inch pastry shell
1 envelope (1 tablespoon) unflavored gelatin
¼ cup cold water
4 egg whites
½ cup sugar

Combine ½ cup sugar and cornstarch. Slowly add scalded milk to beaten egg yolks. Stir in sugar mixture. Cook and stir in top of double boiler over *hot, not boiling* water until custard coats a spoon. Remove from heat; add vanilla. To 1 cup of the custard, add chocolate; stir till melted. Pour into bottom of baked pastry shell. Chill.

Meanwhile, soften gelatin in cold water; add to remaining hot custard. Stir till dissolved. Chill until slightly thick. Beat egg whites till soft peaks form. Gradually beat in sugar and continue beating till stiff peaks form. Fold in custard-gelatin mixture. Pour over chocolate layer and chill till set. Trim with shaved unsweetened-chocolate curls and bias-cut banana slices.

Spicy Marble Coffeecake

½ cup shortening
¾ cup granulated sugar
1 egg

• • •

2 cups sifted enriched flour
2 teaspoons baking powder
½ teaspoon salt
¾ cup milk
2 tablespoons light molasses
1 teaspoon cinnamon
¼ teaspoon nutmeg
¼ teaspoon cloves

• • •

½ cup brown sugar
½ cup chopped walnuts
2 tablespoons enriched flour
1 teaspoon cinnamon
2 tablespoons melted butter

Cream shortening and granulated sugar. Add egg; beat well. Sift together 2 cups flour, the baking powder, and salt; add to creamed mixture alternately with milk, beating after each addition.

Divide batter in 2 parts. To one part, add molasses and spices. Spoon batters alternately into greased 9x9x2-inch pan; zigzag spatula through. Mix remaining ingredients for topping; sprinkle over batter in pan.

Bake coffeecake in moderate oven (350°) 30 minutes, or till done. Cut in 9 squares and serve warm with butter.

A treat—Black-bottom Pie

It's doubly delicious—a dark, rich chocolate layer hides underneath fluffy custard filling

Flaky, butter-rich Danish Kringle is worth the importing—

You're on your way to coffeecake fame when you serve this delicious pastry! It's buttery-tender under almond topper, hides a sweet-and-spicy raisin filling.

For a Continental touch, serve the warm coffeecake with feathery curls of butter and keep coffeepot hot in a cozy.

Danish Kringle

¾ cup butter
¼ cup sifted enriched flour

• • •

1 package active dry yeast
¼ cup *warm* water
1 beaten egg
¾ cup milk
3 tablespoons sugar
1 teaspoon salt
3 to 3½ cups sifted enriched flour

• • •

1 teaspoon ground cardamom
¼ cup soft butter
2 cups sifted confectioners' sugar
2 tablespoons cream
1 cup light seedless raisins

• • •

Beaten egg
¼ cup sugar
½ cup halved almonds

Cream ¾ cup butter with ¼ cup flour; pat or roll the mixture between 2 sheets of waxed paper, to a 10x4-inch rectangle. Chill thoroughly while preparing dough.

Meanwhile, soften yeast in warm water. To beaten egg, add milk, sugar, salt, and softened yeast; mix well. Stir in 3 to 3½ cups sifted flour for soft dough. On floured surface, roll to 12-inch square.

Place chilled butter mixture in center of dough; overlap sides of dough atop butter. Turn dough ¼-way around; roll to 12-inch square. Repeat folding and rolling twice. Wrap in waxed paper. Chill 30 minutes.

Meanwhile mix raisin filling: Add cardamom to soft butter; gradually stir in confectioners' sugar. Blend in cream; add raisins.

Roll chilled dough to 24x12-inch rectangle. Cut lengthwise in 2 strips; spread each with filling. Roll as for jelly roll. Moisten edges, seal. Stretch to 30-inch length, without breaking. Place each roll seam down on greased baking sheet, shaping as shown.

Flatten to ½ inch with rolling pin. Brush rolls with beaten egg; sprinkle with ¼ cup sugar and almonds. Cover with waxed paper and damp cloth. Let rise till almost double, about 25 minutes. Bake in 375° oven 25 to 30 minutes. Makes 2 Kringles.

Light-as-a-feather Puff Pastry

Puff Pastry

1 cup chilled butter or margarine
1¾ cups sifted enriched flour
½ cup ice water

Reserve 2 tablespoons butter; chill. Work remaining chilled butter with back of wooden spoon or in electric mixer just until as pliable as putty. Pat or roll between sheets of waxed paper in 8x6-inch rectangle, ½ inch thick. Chill thoroughly, at least 1 hour in refrigerator or 20 minutes in freezer.

Measure flour into mixing bowl; cut in reserved 2 tablespoons of butter with pastry-blender or blending fork till mixture is like coarse meal. Gradually add ice water, tossing with fork to make a stiff dough. Shape in ball. Turn onto lightly floured surface and knead (step 1, opposite page) till smooth and elastic, about 5 minutes. Cover dough and let rest 10 minutes.

On lightly floured surface, roll dough in 15x9-inch rectangle, ¼ inch thick. Peel top sheet of waxed paper from chilled rectangle of butter; invert on half the dough; peel off other sheet of waxed paper. Fold over other half of dough to cover butter (step 2, opposite page).

Seal edges of dough by pressing down with side or heel of hand (step 3). Wrap in waxed paper; chill thoroughly at least 1 hour in refrigerator or 20 minutes in freezer.

Unwrap. On lightly floured surface, roll dough in 15x9-inch rectangle, ¼ inch thick. (Roll dough from center, *just to* the edges. Don't flatten edges by allowing rolling pin to go over them.) Brush any excess flour from pastry; fold in thirds, turn dough around, fold in thirds again (steps 4 and 5).

Seal edges. Wrap in waxed paper; chill thoroughly. Repeat rolling, folding, and thorough chilling 2 or 3 times more. Now you're ready to make Napoleons.

Napoleons

Roll Puff Pastry into 14x8-inch rectangle, ⅜ inch thick. With floured sharp knife, cut off all edges. Prick dough thoroughly with fork (to prevent uneven puffing while baking). Cut in 3½x2-inch rectangles (step 6).

Place on baking sheets covered with 3 or 4 thicknesses of paper towels. Chill thoroughly. Brush with mixture of 1 slightly beaten egg white, 1 tablespoon ice water.

Bake at 450° 6 minutes, then at 300° 25 to 30 minutes, till lightly browned and crisp. Remove from pan; cool on rack.

Separate each pastry in 3 layers. Fill between layers with Cream Filling and spread top with Confectioners' Glaze (recipes on page 138). Using pastry tube, decorate with 2 lengthwise, wavy strips of Chocolate Glaze (page 138). Makes 16 Napoleons.

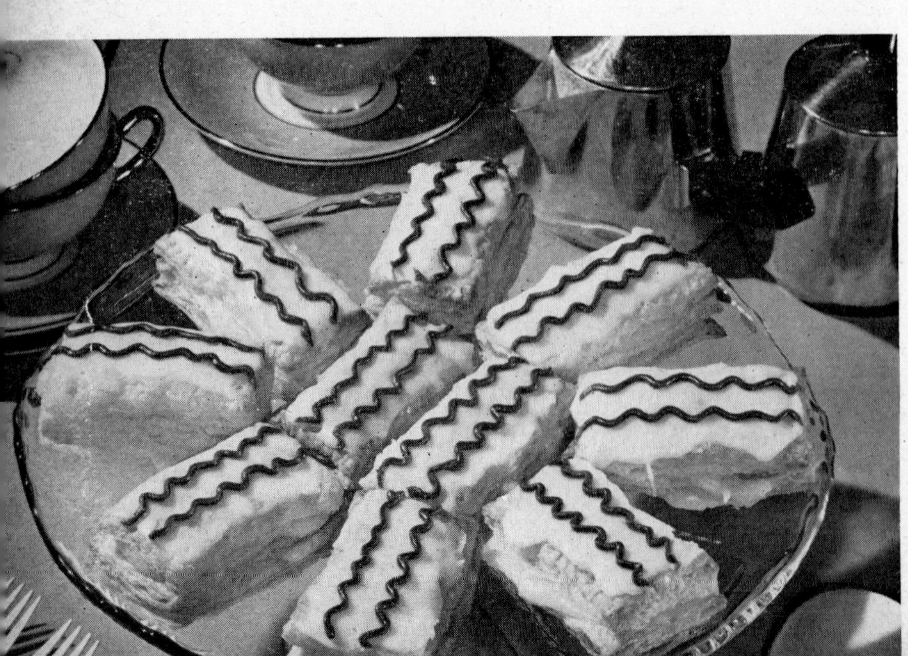

Flaky Napoleons—the ultimate in pastries

Napoleons are layers of flaky pastry, cream-filled, glazed, beribboned with chocolate icing.

These puff pastries are the delight of French pastry chefs — have brought world fame to restaurants. They can make your reputation as a hostess, too.

But Napoleons take attention and time. The key to success is thorough chilling and speedy rolling and folding of dough.

2 Roll dough to a 15x9-inch rectangle, ¼ inch thick. Peel top sheet of waxed paper from chilled rectangle of butter (recipe tells how to prepare); invert on half the dough; peel off other sheet of waxed paper from the butter.

Fold over other half of the dough to cover butter, as shown in picture.

↓

↑

1 When dough is first mixed, knead it thoroughly on a lightly floured surface until a smooth elastic ball of dough is formed. This will usually take about 5 minutes.

After kneading, cover and allow dough to rest for 10 minutes—this makes the dough easier to roll.

↑

3 Seal edges of the dough together by pressing down with side or heel of hand. This helps keep butter enclosed when rolling and folding the dough.

Wrap pastry in waxed paper; chill at least 1 hour in refrigerator or 20 minutes in freezer.

5 Turn folded dough around and fold again in thirds, as shown; seal edges. Wrap in waxed paper; chill thoroughly. Dough is now in 9 layers.

Repeat rolling, folding and thorough chilling (steps 4 and 5) two or three times more.

Puff Pastry is now ready to shape into Napoleons.

↓

↑

4 On lightly floured surface, roll chilled pastry ¼ inch thick, shaping into 15x9-inch rectangle. (Roll just *to* edges, to avoid flattening them.) Always remember to brush excess flour from the dough after rolling and before folding.

Fold dough in thirds as shown in picture. Seal edges of the dough together with side or heel of hand. The dough is now in 3 layers.

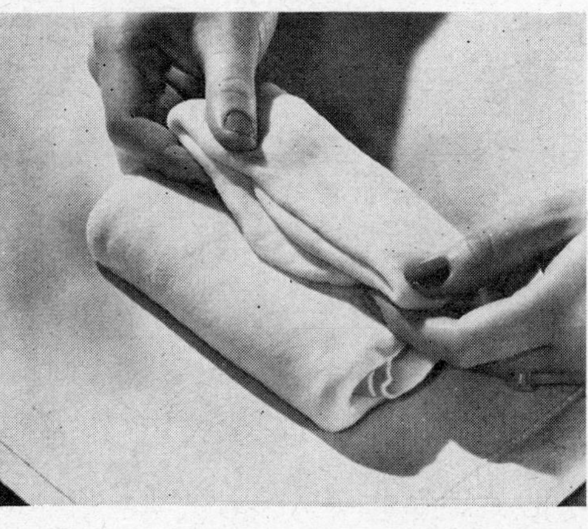

↑

6 To cut Napoleons: Roll dough into 14x8-inch rectangle, ⅜ inch thick. With floured sharp knife, trim off edges; prick entire surface with fork. Cut into 16 oblongs.

Place on baking sheets covered with paper towels and chill thoroughly. Brush with mixture of egg white and ice water; bake and fill as directed in recipe.

Cream Filling (*for Napoleons*)

1 cup sugar
¼ cup enriched flour
¼ cup cornstarch
½ teaspoon salt
3 cups milk
4 beaten egg yolks
2 teaspoons vanilla

Combine sugar, flour, cornstarch, and salt. Gradually stir in milk. Cook, stirring constantly, till mixture boils and thickens.

Stir a little of the hot mixture into the egg yolks; return to hot mixture. Stirring constantly, bring just to boiling. Cool; add vanilla. Chill. Beat with electric mixer or rotary beater till smooth. Makes about 3 cups.

Confectioners' Glaze
(*for Napoleons*)

2 cups sifted confectioners' sugar
Dash salt
¼ teaspoon vanilla
3 to 4 tablespoons boiling water

Combine sugar, salt, and vanilla. Add boiling water, mixing well. Makes ¾ cup.

Chocolate Glaze (*for Napoleons*)

1 1-ounce square unsweetened chocolate
1 teaspoon butter or margarine
3 tablespoons sifted confectioners' sugar
Dash salt

Melt chocolate and butter over hot water. Cool slightly. Stir in confectioners' sugar and salt; mix till smooth. Makes ⅓ cup.

Puff-pastry Pointers

- Chill utensils in refrigerator before each use and work fast so dough won't warm up. If it gets soft during rolling or folding, return to refrigerator till firm again.
- Butter must be firm at all times, yet never so hard it breaks through the dough. If it starts to melt, chill.
- To store Puff Pastry: Wrap in foil or saran; place in a box for protection, and store in freezer.

Even *unbaked* pastry will keep several weeks in the freezer or several days in the refrigerator.

For chocolate fans,

Frankly fancy—Chocolate Leaves

Chocolate Leaves are the easy but elegant trim for fudge-y Red Devil's Food Cake. You'll need real rose leaves. Leave a little of each stem for a handle. Rinse leaves; dry.

Melt candymaking chocolate or semisweet chocolate pieces over hot water till partly melted; remove, stir till smooth. With a new water-color brush, paint underside of leaves with a smooth thick coat of chocolate, spreading *just to edge*. Refrigerate to set chocolate.

To remove rose leaf from chocolate, insert point of paring knife at tip of leaf, then peel it off. Now onto waxed paper with chocolate leaves—be quick but gentle. Chill till ready to use.

Refrigerate decorated cake till party time so leaves will be fresh and perky. (If frosting on cake is too thin to hold up leaves, chill just long enough to do the job.)

triple-chocolate cake

It's a chocolate-on-chocolate treat—inside is feathery, moist Red Devil's Food Cake; outside, swirls of Fudge Velvet Frosting and a wreath of Chocolate Leaves. Another time, array Leaves on peppermint-frosted white cake.

Red Devil's Food Cake

½ cup shortening
1 cup sugar
1 teaspoon salt
1 teaspoon vanilla
⅓ cup cold water
½ cup cocoa

• • •

2½ cups sifted cake flour
1 cup cold water

• • •

3 egg whites
¾ cup sugar
1½ teaspoons soda
⅓ cup cold water

Stir shortening to soften. Gradually add 1 cup sugar, creaming together till light and fluffy. Add salt and vanilla. Combine ⅓ cup cold water and cocoa; beat into creamed mixture. Add flour alternately with 1 cup cold water, beating well after each addition.

Beat egg whites till soft peaks form; gradually add ¾ cup sugar, beating till stiff peaks form. Fold meringue into batter.

Combine soda and ⅓ cup cold water; stir to dissolve soda. Stir into batter. Mix well.

Bake in 2 paper-lined 9x1½-inch round pans in moderate oven (350°) 30 minutes or till done. Frost cooled cake with Fudge Velvet Frosting; trim with Chocolate Leaves in two sizes.

Fudge Velvet Frosting

3 1-ounce squares unsweetened chocolate

• • •

1½ cups sifted confectioners' sugar
3 tablespoons hot water

• • •

3 egg yolks *or* 1 egg
2 tablespoons soft butter
1 teaspoon vanilla

Melt chocolate in mixing bowl over hot water. Remove from heat. With electric mixer blend in sugar and water. Beat in egg yolks (or the whole egg), then butter and vanilla. Frosting will be thin at this point, so place bowl in ice water and beat till of spreading consistency. Will frost tops and sides of two 9-inch layers.

Tips on Chocolate Leaves

- For chocolate-mint leaves, add a few drops of peppermint extract to the melted chocolate.
- Any sturdy, smooth leaf will make a good pattern. Ivy and philodendron leaves, for example, can substitute for the rose leaves shown.
- On a warm day, take the chocolate-coated leaves from the refrigerator just a few at a time, to peel off the real leaves.
- Another use for chocolate leaves: Large ones make a delicious garnish for scoops of ice cream.

French Pastries

2 egg whites
½ cup sugar
2¼ cups sifted cake flour
1 cup sugar
3 teaspoons baking powder
1 teaspoon salt

• • •

⅓ cup salad oil
1 cup milk
1½ teaspoons vanilla
2 egg yolks

• • •

1 recipe French Pastry Frosting
Chopped California walnuts
Toasted coconut

Beat egg whites till foamy. Gradually beat in ½ cup sugar. Continue beating till very stiff and glossy.

Sift remaining dry ingredients into another bowl. Add salad oil, *half* the milk, and the vanilla. Beat 1 minute at medium speed on mixer or 150 strokes by hand, scraping sides and bottom of bowl constantly. Add remaining milk and egg yolks. Beat 1 minute longer, scraping bowl constantly. Gently fold in egg-white mixture with down-up-and-over motion, turning the bowl.

Pour batter in paper-lined 15½x10½x1-inch jelly-roll pan. Bake in moderate oven (350°) 15 to 18 minutes or till done. Cool cake on rack and remove from pan.

With sharp knife, trim edges so they'll be straight. Cut cake in 30 pieces as shown below. If desired, split cakes and fill with jam or jelly.

With a fork, hold each cake firm on board while you frost with French Pastry Frosting—white or chocolate. Press chopped walnuts or toasted coconut against sides. Pipe the tinted frosting around top edge. Center pastry with walnut or pecan half, or piped-on frosting rose, if desired.

French Pastry Frosting

1 cup butter or margarine
1⅓ cups shortening

• • •

2 tablespoons light corn syrup
¼ teaspoon salt
2 teaspoons vanilla

• • •

2 1-pound packages confectioners' sugar, sifted (about 8 cups)

• • •

Milk

• • •

2½ squares unsweetened chocolate, melted

Cream butter and shortening until light and fluffy. Beat in corn syrup, salt, and vanilla. With spoon, gradually blend in confectioners' sugar. Frosts and decorates 30 French Pastries, cut from one 15½x10½x1-inch sheet cake.

White frosting: Thin 2 cups French Pastry Frosting with milk till of spreading consistency. Frost tops and sides of 15 cakes for French Pastries.

Chocolate frosting: To 2 cups French Pastry Frosting, add the melted chocolate. Thin with milk till of spreading consistency. Frost remaining cakes for French Pastries.

Decorator's frosting: To decorate with pastry-tube designs, divide remaining frosting in several parts; tint each a different color. Pipe trims on frosted cakes—edgings, diagonal stripes, rosettes, or dainty flowers.

Cut-ups for French Pastries

Before cutting the cake in pretty shapes, mark the cutting lines with toothpicks. You may want to draw a guide on paper before you start.

Using a sharp knife, cut a 2-inch strip from ends and one side of cake; cut end strips in 5 squares, then the side strip in 4 rectangles. Cut remaining cake in half lengthwise; make 5 diagonal cuts, then 2 lengthwise ones. You get 10 squares, 12 diamonds, 4 rectangles, 4 triangles. Frost and trim as directed.

Just right with a cup of tea—dainty cookies and little fancy cakes

From such a pretty array guests will be tempted to choose one of each kind!

Top tier offers thinly sliced pound cake (buy it frozen), crisp macaroons; center tier, Pecan Tassies and, from bakeshop, tiny cake towers; and lower tier, Petits Fours and Brownies.

Teas and tea luncheons

Perfect Hot Tea

Black tea, green tea, oolong, and exotic perfumed teas differ only in processing. They may come from the same tea plant and are brewed in the same way.

To make tea, heat teapot by rinsing with boiling water. Then add 1 teaspoon tea or 1 tea bag for each cup.

Bring freshly drawn cold water to a vigorous boil; immediately pour over the tea and steep 5 minutes. Be a clock watcher—you can't judge strength of tea by color. Some teas brew light, others dark. Give tea a stir and serve at once or strain into preheated serving pot.

Like a weak brew? Dilute tea by adding a little hot water to the cup. Some folks prefer milk rather than cream with hot tea. And remember to pass sugar and lemon, too.

Hurry-up Hot Tea

In a rush? Keep a jar of instant tea handy for a bracing cup of hot tea. Measure the tea into each cup according to directions on label. Fill cup with boiling water; stir.

**See also tips for serving teas on page 158.*

Tea for a Crowd

Planning a tea?* A tea concentrate makes serving large groups easy. At teatime, all you have to do is pour a little concentrate into each cup and fill with hot, hot water. The tea can be strong or weak—it's the amount of concentrate you use that makes the difference. Or just before serving you can combine the concentrate with the hot water in a large teapot—1 cup concentrate to 6 cups boiling water.

Tea Concentrate for 40 to 45 servings: Bring to a high bubbling boil 6 cups freshly drawn cold water. Remove from heat and promptly add ¼ pound loose tea, stirring in leaves. Cover; steep 5 minutes. Strain into teapot.

Concentrate cloudy? Adding the hot water at teatime will make it sparkle again.

Hot Spiced Tea

To 6 cups water, add 1 teaspoon of whole cloves and 1 inch stick cinnamon. Heat to boiling. Add 2½ tablespoons black tea. Cover and let steep 5 minutes; strain.

Heat ¾ cup orange juice, 2 tablespoons lemon juice, and ½ cup sugar just to boiling; stir; add to hot tea. Serves 6 to 8.

After bridge, a cool salad meal

ACE-OF-TRUMPS TEA LUNCHEON

Shrimp Bowl with Louis Dressing
Herb Pan Rolls Butter
Iced Tea
Pecan Tassies, page 145

Shrimp Bowl

Arrange Fresh-cooked Shrimp on greens in salad bowl (we show tender Bibb and Boston lettuce). Top with a boutonniere of water cress. Serve with Louis Dressing.

Makes 4 or 5 servings.

Fresh-cooked Shrimp

6 cups water
3 tablespoons salt
2 tablespoons vinegar
2 bay leaves
1 teaspoon mixed pickling spices
2 stalks celery

• • •

1 pound raw cleaned shrimp (2 pounds in shells)

Combine first 6 ingredients; bring to boiling. Add shrimp (in shells, or peeled and cleaned). Cover; heat to boiling, then lower heat and simmer gently just till shrimp turn pink, about 5 minutes. Drain. If cooked in shell, peel and remove vein that runs down back. Chill.

Louis Dressing

1 cup mayonnaise
¼ cup chili sauce
¼ cup chopped green pepper
¼ cup finely chopped green onions with tops
1 teaspoon lemon juice
Salt to taste

Combine all ingredients. Makes 1½ cups.

Note: For a mild fluffy dressing, whip ¼ cup heavy cream and fold in last.

Herb Pan Rolls

1 package active dry yeast *or* 1 cake compressed yeast
¾ cup water

• • •

2½ cups packaged biscuit mix
½ teaspoon celery seed
¾ teaspoon poultry seasoning
¼ teaspoon nutmeg

Soften active dry yeast in *warm* water or compressed yeast in *lukewarm* water. Stir in biscuit mix and remaining ingredients; beat vigorously (2 or 3 minutes). Turn out on surface well dusted with biscuit mix. Knead till smooth, about 25 strokes.

Roll in a 14x6-inch rectangle, about ¼ inch thick. Cut dough lengthwise in thirds, then crosswise at 2-inch intervals to make 21 squares. Form each in ball. In greased 8x1½-inch round pan, arrange 13 rolls (not quite touching each other) around edge; arrange an inner circle of 8 rolls, leaving a 2-inch hole in center.

Cover with damp cloth. Let rise in warm place till double (about 1 hour). Bake in hot oven (400°) 15 to 20 minutes or till golden brown. Serve hot.

Iced Tea

To make 4 glasses of iced tea, measure 2 tablespoons (6 teaspoons) tea leaves (or 6 teabags) into teapot. (For large quantity, use a glass or enamelware pan.)

Pour 2 cups fresh, vigorously boiling water over leaves. Cover, let stand 5 minutes. Stir a second or two. Then pour brew through a tea strainer into glass, earthenware, or enamelware pitcher (warm glass pitcher first with hot water so it won't break when you pour in tea).

Immediately add 2 cups cold water and let tea cool at room temperature till you're ready to serve it.

Pour tea into tall ice-filled glasses. Offer juicy lemon wedges and sugar. Trim glasses with mint sprigs.

Cloudy iced tea? Flavor is every bit as good, but to make tea sparkle again, just add a little boiling water.

Light lunch for the girls—
Shrimp Bowl, herbed rolls,
iced tea in frosty glasses

Neat tricks for bridge

No-trump Tower and Joker's Wands are gay decorations for card table or buffet. Make them of construction paper (red, black, and white); 1/8- or 1/16-inch dowels (from hobby shop) or other sturdy thin stick; and for tower, a small box and plastic foam.

Cut plastic foam to fit inside box, then cover box diagonally half-and-half with black and white paper. To make 4 figures for Tower, fold 4x3-inch pieces of paper lengthwise down center —cut two each clubs and spades from black paper; two each hearts and diamonds from red, two of every suit from white.

Now make 4-sided figures. Glue four symbols of a kind (two white and two black or red) back-to-back, joining *half* a white symbol to *half* a red or black one. Paint doweling red; glue 4 figures to it. Poke through top of box into plastic foam. Top with table-number pennant. Make wands by gluing single figures to dowels. Stick wands into clay in bottom of snack bowl or into bouquets of red carnations. Or lay on napkins as favors.

Easy cutups—a perfect theme for your card party. Make figures from colored paper and thin sticks —we tell how.

Teatime sweets and snacks

Pecan Tassies

1 3-ounce package cream cheese
½ cup butter or margarine
1 cup sifted enriched flour

• • •

1 egg
¾ cup brown sugar
1 tablespoon soft butter or margarine
1 teaspoon vanilla
Dash salt

• • •

⅔ cup coarsely broken pecans

Cheese Pastry: Let cream cheese and ½ cup butter soften at room temperature; blend. Stir in flour. Chill slightly, about 1 hour. Shape in 2 dozen 1-inch balls; place in tiny ungreased 1¾-inch muffin cups. Press dough against bottom and sides of cups.

Pecan Filling: Beat together egg, sugar, 1 tablespoon butter, vanilla, and salt just till smooth. Divide *half* the pecans among pastry-lined cups; add egg mixture and top with remaining pecans. Bake in slow oven (325°) 25 minutes or till filling is set. Cool; remove from pans.

Brownies

½ cup butter or margarine
1 cup sugar
2 eggs

• • •

2 1-ounce squares unsweetened chocolate, melted
1 teaspoon vanilla
½ cup sifted enriched flour
½ cup chopped California walnuts

Thoroughly cream butter and sugar; add eggs and beat well. Blend in melted chocolate, vanilla, and flour. Add nuts to batter or sprinkle them over the top after batter is poured into the pan.

Pour batter into greased 8x8x2-inch pan. Bake in slow oven (325°) about 35 minutes. Cool and cut in squares. Makes sixteen 2-inch brownies.

If desired, frost with Fudge Velvet Frosting, page 139, then top each brownie with a walnut half for a party finish.

Petits Fours

¼ cup butter or margarine
¼ cup shortening
1 cup sugar
½ teaspoon vanilla
¼ teaspoon almond extract
2 cups sifted cake flour
3 teaspoons baking powder
¼ teaspoon salt
¾ cup milk
¾ cup (6) egg whites
¼ cup sugar

Cream butter and shortening thoroughly. Gradually add 1 cup sugar, and cream together till light and fluffy. Add extracts. Sift together flour, baking powder, and salt; add to creamed mixture alternately with milk, beating till smooth after each addition. Beat egg whites until foamy; gradually add ¼ cup sugar and beat till mixture forms soft peaks. Fold into batter.

Bake in paper-lined 13x9½x2-inch pan in moderate oven (350°) about 40 minutes. Cool 5 minutes before removing from pan.

When thoroughly cool, cut in 1½-inch squares or diamonds. (For a guide, poke toothpicks into sides of cake at 1½-inch intervals.) Or cut with tiny round biscuit cutter. Line cakes up on rack with cooky sheet below. Pour Petits Fours Icing over cakes. Trim each with candy decoration or, using Ornamental Frosting, page 114, pipe on frosting rose.

Petits Fours Icing

3 cups sugar
¼ teaspoon cream of tartar
1½ cups hot water
1 teaspoon vanilla
About 2¼ cups sifted confectioners' sugar
Few drops food coloring

Cook sugar, cream of tartar and hot water to thin syrup (226°). Cool to lukewarm (110°).

Add vanilla. Stir in sifted confectioners' sugar till frosting is of consistency to pour. Tint frosting with food coloring. Frosts 1 recipe of Petits Fours.

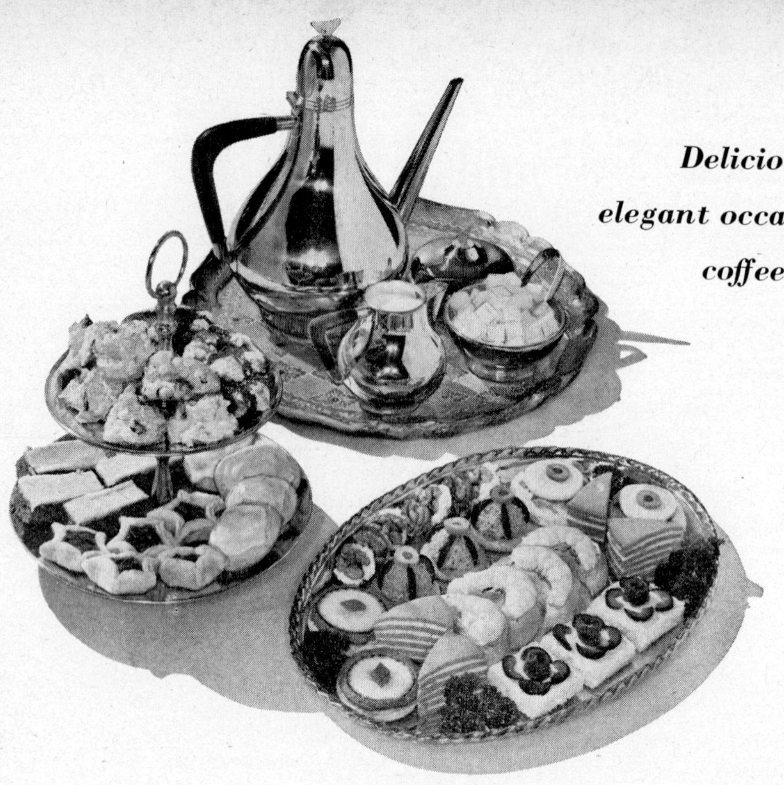

Delicious party fare for elegant occasions—teas, coffees, an open house

Go glamorous *and* skip the forks. Offer dainty cookies, canapes, and hors d'oeuvres, each no bigger than two- or three-bite size.

On tiered dish are Chocolate Crinkles and Polka-dot Macaroons (top); Frosted Molasses Creams, Pastry Star Tarts and Stuffed-date Drops (lower tier).

Around Shrimp Crescents, counterclockwise on tray, are Anchovy Bites, Bologna Stackups, Stuffed-olive circles, Meat-mountain Snacks, Walnut Sandwiches, and Cucumber-Anchovy Circles.

Fancy cookies, nut bread, snacks

Banana-Nut Bread

⅓ cup shortening
½ cup sugar
2 eggs
1¾ cups sifted enriched flour
2 teaspoons baking powder
½ teaspoon salt
¼ teaspoon soda
1 cup mashed *ripe* banana
½ cup broken California walnuts

Cream together shortening and sugar; add eggs and beat well. Sift together dry ingredients; add to creamed mixture alternately with banana, beating well after each addition. Stir in walnuts. Pour into a well-greased 8½x4½x2½-inch loaf pan. Bake in moderate oven (350°) about 1 hour or till done. Remove from pan; cool on rack.

Pastry Star Tarts

Roll out 1 recipe Plain Pastry (page 19). Cut about 1 dozen 2¾-inch rounds with cooky cutter. Pinch sides together to form 5-pointed stars.

Bake on cooky sheet in very hot oven (450°) 10 to 15 minutes. Cool. Fill with jelly, jam, or sharp cheese spread.

Chocolate Crinkles

½ cup shortening
1⅔ cups granulated sugar
2 teaspoons vanilla

• • •

2 eggs
2 1-ounce squares unsweetened chocolate, melted

• • •

2 cups sifted enriched flour
2 teaspoons baking powder
½ teaspoon salt

• • •

⅓ cup milk
½ cup chopped walnuts

• • •

Sifted confectioners' sugar

Cream shortening, granulated sugar, and vanilla thoroughly. Beat in eggs, then chocolate. Sift together dry ingredients; add to creamed mixture alternately with milk, blending well after each addition. Stir in nuts. Chill 2 or 3 hours. Form in 1-inch balls. Roll in confectioners' sugar. Place on a greased cooky sheet 2 or 3 inches apart.

Bake in moderate oven (350°) about 15 minutes. Cool slightly before removing from pan. Makes about 4 dozen.

Polka-dot Macaroons

½ teaspoon salt
3 egg whites
¾ cup sugar
3 cups corn flakes
1 6-ounce package (1 cup)
  semisweet chocolate pieces
1 teaspoon vanilla

Add salt to egg whites; beat till soft peaks form. Slowly add sugar; beat till stiff peaks form. Fold in remaining ingredients. Drop from teaspoon onto greased cooky sheet about 2 inches apart. Bake at 350° 15 to 18 minutes. Let cool slightly before removing from pan. Makes about 2½ dozen.

Frosted Molasses Creams

½ cup shortening
½ cup sugar
1 well-beaten egg
½ cup light molasses
½ cup hot water
1½ cups sifted enriched flour
½ teaspoon salt
1½ teaspoons baking powder
¼ teaspoon soda
1 teaspoon instant coffee
1 teaspoon cinnamon
½ teaspoon cloves

Thoroughly cream shortening and sugar; add egg and molasses; mix well. Add hot water. Sift dry ingredients; add to creamed mixture; beat till smooth.

Bake in greased 13x9½x2-inch pan at 350° 25 minutes. While warm, frost with Confectioners' Frosting, page 64. Cool; cut in bars.

Stuffed-date Drops

1 pound (about 70) pitted dates
1 3-ounce package pecan halves
¼ cup shortening
¾ cup medium-brown sugar
1 egg
1¼ cups sifted enriched flour
½ teaspoon baking powder
½ teaspoon soda
¼ teaspoon salt
½ cup dairy sour cream

Stuff dates with nut halves. Thoroughly cream shortening, sugar; beat in egg. Sift together dry ingredients; add alternately with sour cream to creamed mixture. Stir in dates. Drop onto greased cooky sheet (one date per cooky). Bake at 400° 8 to 10 minutes. Cool. Top with Golden Frosting.

Golden Frosting

½ cup butter or margarine
3 cups sifted confectioners' sugar
¾ teaspoon vanilla
About 3 tablespoons water

Lightly brown butter; remove from heat; gradually beat in sugar and vanilla. Slowly add water till of spreading consistency.

Canapes

Cut bread in fancy shapes; toast or brown in butter in skillet on one side. Spread topping on untoasted side. (Or use crackers.)

Cucumber-Anchovy Circles: Spread mayonnaise on bread rounds; top with cucumber slice, pimiento diamond. Pipe anchovy paste on edge.

Shrimp Crescents: Combine cream cheese with chopped chives; spread on buttered bread crescents and top with whole shrimp.

Anchovy Bites: Spread squares of bread with soft butter and cream cheese. Top each with a rolled anchovy fillet, ripe-olive slices.

Stuffed-olive Circles: Spread mayonnaise on bread rounds; sprinkle with chopped stuffed olives. Stack hard-cooked egg slice, mayonnaise, and slice of stuffed olive atop.

Meat-mountain Snacks: Mound smoked liver sausage or canned deviled ham on rich round crackers; trim sides with ripe-olive slice. Top with stuffed-olive circles.

Hors d'oeuvres

Bologna Stackups: Spread slices of Bologna with mixture of one 3-ounce package cream cheese, 2 tablespoons cream, and 1 tablespoon horseradish. Put six slices together with cheese spread; cut in wedges.

Or, alternate slices of any ready-for-the-table meat and sharp cheese. Cut in bite-size squares. Top each with a stuffed-olive slice and spear on a toothpick.

Walnut Sandwiches: Put halves of California walnuts together with creamed blue cheese or a sharp spreading cheese.

Ham Roll-ups: Marinate 1-inch cooked asparagus tips in French dressing; roll in ham slices narrower than asparagus; toothpick.

Refreshing party punch

Fruit punches are delicious, and colorful, concoctions to star at graduation parties, receptions, open house, or just any time. Ladle your punch from smart crystal or a big salad bowl or soup tureen.

Punch-bowl trims—rosebuds on block of ice; maraschino cherries frozen in ice ring; cherry, orange-slice, lemon-slice floaters.

Fruit Kabobs—For glasses, skewer cherries, pineapple chunks, or melon balls on straws.

Hawaiian Fruit Punch

2 46-ounce cans unsweetened pineapple juice
2⅔ cups orange juice
1⅓ cups lemon juice
⅔ cup lime juice
2 cups sugar
2 large bottles (7 to 8 cups) ginger ale, chilled
2 large bottles (7 to 8 cups) plain carbonated water, chilled

Combine fruit juices and sugar; chill thoroughly. Pour over large cake of ice in punch bowl. Pour ginger ale and carbonated water slowly down the side of bowl. For trim, float twist of sliced orange and sprigs of fresh mint on block of ice. Makes about 9 quarts.

Cranberry Sparkle goes fancy on this holiday snack table. Punch is peppy, simple to fix. Scalloped orange slices, lemon rings, and fresh cranberries sail atop.

Let guests help themselves to punch and choice of fruitcake, tiny popcorn balls, pastry snacks, and pound cake (buy it) ribboned with red and green jelly. Holly makes quick table trim.

Cranberry Sparkle

1 quart bottle (4 cups) cranberry-juice cocktail, chilled
1 cup orange juice, chilled

• • •

2 7-ounce bottles lemon-lime carbonated beverage, chilled

Place cake of ice or ice cubes in punch bowl. Add fruit juices; stir. Pour carbonated beverage carefully down side of bowl. Float scalloped orange slices and whole fresh cranberries, to match picture.

Makes 2½ to 3 quarts.

Rosy Punch

2 cups ½-inch slices rhubarb
1 cup sugar
½ cup water
½ cup unsweetened pineapple juice
¼ cup lemon juice
Few drops red food coloring
2 small bottles (about 2 cups) ginger ale, chilled

Combine rhubarb, sugar, and water; cook till rhubarb is tender; strain. Add fruit juices. Tint with coloring. Chill. Add ginger ale last minute. Serve over crushed ice or ice cubes. Makes 6 to 8 servings, or 1 quart.

Raspberry Ade

1 envelope raspberry-flavored summer-drink powder
1 envelope grape-flavored summer-drink powder
1½ cups sugar
2 quarts water
1 cup orange juice
½ cup lemon juice
1 9-ounce can (1 cup) crushed pineapple

Dissolve drink powders and sugar in water. Add fruit juices and pineapple; chill thoroughly. Makes about 2½ quarts.

Orange-blossom Cooler

2 6-ounce cans frozen lemonade concentrate
1 6-ounce can frozen orange-juice concentrate
9 cups cold water
5 pints pineapple sherbet
1 quart vanilla ice cream

Combine frozen concentrates and water. Place sherbet and ice cream in bottom of punch bowl; break in small pieces with a large spoon. Add juice mixture; stir till sherbet and ice cream are partially melted. On top of punch, float "blossoms" of orange slices centered with maraschino cherries. Makes about 5 quarts punch or 40 one-half cup servings.

Double-orange Fizz

For each serving, scoop 2 balls of orange sherbet into a chilled tall glass, or a scooped-out orange shell. Then fill with chilled orange carbonated beverage.

Golden Banquet Punch

⅔ cup boiling water
2 teaspoons tea leaves or 2 tea bags
1 12-ounce can (1½ cups) unsweetened pineapple juice
1 cup unsweetened grapefruit juice
1 cup orange juice
½ cup lemon juice
1 to 1¼ cups sugar
2 cups ice water
Aromatic bitters to taste (optional)
1 large bottle (3½ to 4 cups) ginger ale, chilled

Pour boiling water over tea; cover and let stand 5 minutes; strain. Combine fruit juices and tea; add sugar and stir till dissolved. Chill. Add ice water. Generously dash in aromatic bitters to taste. Pour mixture over cake of ice in punch bowl. Pour ginger ale slowly down side of bowl. Makes about 2½ quarts or 20 one-half cup servings.

Old-fashioned Lemonade

3 to 4 tablespoons Sugar Syrup
1½ tablespoons lemon juice
1 cup water

For each serving, combine all ingredients. Pour into ice-filled glass. Trim with mint sprig or slice of lemon.

Sugar Syrup: Combine 1 cup sugar and 1 cup water in saucepan. Heat, stirring constantly, till sugar dissolves, then bring to a full rolling boil. Cool; store in refrigerator.

Lime Luscious Sodas

⅔ to 1 cup sugar
1 cup lime juice
1 cup water
1 quart lime sherbet
2 small bottles (about 2 cups) carbonated water, chilled

Combine sugar, lime juice, and water; stir to dissolve sugar. Spoon sherbet into 6 chilled 10-ounce glasses. Add ⅓ cup of the lime-juice mixture to each, then fill with carbonated water.

Limeade Soda: You may make this soda using one 6-ounce can frozen limeade concentrate. Add only 1 to 2 cans water to concentrate. Omit lime juice, sugar, and water in recipe above. Add remaining ingredients as directed.

Tempting fancy sandwiches

Party-sandwich tips

- For neat sandwiches, freeze bread first. Cut and spread while frozen.

- Spread bread with soft butter or margarine to edge before spreading filling, to prevent sogginess.

- If you make sandwiches a day ahead, wrap in foil and seal well; or, wrap in waxed paper, then in damp towel; refrigerate.

- Freezer tip: Make fancy sandwiches up to two weeks ahead and store in freezer at 0°. Wrap in foil or tuck in plastic box. Freeze immediately. Allow about 3 hours for thawing.

Best fillings to freeze are peanut butter, American cheese, sliced or ground meat, fish, chicken, turkey. Skip mayonnaise, lettuce, tomatoes, celery, carrots, egg salad.

Canape Flowerpots

Unsliced enriched bread
1 6½-ounce can (1 cup) crab meat, flaked
½ cup finely chopped celery
¼ cup finely chopped green pepper
¼ teaspoon salt
Dash pepper
1 tablespoon lemon juice
⅓ cup mayonnaise or salad dressing
Sprigs of parsley

Cut bread in 1-inch slices; freeze. Cut out circles from frozen slices with 1-inch round cutter. Hollow out centers with scissors or paring knife, leaving bottom and sides about ¼-inch thick.

Combine crab meat, celery, green pepper, and seasonings. Add lemon juice and mayonnaise; mix well. Chill. Heap filling in "flowerpots." Garnish top of each with a small sprig of parsley.

Carrot-Olive Bars

1 cup finely grated carrots
¼ cup minced celery
½ cup chopped ripe olives
1½ tablespoons minced onion
¼ teaspoon salt
¼ cup mayonnaise or salad dressing
• • •
5 slices enriched sandwich bread
5 slices whole-wheat sandwich bread

For filling, combine first 6 ingredients and chill. Spread on white bread; top with whole-wheat slices. Trim off crusts. Cut sandwiches lengthwise in thirds. Trim with fans of ripe-olive strips. Makes 15 bars.

Cheese-Bacon Bars: Soften one 3-ounce package cream cheese. Blend in 1 tablespoon milk, 4 slices crisp-cooked bacon, crumbled, 1 teaspoon horseradish, and ½ teaspoon Worcestershire sauce. Substitute for filling in above recipe, using 6 slices of each kind of bread. Makes 18 bars.

Dainty snacks for the ladies

With tea or punch, pass a handsome sandwich tray like this. Canape Flowerpots "grow" parsley blossoms. Bar sandwiches rate fillings of colorful carrot-olive mixture or smooth cheese-bacon spread, olive trim.

Frosted Sandwich Loaf sets the pace for summer garden party or patio picnic. Serve with fruit plates, iced tea, dessert

One sandwich serves everyone when it's loaf-style. *And* it's pretty enough to be your centerpiece.

Delicious salad fillings are ham, egg, and chicken. "Daisy" garnish has egg-slice petals and a green-pepper stem. Circle with pineapple rings, stems-on cherries.

In a hurry? Try our quick version—Sandwich Loaf, Sliced-bread Style.

Frosted Sandwich Loaf

Egg-salad Filling:

4 hard-cooked eggs, chopped
3 tablespoons mayonnaise
2 teaspoons prepared mustard
1 teaspoon grated onion
½ teaspoon salt

• • •

Ham Filling:

1 cup ground cooked ham
⅓ cup mayonnaise
1 teaspoon prepared horseradish

• • •

Chicken Filling:

1 5-ounce can boned chicken, chopped
¼ cup finely chopped celery
¼ cup mayonnaise
2 tablespoons pickle relish

• • •

1 unsliced sandwich loaf

Combine ingredients for each filling. Trim crusts from loaf. Slice bread lengthwise in 4 equal layers. Butter slices. Spread first slice, butter side up, with Egg-salad Filling, second slice, Ham Filling, third slice with Chicken Filling. End with fourth slice. Wrap loaf in foil; chill.

Beat three 3-ounce packages softened cream cheese with 5 tablespoons top milk till fluffy; frost loaf. Trim. Makes 10 slices.

Sandwich Loaf, Sliced-bread Style

Egg Filling:

3 hard-cooked eggs, chopped
3 tablespoons finely chopped onion
2 tablespoons chopped stuffed olives
2 tablespoons mayonnaise
1 teaspoon prepared mustard
¼ teaspoon salt

• • •

Ham Filling:

1 2¼-ounce can deviled ham
2 tablespoons finely chopped celery
1 tablespoon finely chopped green pepper
1 teaspoon prepared horseradish

• • •

8 slices regular bread
Soft butter or margarine

Combine ingredients for fillings. Trim crusts from bread; butter. Arrange 2 slices, butter side up, with narrow ends *touching*. Spread with *half* the Egg Filling. Top with 2 slices bread. Spread with Ham Filling. Top with 2 more bread slices; spread with remaining Egg Filling. Top with last 2 bread slices, butter side down. Wrap loaf in foil; chill.

Blend two 3-ounce packages softened cream cheese with 1½ tablespoons mayonnaise. Frost loaf; chill. Trim with stuffed-olive slices. Cut in 6 or 7 1-inch slices.

Make plenty of these sandwiches—they're delicious! Guests will sample several. Between rows of Checkerboards are Fold-ups, open-face Diamonds, Cornucopias, and Date-roll Sandwiches cut in crescents. All are make-aheads.

Dainty sandwiches

Sandwich suggestions

Date-roll Sandwiches—Soften one 3-ounce package cream cheese. Stir in 1 tablespoon milk, 2 tablespoons very finely chopped candied ginger. Slice canned date-nut roll 3/8 inch thick. Spread half the slices with cheese mixture. Top with remaining slices. Cut a crescent from one side of each sandwich. Center piece makes a petal-shaped sandwich.

Diamonds: Combine flaked tuna, crab meat, *or* lobster with an equal part finely chopped celery. Moisten with mayonnaise, adding lemon juice to taste. Spread on diamonds of whole-wheat bread. Trim with pimiento diamonds.

Fold-ups: Trim crusts from sliced white bread. Spread the squares with Orange-Date Filling: Mix 1/2 cup each finely chopped dates and walnuts, and 1/3 cup orange juice. Bring 2 opposite corners together at center and hold with toothpick and sprig of water cress.

Sandwich Butters

Cheese Butter: Mix one 5-ounce jar sharp spreading cheese, 1/4 pound soft butter.

Parsley Butter: Blend 1/4 cup soft butter, 1 1/2 tablespoons finely chopped parsley, and 1/2 teaspoon lemon juice.

1 *How to slice bread* for Ribbon Sandwiches or Checkerboards: Remove crusts from 2 unsliced sandwich loaves—1 white, 1 whole wheat. From each loaf, cut 6 lengthwise slices 1/2 inch thick. (Or have bread sliced at the bakery.) This will make 3 Ribbon Loaves.

2 *Ribbon Sandwiches*—Use Cheese Butter to put 4 long slices of bread together, alternating 2 whole wheat and 2 white. Make three loaves. Wrap in foil, saran, or waxed paper; chill, slice crosswise to make thin "ribbons."

3 *Checkerboards*—Make Ribbon Loaves, as shown. Cut in 6 *lengthwise* slices. Put 4 slices together, alternating colors, to make checkerboard. Wrap and chill. Slice *crosswise*. Two Ribbon Loaves make three Checkerboards.

—let folks choose from a gay assortment

Pinwheels on parade! They take to a variety of fillings

1 *Parsley Pinwheels*—Trim crusts from 1 loaf unsliced sandwich bread. Cut loaf in lengthwise slices ¼ inch thick. Spread with Parsley Butter.

For pretty centers, line up a row of stuffed green olives near end of each slice as shown. For variety, make some pinwheels with Cheese Butter, no olives.

2 Roll as for jelly roll. Wrap in waxed paper; chill. At serving time, place roll seam side against board; cut in ⅜-inch slices. *Pepper Pinwheels*—Spread long bread slices with pimento-cheese spread. Lay *thin* green-pepper strips across bread at inch intervals. Roll up; chill. Slice as above.

Cornucopias—quick

Trim crusts from bread slices. Top with softened pineapple-cheese spread. Roll in cornucopias. Trim with ripe-olive petals. Chill seam side down.

Diplomas and Caps—for graduation parties

Diplomas—Trim crusts from white-bread slices; spread with chive cream cheese. Roll; tie with ribbon. *Caps*—Cut slices of dark rye bread in 2-inch squares and 1½-inch circles. Put together in form of caps with canned deviled ham. Tassels are pimiento strips. Serve with a pretty fruit salad, sparkling punch, a fluffy cake.

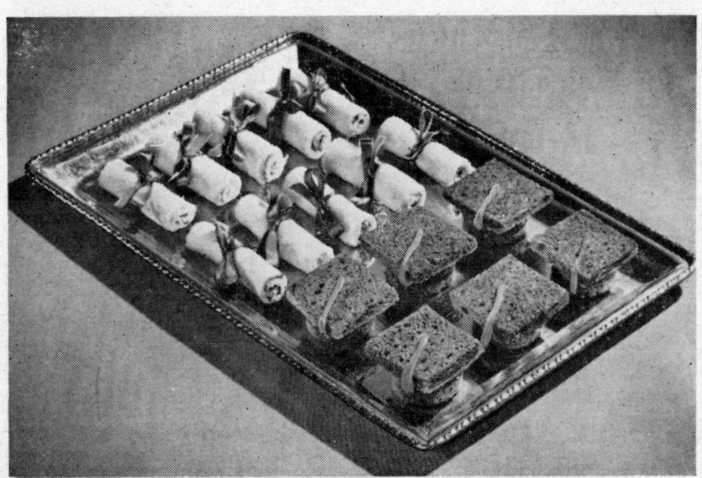

Smart entertaining—an elegant buffet that's easy on the hostess

Serving problems, eliminated! You will fairly glide through dinner served buffet-style—guests will remember your party as "lovely."

From the buffet, below, guests help themselves to the main dish—here it's piping hot in chafing dish—and to other foods set out for easy pickup. They carry their plates to places set at dining table (closeup at left).

Serving cart holds the dessert, coffee. When guests finish the main course and put their plates on the buffet, serve dessert at the table or have guests help themselves.

Table settings

Having a buffet . . . tea for 5 or 50 . . . an informal luncheon? Here are pointers for a perfect party

Buffet-style serving is fun! You, the hostess, can enjoy your party without running back and forth to the kitchen; you'll have time to chat with your guests and they'll relax and have a good time.

Buffet serving is a natural when guests outnumber the places at your dining table. Set up card tables or small tray tables. Or let guests eat lap-style from trays—place a stack of trays near the serving table.

If guests are to sit at the dining table as at left, or at card tables, have the places all set with linens, silver, glassware, and salt and pepper shakers.

For a buffet, you can go fancy and use your best china; or keep it casual with simple accessories. It's all up to you.

There's no hard and fast rule for setting a buffet. Most important: Arrange it attractively—no crowding; place serving dishes to make it easy for guests to help themselves. Often big dishes are placed in center at each end. Include serving fork or spoon with each food.

Serving a crowd? Make twin arrangements of food, one on each side of table.

Decide exactly how many forks, spoons, plates, and cups you'll need and put out just that number. The food and tableware can go on dining table, sideboard, or both.

In the drawings, below, guests would begin by picking up plates and napkins. (Here, napkins are stacked with plates to save room on the table; but they might be arranged beside the plates or placed with the silver.) Guests would go around the table, helping themselves to meat, vegetables, relishes, salad, rolls, and silver. If you like, you or your husband may serve the main dish.

When it's time for dessert . . .

Have dessert arranged on side table; or clear buffet and arrange dessert, plates, and silver—let guests help themselves. Or pass tray of desserts to guests seated at tray or card tables. Serve coffee with either the meal or dessert, or both. Usually any beverages go on buffet or a side table.

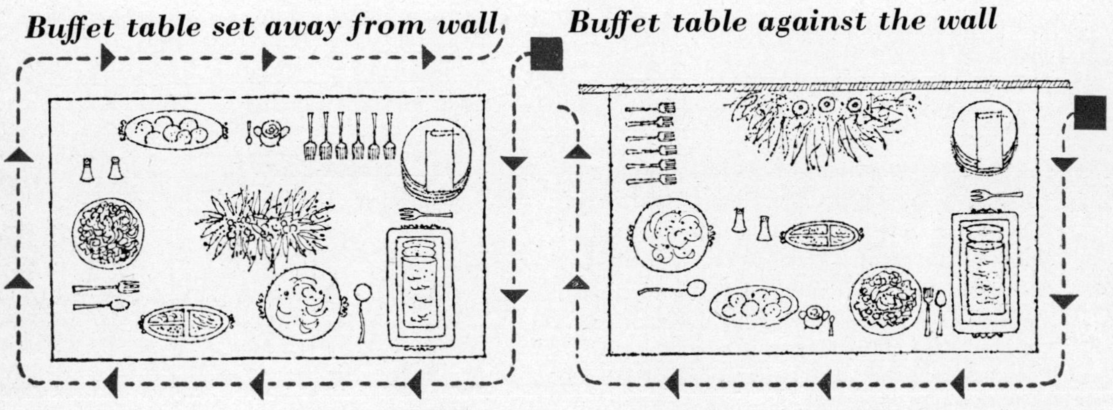

Buffet table set away from wall

Buffet table against the wall

Follow these table-setting rules for a formal dinner

We show how to set a formal dinner table—many of the rules for informal settings are based on the more formal ones (now rare except perhaps in diplomatic circles).

A formal dinner menu would consist of these courses: 1-soup or other first course, 2-fish, 3-roast, 4-salad, 5-dessert, 6-after-dinner coffee. The drawing, right, shows how to set the table for this dinner.

Silver is placed in the order it will be used, from the outside in. Spoons and knives go at right; sharp knife edge faces plate. Bouillon spoon is at extreme right, then fish knife (used infrequently); next, dinner-size meat knife. Forks are at left of plate; from outside in: fish fork, meat fork, salad fork. Your table will be prettier if you limit the silver at each place to six pieces—three on each side of plate. Additional silver, if needed, may be brought in when the course is served.

Line up silver and plate about 1 inch from table edge. For comfort, allow 24 inches from plate center to next plate center.

Water and then wine glasses are placed left to right above knife and spoon. Coffee is served after dinner in the living room.

Dessert—two ways to serve it

Plate with fork and spoon is set before guest who removes silver; now dessert is served. After dessert, finger bowl is brought on a plate.

Or, finger bowl may be on the dessert plate with silver. Guest removes all from plate, then is served dessert.

Breakfast on a pretty table starts the day right

Take time to have the table look as nice for breakfast as for any other meal. Use gay place mats, correct table setting, a centerpiece of garden flowers or green plant—folks will be glad they got up!

Your breakfast setting will vary with what you're serving, of course. In our drawing at right, silver consists of fork and knife—could be for bacon and eggs; next to the knife is a dessert-size spoon for cereal; then a teaspoon for fruit. (Place dry cereal above the plate; or if a hot cereal, serve when folks are ready.) Coffee spoon is on saucer at the right of cup. Butter spreader goes on the bread-and-butter plate as shown, or place at left of the fork.

How to set the breakfast table—for company or just the family

Informal table setting plus course-by-course service

Today many folks prefer informal table settings. Your table can look elegant even though inconvenient formal customs may be omitted. Important for an attractive table—a neat, orderly arrangement of everything needed for the meal.

In drawing, forks are arranged at left, knives and spoons at right, from outside to plate in order of use. (Here, cocktail fork is brought with first course.) Set bread-and-butter plates left of plate above forks, spreader square on plate. If coffee is to be served with main course, cups would be in place (handles out from plates).

Appetizer starts off the meal. Serve in crystal sherbet; place cocktail fork on crystal plate; set on china service plate. (Or cocktail fork may go at extreme right, outside knife and spoons.) Later, service plate is removed for main course.

Soup is usually served before main course in soup bowl or consomme cup. Place directly on service plate. Note position of soup spoon. (You may want to omit soup course, especially if serving appetizer.)

Meat course. Remove the service plate; serve main course on large dinner plate. Dinner knife, fork are on right, left; the bread-and-butter plate goes above the forks.

Salad may follow meat course — remove dinner plate, used silver. If salad precedes main course, place salad fork to left of dinner fork. (Or serve salad *with* main course.)

Dessert. Bring dessert fork and spoon in on plate; guest should place spoon on right next to plate, fork on left. Serve coffee with dessert at table or later in living room.

Invite a few friends for informal afternoon tea

Tea tray, all set for a party

On tea tray, place teaspoons, plates stacked with napkins, cups on saucers, hot water, teapot on warmer, tea accompaniments.

Pick a pleasant spot—in front of the fireplace or a shady corner of the porch or patio. Before guests arrive, set tea tray as shown, left; place on convenient table.

Just before serving, fill container with *boiling* water and teapot with freshly brewed tea. You may want to use a concentrated brew; see our tea recipes, page 141.

Pour tea brew; then dilute with hot water, add sugar, cream (really milk), and lemon as guests request. Guests help themselves to simple snacks placed near by. (If forks or knives are needed, arrange on tray.)

More formal tea for large group, decidedly an event

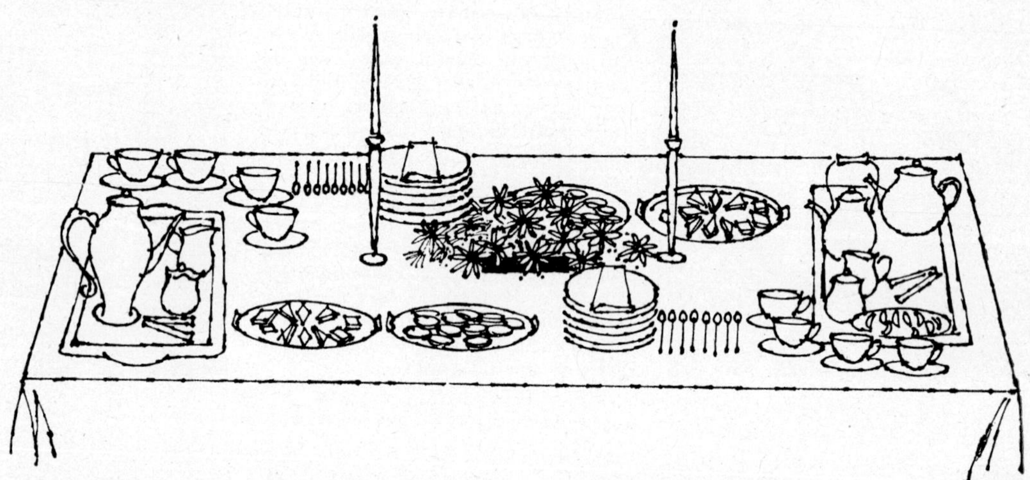

Tea table arranged for many guests. When your tea is a big affair, it's a good idea to set the tea table for "two-way travel." This will speed things along. Place similar plates of tea dainties on both sides of the table; offer a beverage at each end. Guests preferring coffee, punch, or chocolate take one side of the table; tea fans take the other side.

The occasion for a more formal tea is usually to honor someone—a speaker, a new neighbor, or perhaps visiting club members.

Before the day of the tea, ask a friend to pour. Or two friends, one at each end of the table. You'll be free to make guests feel at home and replenish tea and food.

Make the table attractive—as beautiful as gleaming silver, exquisite china, dainty food, and a pretty centerpiece.

Suit the setting to the table, the room, the number of guests. You may want to serve from only one side of the table, or offer beverages at only one end. Watch details—it's the little things that count. Are cup handles parallel, plates and spoons same distance from table edge?

Tea tray holds tea (page 141), hot water, cream, sugar, and lemon. Cups and saucers go near tray—at back and side. Spoons are next. Stack napkins between plates, or arrange near by. (Use plates large enough to hold cup and saucer plus a snack. Or you may use smaller plates and no saucers.)

Person pouring hands beverage to guests, who then help themselves to other refreshments. They may eat standing, or you may have chairs grouped for easy conversation.

Index